Ground Rules for
Social Research

Ground Rules for Social Research

Guidelines for good practice

Second Edition

Martyn Denscombe

 Open University Press

Open University Press
McGraw-Hill Education
McGraw-Hill House
Shoppenhangers Road
Maidenhead
Berkshire
England
SL6 2QL

email: enquiries@openup.co.uk
world wide web: www.openup.co.uk

and Two Penn Plaza, New York, NY 10121-2289, USA

First published 2010

A catalogue record of this book is available from the British Library

ISBN-13: 978 0 335 23381 6 (pb)
ISBN-10: 0 335 23381 3 (pb)

Library of Congress Cataloging-in-Publication Data
A catalog record for this book has been requested

Typeset by RefineCatch Limited, Bungay, Suffolk

Printed and bound by CPI Group (UK) Ltd, Croydon, CR0 4YY

The **McGraw·Hill** Companies

Overview

Contents

Acknowledgements

This book owes much to my family who have enabled me to embark on the path of writing and who have provided love and support over the years. Thanks especially to Viv.

INTRODUCTION

People who undertake research projects as part of an educational qualification or as part of their job do not necessarily regard themselves as 'researchers'. Research is likely to be just one among many tasks they need to complete as part of their course of study or their professional work. Their research project will need to fit in with a host of other competing demands and, though being committed to doing a good job on their project, they will not necessarily have the time or inclination to immerse themselves in the research methodology literature. These are people for whom research is something they do, not something that defines their identity. These are *'project researchers'* who, quite reasonably, will prefer to focus on 'the bottom line' when it comes to preparing for their research. They will want clear guidelines about what they can do and what they cannot do if they are to produce a piece of research that is worthwhile.

Such clear guidelines have not been easy to find because social research is a 'contested' area with plenty of controversies and disagreements among the experts. One reason for this is that social research spans a wide range of subjects. It operates as an umbrella term covering research in areas like education, health, business studies, social work, housing and media studies, and it draws on a number of different disciplines, such as sociology, psychology, economics and politics, each with a distinctive way of seeing the social world. What complicates matters more is that these disciplines and subject areas include a variety of approaches that have different visions of the nature of the social world and the best ways of investigating it. Within the social sciences, there are broad divisions between positivist approaches and interpretivist approaches, between realists and constructionists, between those favouring quantitative data and those advocating the use of qualitative data. There is no single approach that is universally accepted.

For project researchers this poses a particular difficulty. They might ask: 'How can I conduct a piece of good research when there is such a lack of agreement among the experts? Surely, what will please one set of experts will only lead to criticism from another set of experts?' They might be worried that what qualifies as a 'good' piece of research will depend entirely on those who evaluate the work and the specific beliefs that these people hold about the right and proper way to conduct enquiries.

Ground Rules for Social Research addresses such concerns by focusing on areas of agreement that lie behind the debates and disagreements. It does not deny the importance of different subject areas and disciplines or the fact that particular audiences for research will tend to have a preference for 'their own' approach rather than others. But rather than concentrate on the differences, it highlights the areas of common ground and tacit agreement that exist and the fact that there are some general principles of social research that are widely shared. For example, the vast majority of social researchers will agree that the use of 'precise and valid data' forms an essential ingredient of good research. Although researchers from different backgrounds might disagree about the exact meaning and implications of what constitutes 'precise and valid data' they will share the view that findings based on data that are not precise and valid are really not much use at all.

Such areas of common ground provide the foundation for this book. Twelve 'ground rules' are identified and the book provides practical guidance on how to comply with each of them. As well as specifying items of *good practice* and providing *examples* of how these can be applied, there are *checklists* at the end of the chapters that help the project researcher to cover the crucial points and include the main ingredients necessary for good research. The book does not claim to provide a solution to the various debates. It does not attempt to synthesize the alternative approaches within social research or to offer a set of guidelines that will satisfy everyone. A grand solution such as this remains an elusive goal for social science at the start of the twenty-first century. What it can do, however, is alert project researchers to the ground rules for social research and the criteria by which their investigations will be judged. It can enable them to understand the main areas of controversy and help them to predict the kinds of criticism that might be levelled at their work. Forewarned is fore-armed and by addressing potential criticisms before they arise the investigation can be defended and justified to would-be critics.

Key point

There is no such thing as perfect research and 'you cannot please all the people all the time' when it comes to doing social research. However, an awareness of the ground rules can help the project researcher to complete a successful piece of research – one which addresses the 12 key issues that are likely to be in the minds of those who judge the quality of the end-product.

Ground Rules for Social Research: guidelines for good practice

	THEME	Related topics
The research topic needs to:		
▶ have clearly stated aims and questions	PURPOSE	Aims, research questions, hypotheses, descriptive research, exploratory research, explanatory research
▶ relate to existing knowledge and needs	RELEVANCE	Literature review, practical problems, development of theory, timeliness, personal agenda
▶ fit the resources available	FEASIBILITY	Costs, access to data, time-planning, self as resource, cooperation by participants, trust and good will
The research approach needs to:		
▶ protect the interests of participants	ETHICS	Morality, researcher integrity, avoidance of harm to participants, informed consent, ethics approval, data security
▶ be open-minded and self-reflective	OBJECTIVITY	Bias, social values, impartiality, reflexivity, relativism
The research design needs to:		
▶ be coherent and fit for purpose	DESIGN	Blueprints and plans, fit for purpose, pilot studies, consistency, limitations
▶ be aware of its underlying assumptions	PHILOSOPHY	Ontology, epistemology, positivism, interpretivism, critical realism, pragmatism, research paradigms
The research methods need to:		
▶ produce precise and valid data	ACCURACY	Validity, reliability, precision, truth and reality, normality of settings
▶ be collected and used in a justifiable way	ACCOUNTABILITY	Writing about research, record keeping, audit trail, replication, verification, evaluation, web-sites
The research findings need to:		
▶ apply to other situations	GENERALIZATIONS	Sampling, representativeness, generalizability, transferability, theory relevance
▶ contribute something new to knowledge	ORIGINALITY	Difference, new topics, alternative methods, unique information, new analysis, plagiarism
▶ be cautious about their claims	PROOF	Verification, falsification, theory testing, causation, uncertainty

I
TOPIC

1

PURPOSE

Ground rule: **Research should have clearly stated aims and questions**

Questions: What is the research trying to achieve?

What is the point of carrying out the research?

Answers: The purpose of the research is stated clearly and explicitly in a format appropriate for the style of investigation.

Information about the focus and direction of the research is sufficiently precise and detailed to provide criteria for the evaluation of the research.

The need for clarity of purpose

A *clear* vision of the purpose of research is very important. There are three main reasons for this. First, it allows readers to understand the research better. It addresses the sometimes reasonable, sometimes cynical, question that is likely to be posed by anyone looking at the research: '*What is it all about?*' The provision of an explicit and precise description of the purpose answers the question by allowing 'outsiders' to *see* the intentions of the research. It might seem obvious that researchers should supply this kind of information but, to those involved with the investigation, the point of doing the research might seem so obvious that it hardly warrants much attention. The danger, here, is that researchers launch into a description of the methods and findings without paying sufficient attention to explaining what exactly motivated the investigation and what precisely they were trying to find out. For those who read and use the findings from the research, though, *the purpose of the research is something that needs to be understood concisely, precisely and right from the beginning*.

Second, a clear vision of the purpose of research provides a crucial basis for evaluating the research. From the reader's point of view, the quality of a piece of research can be better gauged if there is a clear statement about what the research has set out to achieve. This allows readers to *evaluate* the research by providing benchmarks against which to judge the extent to which the research has been successful.

Third, a clear vision of the purpose of research provides a good platform from which to conduct the investigation. This applies whether the research uses a quantitative, a qualitative, or a mixed methods approach (Leedy and Ormrod 2005; Marshall and Rossman 2006; Creswell 2009). The clarity of the statements of purpose will reflect the clarity of the researcher's preparation and thinking on the topic and this, in turn, will do much to streamline the research process by allowing a suitable research design to be produced. To get a clear vision of the purpose, the researcher will have sifted through a range of possibilities and given careful consideration to alternatives before arriving at conclusions about what is to be investigated and the methods by which it can best be researched. Clarity of purpose also calls on the researcher to identify a relatively narrow and precise area for investigation rather than setting out to investigate some general area of interest. It requires the researcher to focus attention on specific aspects, specific questions, specific issues within the broader area of interest. And this is vital because, unless some quite specific topic is pinpointed, there is the very real danger that:

- researchers will 'bite off more than they can chew';
- researchers will flounder in a sea of vast quantities of issues and data;
- time will be wasted on the collection of unnecessary information;
- time will be wasted on meanderings up blind alleys before a clear direction becomes evident;
- vague questions might lead to vague answers.

> **Key point**
> A lack of clarity and detail in the statement of purpose can be a recipe for sloppy research – research that will suffer later through a lack of forethought about the details of who, what, when, where and how many things are to be covered by the research.

Suitable purpose

There are some things that do not lend themselves to being studied using conventional social research methodologies and, right from the start, the researcher needs to address the question: 'Will the use of a social research methodology be suitable for the investigation of this topic?' The researcher needs to be sure that the questions, results and conclusions fall within the realms of social *science* and are not questions that are better suited to the realms of aesthetics or religion/faith, where different criteria of research and proof operate. A key criterion here is whether the questions, results and conclusions are of the kind that lend themselves to the possibility of being investigated through empirical inquiry and/or rational argument. Social research questions must be, in principle, testable. Explanations and theories must be open to proof or disproof – not a matter of private belief, blind faith or simple assertion.

Link up with **PROOF**

The research should also offer something new. Apart from those relatively rare instances of social research that set out to repeat a piece of previous research in order to check its findings, the research should contain some element of originality or uniqueness. The notion that the research should contain an element of originality might seem daunting. However, it merely means that the purpose of research needs to include some element that is different from other investigations on the topic, some new twist, some new angle that marks the research out as different.

Link up with **ORIGINALITY**

The literature review is particularly important in this context. To offer something new or different, the research needs to build on existing knowledge and link to what is already known on a particular topic or issue. There must be some effort to find out what has already been written on the area so that both the researcher and the audience for the research feel confident that the research is not 'reinventing the wheel'.

Link up with **RELEVANCE**

There is also the practical matter of resources. Research projects are always constrained by the amount of time and money available and the purpose of any piece of research ought to reflect this. Good research avoids the pitfall of being over-ambitious in terms of its scale and its scope.

Link up with **FEASIBILITY**

Last, but not least, it is essential that the research does not set out to do something that is illegal or immoral. Of course, laws vary from country to country and matters of morality will differ from society to society but the project researcher should ensure that his/her activities accord with ethical standards and codes of conduct that operate for the discipline, the profession and the country in which the research is located.

Link up with **ETHICS**

Different types of purpose

Within the spectrum of the social sciences, with its array of disciplines and styles of research, there are differing notions about what social research should be trying to do. Often a distinction is made between:

- *descriptive* research, which provides detailed accounts of events or situations in order to gain a clearer picture of *what* is going on.
- *explanatory* research, which is mainly concerned with cause–effect relationships. It builds on well-established theories with a view to developing them and using them to make predictions that can be tested. It aims to explain *why* things happen.
- *exploratory* research, which investigates new areas and which seeks to generate new theories and concepts.

The purposes listed below expand on these. It is worth emphasizing, however, that the alternatives are not necessarily mutually exclusive. It is quite possible that any given research project might contain elements of more than one category, and this is quite reasonable. It is important, though, that their different ambitions are recognized at the start of the research because they have strong implications for the overall design of the investigation.

Link up with **DESIGN**

Forecasting an outcome (what will happen in the future?)

Very much in line with positivistic approaches that emulate the natural sciences, the purpose of an investigation might be to make predictions about future events on the basis of existing theories and knowledge. The point of doing the research, in this case, is to arrive at conclusions about future events or situations. So, for example, economists might attempt to predict economic growth or patterns of trade and will use models and theories as the basis for making the forecasts. This kind of aim is firmly part of applied research, where the value of the research rests on how well it manages to predict events and supply useful forecasts to those who will use the knowledge. Within the social sciences such *predictive research* can be used to provide forecasts to be used by planners who might need to predict things like the future demand for health, education and housing. Equally, they might have commercial applications and help to inform decisions about investments, marketing and production.

Explaining the causes or consequences of something (why do things happen?)

This kind of purpose is more likely to be associated with pure research than applied research. The main aim is to understand the relationship between events and phenomena, and to move towards theories or models that explain the way things work. Researchers might have an eye on how well they can predict outcomes (as with forecasting) but the primary purpose of research is to improve our understanding of *why* things happen as they do. Such research focuses on theory testing and theory development, or more broadly on improving explanations of economic, political, psychological and social phenomena.

Criticizing or evaluating something (how well does something work?)

Although many types of research, possibly most, will incorporate judgements about the relative merits of alternative explanations, in some instances this can be the principal focus of attention and the *raison d'être* of the research. Such research is driven by the desire to arrive at conclusions about the value of one thing when compared with alternatives. *Evaluation research* is an example of this. Researchers investigate particular programmes or policies with the specific intention of weighing up their strengths/weaknesses and considering how things might be improved.

Describing something (what is it like?)

For many researchers the main purpose of conducting an investigation is to discover information that did not exist before. They are breaking into new territory to explore things and report back on what they find. *Exploratory research* of this kind sets out to collect facts and to describe situations/events. The purpose in this instance is primarily to describe how things *are*, rather than how they will be, or how they should be, or even why they are as they are. Ethnographies, case studies and surveys are sometimes used to provide such information.

Developing good practice (how can it be improved?)

The main driving force behind a piece of research is sometimes the desire to solve a practical problem or to improve procedures. Particularly in the context of organizations and the work environment, the aim of the research is to arrive at recommendations for good practice that will tackle a problem or enhance the performance of the organization and individuals through changes to the rules and procedures within which they operate. This is very much *applied* research. A good example of this approach is *action research*, where the agenda for the investigation tends to be set by the researcher's own working environment and the need to make improvements to that environment through rigorous research.

Empowerment (how can it help those who are being researched?)

Most social research treats the people or things that are investigated as the objects of research. Research is conducted *on* them and *about* them. An alternative, and controversial, approach is to conduct research *for* them, casting aside the stance of neutrality and openly conducting research with the aim of helping those who are collaborating with the research. The aim is to empower those who are the subject of the investigation, and the principal motive for conducting the research is the welfare of those involved. Feminist research is one example of such a 'partisan' approach. Feminist researchers make no apology for their concern with the position of women in society or their stance that research should be conducted in a way that promotes the interests of women. *Anti-racist* and *post-colonial research* parallels feminist research in the sense that it too sets out to redress an inequality through research. In this case, it is research that explicitly sets out to empower those specific social groups adversely affected by racism and the legacy of colonial values.

 Caution

Conducting research with the intention of benefiting the subjects might appear to violate the conventional wisdom that researchers should be detached, impartial and dispassionate.

Link up with **OBJECTIVITY**

Personal interest in the choice of topic

The image of scientific enquiry carries with it the idea that research should be shaped purely and simply by the questions arising from efforts to advance existing knowledge. Good research, following this image, is research whose topic and direction is a direct consequence of working at the cutting edge of knowledge, driven by theoretical issues and practical problems that the community of scholars identify as necessary for the further advancement of the discipline. Researchers' *personal* preferences have no part to play in this. In the real world of research, however, decisions about what to investigate frequently reflect the personal interests of the researcher. Particularly with small-scale project research, it is evident that past and present *personal experiences*, good and bad, often act as a major influence on the choice of topic. The desire to research a particular topic can stem from things like:

- a point in a career;
- an incident in personal life;
- domestic experiences;
- a health crisis;
- a political commitment;
- the development of a leisure interest.

Any such experience can generate the incentive to investigate specific things rather than others. Research on feminist issues offers a good example. The vast majority of writers in this area are women. This is not a coincidence, but a reflection of the way their personal history and identity have spurred them to a particular interest in topics that concern the lives of women.

Link up with **RELEVANCE**

A personal interest in a topic is not necessarily a bad thing as far as social research is concerned. It need not be at odds with the advancement of knowledge in a specific discipline and, indeed, it can be a factor that complements other reasons for deciding to focus an investigation in a specific area. It can operate alongside the 'scientific' factors rather than instead of them. Furthermore, of course, a personal interest in a topic has the benefit that it can supply the passion and commitment for the researcher to stay with the project even when the going gets tough. It is a basis for *self*-motivation and gives the drive, the grit and determination that are needed to see things through to completion.

A personal interest, however, should not blind researchers to things that challenge their expectations. It is crucial to distinguish between the positive and healthy influence of having a personal interest in a topic which will operate to sustain the researcher through hard times, and the detrimental impact of having such a commitment and passion for a topic that the researcher approaches the area with conclusions already set in mind and an unwillingness to discover what is not desired. It is important to recognize that a personal interest in the topic should not act as a blinker that unduly narrows the focus of research. It should not act to close the mind of the researcher, to shut out alternatives and criticisms.

Link up with **OBJECTIVITY**

Box 1.1 Purpose	
The key issue	**Things to be considered**
What is the research trying to achieve?	Do social research methods provide a suitable means for investigating the topic? Has the purpose of the research been described appropriately in a conventional format? Is it clear which kind(s) of purpose the research is trying to achieve: • forecasting some outcome? • explaining the causes of something? • critically evaluating some theory or belief? • describing an event or phenomenon? • developing good practice? • empowering a social group? • contributing to personal or professional self-development?

Aims (the basic reasons for conducting the research)

Near the beginning of any research report there ought to be a fairly succinct summary of the aims of the investigation. These should take the form of broad statements about the overall goals of the research – the target it hopes to achieve. Normally, the aims consist of general statements that incorporate phrases like:

- to analyse the relationship between . . .
- to describe the incidence of . . .
- to critically examine the concept of . . .
- to test the hypothesis that . . .

The number of aims contained within any single piece of research should be kept relatively small. There might just be one aim, but more usually there are three or four aims. The three or four will not normally be parallel in terms of their importance. If they were, it would suggest that three or four almost separate topics were to be investigated, which could prove to be unduly complex in terms of its operation and analysis. It is better practice for the aims to be *hierarchical*, with the first one being the overall main aim and the subsequent two or three developing from this initial aim – focusing on specific instances or refining in some other ways the nature of the investigation.

Research questions (the specific things that will be studied: the 'measurables')

The research questions should draw upon a review of the existing literature. The exact questions to be investigated will relate to what is already known about the topic and will address one or more of the issues arising from a review of the research results that already exist. For this reason, the research questions tend to be presented in full after the literature review and before the methods section in a report. This follows the logic that precise details of what is to be investigated (the research questions) should emerge from a study of what is already known (the literature review) and be investigated in a suitable manner (methods section).

Research questions specify exactly what is to be investigated. They are not the broad goals of research (as outlined in the *aims*). They are things that are directly investigated by the research – specific things that are to be observed, measured, interrogated in order to shed light on the broader topic. From the researcher's point of view, this means that the ideas and concepts that form the backdrop to the research need to be 'operationalized'. The researcher needs to identify specific things that can be used as 'indicators' of the ideas or concepts, and these indicators need to exist in a form that can be observed or measured for the purposes of the research. So, for example, in the illustration below the general purpose of the research is to investigate the possibility of a 'mode effect'. The mode effect is a concept. It revolves around the idea that research tools, rather than being neutral, might have an impact on the findings; in practice, respondents might provide different answers depending on the mode of data collection that is used. This concept is operationalized by identifying 'observable' things that can serve as indicators of the mode effect – things that the researcher can 'measure' in order to arrive at conclusions about whether or not a mode effect exists. In this case the indicators are: (1) the number of words per response to open-ended questions; and (2) the responses to fixed-choice items on the questionnaire. These indicators can then be integrated into the research questions in a way that provides the reader with a clear understanding of exactly what data are to be collected and analysed in order to address the aims of the research.

Research questions can take a number of forms. They can, for example, consist of *hypotheses* that build upon previous theories and are deliberately formulated in a way that allows them to be tested. The possibility of proof/disproof is built into the whole notion of an hypothesis. It takes the form 'If (theory X) is true, then (under conditions Y) we might expect to find (result X).' The test of the hypothesis 'If . . ., then . . .' lies in finding (or not finding) the expected outcome.

Not all styles of social research, however, lend themselves to the use of hypotheses in the strict sense of the word. Indeed, it is probably fair to say that most approaches to social research present their research questions in a rather less rigorous format than the classic hypothesis. In many cases, the research question is still referred to as a 'hypothesis' even when it does not fulfil the strict conditions for a true hypothesis. These are generally research *propositions*. Propositions do not set out precise findings that are to be found (or not found) in support of the theory but they do specify certain basic conditions underlying the approach of the research and they do point towards some general area of findings that might be expected.

Hypotheses and propositions are suited to those styles of research which are involved with prediction of the results and with explaining the causes of phenomena. Where researchers have other purposes, such as evaluation or critique, they tend to feel less comfortable with the idea of establishing hypotheses or propositions in relation to their research. Instead, they prefer to use *specific research questions*. The emphasis continues to be on detail and direction. The specific research questions are expected to provide a picture of exactly what is to be investigated and to give a full, precisely detailed, account of the nature of the work that is to be undertaken.

Some approaches to social research, such as 'grounded theory' and qualitative research, are wary about the specification of research questions in the form of hypotheses or propositions – at least at the initial stages of research. Such approaches regard the purpose of social research as the *discovery* of social theory rather than the *testing* of social theory. Research whose main purpose is description or discovery is less amenable to the provision of clear-cut testable statements at the outset. However, even here good research depends on having a clear vision of the aims of the investigation and the salient issues that the researcher would hope to probe. Certain broad issues and agendas can operate as a starting point and, while they do not close down the options and force the researcher away from the preferred path of discovery, can provide a benchmark against which the research can be evaluated.

Outcomes from the research (the end-products that are anticipated as a consequence of conducting the research)

The word 'purpose' involves the notion of doing something specifically with a target or end-product in mind. The purpose of an activity automatically directs attention to the outcome of the action and the way it relates to the activity in question. There is the idea of something being a means to an end – a rational action designed to produce a specific outcome. It is reasonable, then, that the purpose of research ought to include some reference to the kind of end-product that it is envisaged will result from the investigation.

Outcomes, in this sense, are not the same thing as results or findings, and it is important to recognize the distinction. Results or findings are based on the analysis of the data that has been collected. Outcomes refer to the outputs from the research – the things that are produced by the research which are part of the overall purpose for doing the investigation in the first place. They can take the form of:

a body of new information	}	Facts
a contribution to theory and knowledge clarification of concepts or issues	}	Theoretical development
answers to a practical problem recommendations or guidelines for good practice	}	Applied knowledge
publications such as reports, articles, books other dissemination of findings (e.g. research home page on the web)	}	Communication

Describing the purpose of research

There are differences across the disciplines in terms of how rigidly researchers are expected to adhere to standardized ways of describing the purpose of their research but the example below provides an indication of the kind of content and style that might broadly be expected. The research topic used for the example is that of 'web-based questionnaires'. A review of the research literature on Internet surveys reveals that surveys using web-based questionnaires tend to be cheaper and faster than surveys using conventional paper questionnaires. There would seem to be good reasons, then, for researchers to shift from the use of paper questionnaires to the use of web-based questionnaires. However, the literature also points to some method-ological issues that need to be considered by researchers if they are thinking of making this change. One of these is a concern that respondents might give different answers depending on the kind of questionnaire used – paper or web-based. New research intended to provide evidence on the possibility of such a 'mode effect' might have its purpose expressed as shown in Box 1.2.

Box 1.2 Describing the purpose of a research project – an example

Aims

- To examine the implications for social research of using the Internet to collect survey data.
- To investigate the existence of a mode effect linked to the use of web-based questionnaires distributed via the Internet.
- To assess the reliability of web-based questionnaires in the context of social surveys using the Internet.

Research questions

- Do matched samples of respondents completing near identical question-naires in different modes produce the same findings?
- In terms of qualitative data, is there a significant difference in the mean length of responses to open-ended questions produced by web-based questionnaires compared with the data produced by paper-based question-naires? (Do web-based questions produce longer or shorter answers to open-ended questions?)
- In terms of quantitative data, is there a significant difference in the answers to fixed-choice questions on web-based questionnaires compared with identical questions on paper-based questionnaires? (Do respondents supply different answers depending on which type of questionnaire they complete?)

Outcomes

- A contribution to methodological knowledge relating to the use of Internet surveys and the use of web-based questionnaires.
- Dissemination of this knowledge through publications in refereed journals and the presentation of findings at local and national conferences.
- Development of a research web-site allowing wide access to details about the background of the project, the researchers' expertise, and various findings from the research.
- Creation of a web-based resource to enhance knowledge transfer and communication between researchers in this field.

How precise can statements of purpose be at the start of the research?

For those social researchers who prefer to model their investigations on the traditional scientific approach (positivists and those using quantitative data), there is a presumption that the researcher should be able to be very precise and detailed about the purpose of the enquiry right at the outset – before any data are actually collected. On the basis of existing knowledge, previous theories and established methods, the researcher is expected to be able to say in advance exactly what will be investigated, for what reason and using what data.

Now there are obvious benefits to this approach. Everyone should be clear about the scope of the investigation and, from this, the time, the numbers and the costs involved in conducting the research. Before the investigation proper gets under way, the proposal for research can be evaluated by experts to see if it deserves support. And after the completion of the research, people can refer back to the original purpose and make judgements about how well the research findings match the intentions of the researcher at the beginning of the project.

There are styles of social research, however, where it might seem inappropriate to expect such precision of purpose. Research that is more exploratory and that uses qualitative data does not lend itself as readily, if at all, to the expectation that the researcher should be willing and able to be absolutely precise about the direction and scope of the investigation at the outset. Where the research is more exploratory, setting out on a journey of discovery in which the researcher follows up leads and avenues of enquiry as they emerge during the course of the investigation, it becomes effectively impossible to be precise at the start about exactly when, how many, who and what will be included in the study. Glaser and Strauss's (1967) 'grounded theory' approach tends to be referred to widely as the rationale behind the alternative approach, which argues that not only is it difficult for some styles of research to map out in advance exactly what their investigation will entail, to do so would actually stultify the research by channelling it in one direction and blinding it to the discovery of the unexpected.

 Caution

Exploratory and descriptive types of social research do not sidestep the need to provide a statement of purpose for the research (Mason 2002; Creswell 2007). It might mean that the researcher can be less specific about the design of the research, the route it may take and the exact numbers involved, but it does not absolve the researcher from the need to spell out in advance an agenda for research and some reasonably precise intentions concerning the scale and timing of the investigation.

Guidelines for good practice

Some people will have a burning desire to investigate a particular thing. For them, the purpose is self-evident and straightforward. A vested self-interest might see them selecting a topic for research that has a personal pay-off. Others will want to undertake research in a particular area because the findings are perceived as solving a practical problem – for example, something connected with their employment. Or, knowing something about previous research in an area, the person might be spurred on by what they can see is a gap in existing knowledge and the need to fill that gap. Whatever the initial reason for being interested in a particular area for research, there are some crucial factors that the researcher needs to bear in mind when proceeding to identify the purpose of a research project.

The purpose of the research needs to be suitable

Researchers should be able to respond positively to questions about purpose of their research. They should be able to argue that the choice of topic addresses particular theoretical issues or that it meets specific practical needs. But, more fundamentally, they should also be able to defend the nature of the overall research project as something that is suitable for investigation:

- The purpose needs to be appropriate for investigation using social research methods.
- There needs to be some element of originality in the purpose.
- The purpose should reflect what is feasible in terms of the available facilities (time and resources) and access to necessary sources of data.

Good social research calls for a clear and precise vision of the purpose of the research

This vision is needed at the beginning of the research because, without it, the research will lack direction and it will be difficult to get an appropriate research design. This need applies as much to qualitative research as to quantitative research, and as much to interpretivist research as positivistic research.

- The purpose needs to be specific and focused (not vague or too broad).

Statements about the purpose of the research need to be explicit and prominent in any report on the research

Having a clarity of purpose is one thing, conveying it to the audience for research is another. Not only does good research rely on having a clear purpose in mind, it also depends on declaring that purpose to the readers and encapsulating it in a way that is easily identifiable and recognizable. The purpose of the research, to this end, needs to be packaged appropriately. The conventions can vary slightly according to the discipline and style of the research involved but it is fair to say that the purpose is generally described in relation to:

- the *aims* of the investigation;
- the specific *research questions* to be investigated;
- the type of *outcomes* emerging from the investigation.

The purpose of research needs to tie in closely with the research design and the outcomes

A research project needs to be presented as a coherent package in which the purpose (to forecast, explain, criticize, etc.) matches the design and the anticipated end-product of the investigation. The components need to be consistent and integrated. So, for example, if the primary purpose of the research is to develop good practice, then an action research approach would fit nicely and the production of guidelines for good practice would be an appropriate outcome from the research.

Further reading

Creswell, J.W. (2009) *Research Design: Qualitative, Quantitative, and Mixed Methods Approaches*, 3rd edn. Thousand Oaks, CA: Sage, Chapters 6–7.
Green, J. and Browne, J. (2005) *Principles of Social Research*. Maidenhead: Open University Press, Chapter 3.
Leedy, P.D. and Ormrod, J.E. (2005) *Practical Research: Planning and Design*. Upper Saddle River, NJ: Prentice Hall, Chapters 2–4.
White, P. (2009) *Developing Research Questions*. Basingstoke: Macmillan.

Checklist for PURPOSE

When considering the purpose of the research you should feel confident about answering 'yes' to the following questions: ☑

1   Has the purpose of the research been clearly described within the:
    Aims?   ☐
    Research questions?   ☐
    Outcomes?   ☐

2   Is there a clear statement about which one or more of the following purposes the research is trying to achieve:
    Forecast some outcome?   ☐
    Explain the causes or consequences of something?   ☐
    Criticize or evaluate something?   ☐
    Describe something?   ☐
    Develop good practice?   ☐
    Empower a particular group?   ☐

3   Have the research questions been specified in one of the following formats (appropriate for the style of research):
    Hypotheses?   ☐
    Propositions?   ☐
    Specific questions?   ☐
    Issues or agenda?   ☐

4   Is there a clear link between the purpose of the research, the design of the research, and the outcomes?   ☐

5   Does the purpose of the research:
    Lend itself to investigation through conventional methods of social research?   ☐
    Offer something new and original?   ☐
    Fit within the available resources?   ☐
    Accord with ethical standards?   ☐

© M. Denscombe, *Ground Rules for Social Research*. Open University Press.

2

RELEVANCE

Ground rule: **Research should be related to existing knowledge and needs**

Questions: What is to be gained from the research?

Is the research of any significance? So what?

Answers: The research is worthwhile because it makes a contribution to the development of existing knowledge and/or addresses specific practical needs.

A review of the relevant literature shows that the research addresses important gaps in existing knowledge.

There is a crushing question that can be put to researchers about their work. It is remarkably simple, but it can be equally devastating. It is the question 'So what?' Contained in these two words there is the suggestion that the research might be trivial, unimportant and inconsequential, and the question implies that the world might gain nothing from the work. Of course, these are implications that researchers should be anxious to reject. After all, research takes time and money. It often involves participation and help from other people and depends on their good will. There are personal and financial costs for researchers and others whose support and cooperation are required. People have the right, therefore, to ask why the research is being conducted and what is to be gained from the research.

Answers to such questions normally depend on demonstrating that the research is of *relevance* to things that matter. Specifically, good research should be able to demonstrate its relevance in terms of:

- *Existing knowledge*. In this case, the research can be justified as worthwhile to the extent that it contributes something to existing theories, ideas or information – in some way, however modest, extending the boundaries of knowledge. This is sometimes referred to as *'pure research'*.
- *Practical needs*. The value of conducting the research, equally, might be the way it addresses practical problems. Its findings could be of particular relevance where there is a problem that needs solving or an issue that needs clarification. As *'applied research'*, the research could well produce recommendations in relation to things like organizational rules and practices, social policies or agendas for change.
- *The timeliness of the research*. All kinds of social research can lay claims to being more worthwhile if their findings deal with matters that are of relevance to current concerns. This may not be absolutely essential, but where researchers can demonstrate that their research meets needs that are of special importance at that particular time, there is an extra dimension to the research which makes it all the more worthwhile.
- *The researcher's personal agenda*. It can be argued that the research is worthwhile not only in terms of its potential to enhance existing knowledge and address practical needs but also through the way it fits in with the interests and abilities of the researcher. The value of the research, in this sense, can be gauged by what it does for the person who conducts the research and what perceived benefits there are for him or her.

The need for clarity about the relevance

Social researchers differ in the extent to which they believe that existing knowledge, practical problems or personal interest ought to provide the springboard for research. Some would expect research topics to emerge from a careful reading of existing research knowledge with a view to identifying gaps in the knowledge which need to be investigated. Others would expect the research to be initiated to meet the needs of society and to address current issues of policy and practice. Still others would adopt a more relaxed attitude to the origins of the research topic, placing more emphasis on the right of the researcher to focus on things that are of personal interest. However, although there are these divergences about where the idea comes from – existing knowledge, practical need, personal inspiration – there is agreement that when it comes to the investigation itself, researchers need to be aware of how the investigation ties in with other work that has been done in the area. Without this there is the danger that the research might:

- unnecessarily repeat work that has already been done;
- miss useful ideas and practices already developed elsewhere;

- miss the opportunity to criticize earlier work and reveal the shortcomings of alternative approaches.

Having a clear idea of how their work fits into, and is shaped by, the context of ideas and practices within which it occurs is of obvious benefit for those who conduct the research. Equally, though, the users of the research stand to gain much by being presented with clear statements about the relevance of the research. It allows those who read the research to get a feel for the approach that is being adopted and its underlying assumptions. They should be able to see what values and what vision of social research are being used. They should also become aware of which sources of published research have been influential. Both things put the reader in a better position to evaluate the research and arrive at judgements about whether the research is well conceived, is fairly conducted and achieves its objectives.

Link up with **ACCOUNTABILITY**

Links with existing knowledge

The idea that research should provide an explicit account of how it is related to previous studies owes much to the model of scientific research that adopts a building-block approach to the development of knowledge. Each investigation, according to this model, should use the existing knowledge as its starting point and then build upon it. There is a nice orderliness to the process and an obvious rationale. Research should not waste time and resources by looking into areas where information already exists; there is no need to 'reinvent the wheel'. Researchers should start with what is already known and then proceed to build upon this in the spirit of scientific discovery – a spirit of progress, development, addition and contribution. There is a sense of *value-added* through research, forever pushing the frontiers of knowledge forward through the accumulation of more and more knowledge, using ever-refined methods and increasingly sophisticated theories.

This vision of research is not without its critics. It has been argued by some that it presents a rather over-simplified picture of the way that scientific knowledge actually progresses. Philosophers of science have debated whether, in fact, the progress of science has actually followed a smooth, incremental path or whether it has been characterized by periodic massive changes in its basic ideas about how the world operates – what Kuhn (1970) called 'paradigm shifts'. More radically, some people have argued that the whole idea of this orderly advancement is a myth and that a careful look at the history of scientific discoveries reveals that the accumulation of knowledge has actually been a very haphazard affair. The new discoveries that shape the development of scientific knowledge, according to writers like Feyerabend (1975), are rarely, if ever, the product of a building-block approach. They are the outcome, instead, of a rather anarchic and messy world of scientific discovery which, in practice, is riddled with inconsistencies and contradictions.

This critique has not caused the research community to abandon its commitment to the idea that good research uses existing knowledge as the basis for the design and direction of new research. What it *has* done is shift the emphasis from 'building upon' previous research to a stance that requires the researcher to demonstrate how the current research 'relates to' previous research. There is now a general acceptance that research should be *related to*, not simply built upon, existing knowledge. The past is not ignored. Indeed, it is regarded as crucial for understanding the roots of any piece of research and 'where it is coming from'. But rather than treating existing knowledge as a straitjacket constraining the nature and direction of any new research, it is regarded as a starting point which can be challenged and tested.

Significance in terms of practical needs

Social research can be driven by the desire to tackle some practical problem. Such 'applied' research responds to a need for action and change in relation to things like organizational rules, work practices and policy agendas, rather than being driven specifically by the needs of theory development. However, to justify such research as worthwhile, it is not sufficient simply to argue that it is aimed at a specific practical problem, and leave things at that. The problem itself needs to be placed in context.

- *The problem needs to be considered within the context of what is already known about similar problems.* Although this kind of research may not be theory-driven, it still needs to take into consideration the existing knowledge that might shed light on the nature of the problem, the appropriate ways of investigating it and the kinds of suggestions for change that might be successful.
- *The problem should be located within its social and historical environment.* Problems do not arise in a social vacuum. They reflect, to some extent, the culture and circumstances of the time. Some account is needed of how the problem came into existence and how it comes to be defined and perceived as 'a problem'.
- *The problem needs to be understood as 'one of a type' rather than totally unique.* The problem itself needs to be explained as part of a more general set of issues. Describing the particular aspects of a problem – its unique characteristics – is helpful to a degree but, in order to tackle the problem in some

way that will have implications beyond the individual case, the researcher needs to identify how the practical problem can be seen as part of a wider set of concerns and issues.

- *The significance of the problem needs to be established.* Based on the previous three points, a case should be made that the problem is one of some significance and that it is worth spending the effort, time and money to investigate. This does not mean that any problem that inspires social research has to be huge. Far from it, research can justifiably focus on problems that are of local concern (an organization, an area) and that might have fairly modest benefits if remedied. It is more a matter of establishing for whom the problem is important and in what respects it is significant.

Timeliness of the research

By virtue of appearing at just the right time, some research achieves more impact than other research. Quite separate from how well the research has been designed and conducted, research that takes place at an appropriate moment has an added dimension to it that serves to increase its value and make it all the more worthwhile. Such research is *'timely'*.

- *Research will be perceived as more worthwhile to the extent that it relates to matters that are high on the agenda of current concerns.* Research benefits from being able to demonstrate how its topic and approach fit with contemporary concerns. Such concerns might be things that have a high public profile dealing with social, health, political and economic concerns that hit the headlines and assume great importance for the public and politicians. Equally, they might be theoretical issues that have captured the attention of the research community and are of special concern for the time being. Being timely can be as true for 'pure' research as it can be for 'applied'. There are things to be investigated that emerge as high priority because of their implications for theory, ideas and information, and research in these areas can be just as timely in the way it meets the needs of the moment.
- *Research needs to be 'on time' and 'in time'.* Whereas being timely is something of a bonus, being poorly timed can be a disaster. Research that misses a golden opportunity to study a rare event is one example. Research whose findings are produced too late to be of any value is another. Research that is 'overtaken by events' and whose findings are rendered redundant, and research that becomes impossible to conduct because of a change in circumstances that are beyond the control of the researcher, are other examples of poorly timed research. Whatever the reason, such research is not likely to be seen as worthwhile.

Caution

This does not mean that, in order to qualify as worthwhile, all social research has to establish its credentials as meeting the needs of the moment. This is not the case. It is quite reasonable for research to be undertaken which deals with fundamental issues in a discipline or long-term concerns that do not relate to any particular, possibly fleeting, trend.

Personal interests of the researcher

This is a controversial item to include in a list of reasons to justify research as worthwhile. In a very practical sense, though, most social researchers become involved in research that centres on topics in which they have a particular interest. They choose topics that are of relevance to them in terms of:

- their own personal identity (e.g. age, sex, ethnicity);
- their social background (culture, religion, social class);
- their qualifications and career path (job-related issues, professional development);
- their personal biography (health, family, lifestyle, interests).

Link up with **PURPOSE**

Given the amount of personal effort and commitment that is demanded for the successful completion of research this is possibly no bad thing. But whether it is regarded as good or bad, there is one thing for sure: in reality, social researchers, particularly those doing small-scale one-off projects, tend to choose topics that are of relevance to them and to their own personal agendas. What makes the research worthwhile, in this respect, is the contribution of research for the researcher as a person, separate from any contribution it might also make to existing knowledge or practical needs.

Acknowledging the role of personal interests is controversial because it seems to run against the idea of the researcher as dispassionate and impartial. Some social researchers, particularly the more positivistic ones, would rather emphasize the objectivity of research and keep matters of personal identity, beliefs and predispositions as distant as possible from the process of collecting data and analysing the results. They would stress the need for scientific detachment. On the other hand, interpretivists tend to be more comfortable with the inclusion of the researcher's self as an inescapable factor in all social enquiry – an active ingredient in the collection and analysis of data. Indeed, some would go as far as to insist that some consideration of the researcher's background and values ought to be integrated into any account of the methods and analysis involved in the investigation.

Link up with **OBJECTIVITY**

 Caution

A word of warning is warranted at this point. The fact that research can be worthwhile in terms of its relevance for the researcher himself or herself is not, on its own, enough to justify research. It may well account for the choice of topic in the first place and it may well have a bearing on matters concerned with the data collection and interpretation which will need to be considered at some point in relation to interpretivist research. However, *for the purposes of research, it is the relevance in terms of existing knowledge and practical needs that need to take priority.* Establishing that the investigation is important in terms of what it means for 'me' the researcher, without also establishing how the research relates to existing knowledge and/or practical needs, will not satisfy most audiences.

Box 2.1 Relevance	
The key issue	**Things to be considered**
Does it really matter whether the research takes place?	• Will the research enhance existing knowledge about the topic (theories, ideas, information)? • Will the research address specific needs (practice, policy, recommendations, personal agenda)? • Will the research be timely in respect of current issues? • Will the research correspond with the personal agenda of the researcher?

The literature review

The literature review puts the research *in context.* To be more precise, it locates the research within the context of the published knowledge that already exists about the area that is being investigated. It demonstrates the relevance of the research by showing how it addresses questions that arise from a careful and considered evaluation of what has been done so far, and how the current research aims to 'fill in the gaps' or 'take things further' or 'do a better job than has been done so far'.

The literature review, then, uses the existing material as the basis for show-ing how the current research has *something valuable to offer*. For some researchers this can be a matter of *building upon* what has gone before, using the existing findings as a platform for deciding where to go and what new bits of knowledge are needed to move things forward. Other researchers concen-trate on identifying areas that have been overlooked so far and use the review of the literature to show that their research *fills a gap* in existing knowledge. And still other researchers adopt a *critical stance*, reviewing the existing material to show its inadequacies. Their literature review tries to point to the flaws in earlier investigations and to produce an argument that their research does a better job. Whichever approach the researcher takes, the literature review tends to serve four main functions. These are to:

1 *Identify the intellectual origins of the work*. The studies included in the literature review act like signposts telling readers which works are regarded as the most important intellectual roots of the research. This locates the research within the range of existing theories and practices and, at the same time, provides the opportunity to acknowledge the contribution of others and the way the current research has been influenced by the writings of other people.
2 *Show familiarity with existing ideas, information and practices related to the area of interest*. For research to have any credibility, there is a reasonable assumption that those conducting the research will have done some background preparation and have developed some proficient awareness of what counts as good practice and theory in the area of the investigation. Without necessarily purporting to be experts, researchers can be expected to know something about the main issues and debates in the field. The literature review provides the opportunity to demonstrate such familiarity and thus enhance the credibility of the research in the eyes of those who read it and who might be influenced by its findings. This is, of course, particularly important in connection with academic dissertations and research theses.
3 *Justify the choice of research topic and approach as necessary and timely*. A crucial purpose of the literature review is to justify the research as something that is worthwhile and valuable in terms of what it can contribute to the existing material. The contribution might be in terms of something practical or it might be something theoretical. Whatever it is, the literature review ought to demonstrate the *need for the research* and convince the reader that the research addresses an area that warrants investigation. As part and parcel of this, the literature review needs to argue the case that its contribution involves some element of *originality* and involves, in some way, something that has not already been done. It can also show how the research is *timely* in the sense that what it investigates and what it finds are of particular significance in relation to contemporary events.

Link up with **ORIGINALITY**

4 *Develop and refine the research questions and aims of the research.* Reviewing the work that has already been done by others allows the researcher to reach a decision about precisely what needs to be investigated. Moving from broad areas of interest, a review of the literature should channel the investigation towards a series of quite specific research questions. This is an important purpose of the literature review. Having looked at what is already available, the researcher should move beyond this and take things forward by noting focused, finite and feasible questions to investigate which will relate directly to the issues and debates in the broader field.

Link up with **PURPOSE**

> **Key point**
>
> *All* research can be linked with predecessors. Even if the idea for the research has been plucked out of thin air by the researcher in a moment of inspiration, and therefore is not an obvious building upon earlier theories, by the time the idea has been translated into a research project some consideration needs to have been given to how it fits in with established paths of research. It does not matter exactly how the idea for the research was conceived, before it comes to fruition the idea for the research needs to have been contextualized in terms of existing relevant knowledge.

Critically reviewing the literature

The business of critically reviewing the literature is one that calls for judgement and insight on the part of the researcher. To this extent, it is a creative exercise, not a mechanical chore. The success, or otherwise, of a literature review hinges on the latter of the two words – the review. The point is not just to identify the literature that is relevant to the topic of investigation. Nor is it just to describe the contents of these works. The key to success lies in doing more than these things. It calls on the researcher to do the following:

• *Identify the key sources of documented ideas, information and practices.* Reference should be made to the most important literature pertaining to the proposed research. This, of course, calls for a judgement, based on reading the literature, about what is relevant and what is important.

Initially such a judgement will be guided by expert opinion and the works that are most frequently cited. As things develop, researchers may need to make their own judgements – particularly where expert opinion is divided.

- *Evaluate the ideas, information and practices contained in the various works.* Providing a timid, sit-on-the-fence descriptive account of the literature is not really in keeping with the spirit of providing a review. It is obviously difficult for the newcomer to an area to criticize the experts but it is necessary nevertheless to arrive at conclusions about the relative merits and failings of alternative ideas and practices that are contained within the existing literature. The works need to be compared and contrasted.
- *Look for key issues and themes running throughout the works.*
- *Take a holistic view of the relevant literature to provide an overview of what it says to the researcher as a totality.* The review is not just about the contributions of each separate item but is about the relevant literature as a whole and what can be gleaned from it in terms of guiding the research.
- *Discuss how the research addresses issues, questions or needs identified through reviewing the existing literature.* This can include any neglected areas or ones seen as being addressed in a biased way.
- *Arrive at research questions, propositions, etc.* These should subsequently be used to shape the methods, the analysis and the discussion of findings as they appear in the research.

Key point

The literature review should not consist of a sequence of summaries of relevant published work. The review is more than a catalogue or inventory of items. The ultimate aim is to provide an *analysis* of the various components – not just a list of their contents.

Completing the literature review

The literature review paves the way for research. However, as Silverman (2005) argues, it is likely to continue as an activity during the rest of the research as well. Despite the assumption contained in many textbooks that the literature review should be completed and written up prior to the actual research, in practice, the literature review tends to continue for the duration of the enquiry. Newly published works need to be considered; new sources are discovered; different things become relevant as the research progresses. The result is that the literature review is not finally pulled together and put into shape until the writing-up phase of the research at the end of the project.

This does not mean, though, that research can be instigated without having already engaged with the relevant literature and gained some direction from having read around the subject. This is worth stressing. *Good research depends on good preparation and a cornerstone of this is familiarity with existing ideas and findings that have been published on the area of the proposed investigation.* What is at issue is the point at which there is some closure on the critique of the literature and the stage at which researchers produce their finalized review.

Box 2.2 The purposes of the literature review

To identify the contribution that can be made by the new research

Having reviewed the *findings* from existing research, it should be possible to indicate how the new research might contribute to the existing research and debates. This contribution should be specified clearly and concisely as part of the conclusion to the literature review.

To justify the research approach that has been chosen

On the basis of reviewing the *theories and methods* previously used to study the topic it should be possible to draw conclusions about the approach that is likely to be best suited to the investigation. These should be summarized towards the end of the literature review.

To arrive at specific research questions

Having considered the relevant debates and their particular *focus* of attention, it should be possible to conclude that it will be valuable to conduct research into specific questions. The research questions are effectively the end-product of the literature review and should be stated explicitly at the end. They provide a platform for a discussion on how data on the specific questions will be collected and analysed (which is normally contained in the methodology section that follows on directly from the literature review).

The literature search

When conducting a literature review any researcher is faced with the task of identifying the relevant sources to include in the review. This is done through *the literature search*. Each discipline within the social sciences has its own specialist resources to help researchers to identify the relevant material and there is no point in the context of this book in attempting to list such resources. The list would be very extensive. It would also become out of date very quickly. There are, however, basically four ways of tracking down the published material on a specific topic and it is these routes for identifying the relevant publications that the researcher needs to be aware of.

Indexes, and the use of key words

For an index to be of any value, the researcher needs to have certain *key words* in mind that capture the essence of the topic he or she wishes to investigate. This calls for a clarity of purpose. Fuzzy thinking and a lack of clarity about the topic are likely to produce key words that are too broad to be of much value for a search or, at worst, key words that are simply irrelevant. Neither helps the quest to identify existing published works that will guide the enquiry in a useful direction. Having given considerable thought to the matter, the researcher should be able to approach indexes armed with four to six key words, preferably in some hierarchical order of importance in relation to the area of enquiry. Suitably prepared, the researcher is then able to make the most from widely available resources such as library indexes and a whole host of databases available through the Internet.

Internet searches

The simplicity of conducting searches using the Internet makes it an attractive option for researchers. It can also be highly productive, opening up access to relevant literature on a global scale and including the latest research from a huge variety of sources. Of course, searching on the Internet illustrates the need for suitable key words. This will soon become apparent to anyone who tries a search that is not based on precise terms, as they become inundated with far too many hits to include or even look at. Internet searches are, in a sense, indiscriminate. They do not weed out the bogus or suspect material, they cannot make judgements about the quality of the sources that are reported by the search. Perhaps more than with the other methods of identifying key sources, which have already been vetted through the conventional publishing procedures, Internet sources come with no guarantees about the accuracy of their arguments or research findings. Consequently, they need to be used with caution.

Bibliographies

Bibliographies, in the sense of compiled lists of books, articles and other sources, already exist for many subjects, and the researcher ought to check early on whether there is a bibliography already in existence which covers the topic that is to be investigated, or one very close to it. Libraries are the obvious place to check first, but the researcher can also look out for more specialist 'in-house' bibliographies compiled for the purpose by colleagues working in an organization or possibly by tutors where the research is to be undertaken as part of an academic course.

References

A useful way of identifying key sources is to follow up references in books and articles to other works – works that would appear to be particularly important and relevant. The discussion within the original source will be likely to pinpoint certain sources as being significant and the researcher can pursue these by using the *references* section in that article or book to locate and retrieve the sources. It should soon become apparent that a relatively small number of sources are referred to frequently. These can be taken to be significant works in the field and ones that have been influential in terms of their findings and arguments. Even if they are consistently criticized by those who refer to them, they are evidently considered to be important enough to warrant attention and should, therefore, be included in the array of key sources – included not so much for what they advocate but as signposts for discredited ideas or bad practice. There is obviously an element of judgement on this score to be exercised by the researcher in the way he or she interprets such key works.

How many sources?

The literature search is liable to reveal a large number of potential sources that could be included in the literature review and the researcher is always faced with the problem of deciding how many to include from the huge volume of material that might be available on the topic. There is no formula that can be applied to all cases on this matter.

One criterion for deciding the appropriate number to include is the nature of the research and the purpose for which it is conducted. Expectations will differ according to the context, and the numbers can range from a few to over 100 sources. Research that has been conducted to meet an immediate practical problem – for example, as part of a short in-house action research project – might include only a small number of items and, in any reports arising from the investigation, might place little emphasis on the background literature or the ideas that shaped the enquiry. At the other end of the continuum, a PhD thesis will be expected to contain a detailed and extensive literature review. This is where it is not unusual for the literature review to cover more than 100 sources. In between, there are journal articles and technical reports that will, as a very broad guideline, cover somewhere between 5 and 30 sources, depending on the nature of the journal. It should be stressed, though, that such figures are not presented as concrete targets to be aimed for but as 'ball-park' figures that reflect the number of sources that researchers tend to cover. What could be said is that a social science PhD that included a literature review covering just ten items would be unlikely to prove satisfactory to the examiners. By contrast, most editors of journals and executives of companies would not appreciate research reports containing a detailed literature review of 100 sources; constraints of space in a brief report and the time taken to read such a review would make it inappropriate.

Guidelines for good practice

Good research can justify itself as being worthwhile by demonstrating its relevance to theoretical issues or practical problems. Researchers need to ensure that their research does not get criticized as trivial and inconsequential, and the following guidelines can help in this respect.

Make the connections with other work in the field early on in the planning and design of the research

Even if the research question comes 'out of thin air' in a moment of personal inspiration, the task for the researcher is to locate work that has already been done in the area: (1) to make sure the proposed investigation does not simply copy something that has already been done; and (2) to identify how the proposed research compares and contrasts with the other work in the field. Good research should always be aware of how it connects with theories, practices and problems that already exist.

Demonstrate the relevance of the research in an explicit manner

It is the duty of researchers to make sure that readers of the research are left in no doubt that the research they are reading addresses particular areas that are of interest, particular topics that are of significance and specific issues that are of importance. Researchers need to show how their work relates to things that matter, and it is in this sense that good research calls upon researchers to *demonstrate* the relevance of their work. The relevance should never be taken for granted; it should never be assumed to 'speak for itself'.

Be clear about the kind of relevance that is most important for the research

It is quite feasible for the research to involve more than one kind of relevance, but it helps both the researcher and the reader of the research reports if there is clarity about where the focus of attention lies. It helps to be clear whether the relevance is mainly concerned with:

- a contribution to knowledge;
- meeting urgent and timely requirements;

- having potential for practical applications;
- fitting the researcher's personal agenda.

Use a preface to link the research topic to your personal biography

The *preface* provides a place to make a statement about the way the research links with personal experience, expertise and interests. It can be used to include some information and views about how the researcher's background and self-identity link with the research. Readers benefit by being allowed to know something about the researcher, and this might inform their subsequent evaluation of the research. Being a separate preamble to the main research report, this short personal statement can satisfy the interpretivists' desire to know how the personal biography of the researcher links with the nature of the investigation while, at the same time, allowing the main body of the report to be presented more in line with the impersonal tone and formal style preferred by positivists.

Use the literature review to demonstrate how the research relates to existing theories, practices and problems

The literature review provides the conventional means by which the researcher is expected to show to the readership how the research is related to existing knowledge and practical problems. In a longer report the literature review might be a separate section or chapter. In shorter reports it might appear under a subheading or might simply form part of the introductory discussion.

Critically review the literature

It is important to avoid the trap of only listing a series of summaries of works. Their content may indeed be relevant, and the summaries might be accurate, informative and clear. The listing might show that the researcher has read the relevant material, however, what is required is something over and above all this. It is an analysis of the overall picture which highlights the main features and which provides insights about the strengths and weaknesses of the available knowledge on the topic. Ultimately, the review is about the totality of the works included rather than each separate piece.

Regard the literature search as an essential component of the research process

It is part of the research process itself and, like the data collection procedures, the process should be:

- rigorous – the approach needs to be systematic and thorough;
- recorded – some details of the search should be logged for reference.

The number of indexes, catalogues, etc. that are searched and the eventual number of sources incorporated into the literature review will depend on both the scale of research and kind of topic that is being dealt with. There is no simple formula to tell researchers how many sources they ought to aim to include. The best advice on this point is to check on the number of sources that tend to be used in similar research reports and use this as guidance.

Citing works

The works that have been used as sources of ideas and information relating to the research must always be cited appropriately. They must be cited in a fashion that carefully follows a recognized convention (e.g. Harvard system, numerical system).

Further reading

Bell, J. (2005) *Doing Your Research Project: A Guide for First-time Researchers in Education, Health and Social Science*, 4th edn. Maidenhead: Open University Press, Chapters 4–6.

Fink, A. (2005) *Conducting Research Literature Reviews: From the Internet to Paper*. Thousand Oaks, CA: Sage.

Hart, C. (1998) *Doing a Literature Review: Releasing the Social Science Research Imagination*. London: Sage.

Neville, C. (2007) *The Complete Guide to Referencing and Avoiding Plagiarism*. Maidenhead: Open University Press.

Ridley, D.D. (2008) *The Literature Review: A Step-By-Step Guide for Students*. London: Sage.

Rumsey, S. (2008) *How to Find Information*, 2nd edn. Maidenhead: Open University Press.

Checklist for RELEVANCE

When considering the relevance of the research you should feel confident about answering 'yes' to the following questions: ☑

1   Does the research have clear relevance in
    terms of at least one of the following:
    Existing knowledge? ☐
    Practical needs? ☐
    Its timeliness? ☐
    The researcher's personal interests? ☐

2   If the research is 'knowledge-driven', does it
    aim to do one or more of the following:
    Build upon previous research? ☐
    Fill a gap in what is already known? ☐
    Show the inadequacies of previous research? ☐

3   If the research addresses specific practical needs or
    problems, does it do one or more of the following:
    Incorporate knowledge about similar problems? ☐
    Place the problem in its social and historical context? ☐
    Identify the general characteristics of the problem? ☐
    Highlight the significance of the problem? ☐
    Lead to specific recommendations? ☐

4   If the research is driven by the personal interests of
    the researcher, does it reflect one or more of the following:
    Personal experience? ☐
    Social background? ☐
    Professional development? ☐

5   Does the literature review:
    Identify key texts? ☐
    Identify themes in the literature? ☐
    Provide an overview of the literature? ☐
    Evaluate the literature? ☐
    Arrive at precise research questions? ☐

6   Has the literature search:
    Identified the most appropriate databases, etc.? ☐
    Revealed a suitable number of relevant sources? ☐

3

FEASIBILITY

Ground rule: Research should be tailored to fit the resources available

Questions: Is the research feasible in terms of the available resources?

Will it be completed on time?

Answers: The scale of the research reflects the resources available for the project.

The scope of the enquiry reflects the opportunities for access to relevant data.

The planning of the research has taken into account both the deadline for completion and the amount of researcher-time available for work on the project.

Money is important when it comes to doing research. It is, however, not the only resource that needs to be taken into consideration. *Time* is another crucial factor. Deadlines limit the time available for collecting and analysing the data and impose a finite time resource within which the research needs to operate. In this sense, time impacts on the design of the research and has a direct bearing on the methodology to be used. *Good will* from people who are called upon to provide information or allow access to sources of information is another resource factor that goes beyond simple matters of money. And then there is the time and effort put into the research by the person who conducts the investigation and by those whose cooperation is needed at various times during the stages of data collection and analysis. There is an *opportunity cost* for all these people – the value of what they might have been doing during the time they were actually involved in the research and contributing to its completion.

Bearing these points in mind, research design involves more than simply choosing the best possible approach to the topic. In the real world, good research is a matter of choosing the best possible approach *within the given resource constraints*. It is a matter of what is realistically possible rather than what is desirable in an ideal world.

Link up with **DESIGN**

Money

The question of money does not figure as prominently as it ought to in considerations of research methods. Perhaps it is regarded as rather tacky to consider money when hacking at the frontiers of knowledge. Yet money is, and always has been, a fundamental consideration. It sets parameters to the scale and scope of an investigation. And the absence of funding can make it impossible to carry out certain kinds of research in the social sciences.

The costs of conducting research, of course, will vary according to the nature of the research that is being conducted. Experiments conducted in a laboratory will incur the costs of specialist equipment and possibly expenses arising from the use of the laboratory itself. Surveys that involve the distribution of postal questionnaires need funding for the printing and distribution of the questionnaires. Longitudinal research will carry a lot of administrative costs to allow for the investigation to be pursued over a long period of time. Ethnographic research might require little by way of equipment or administrative overheads, but require the funding of travel and release from some employment to allow the fieldwork to be conducted.

The costs will also reflect the scale of the investigation that is being undertaken. Research conducted by a single researcher operating alone, using interviews with informants who live locally, will obviously cost less than research conducted by a commercial team covering informants located throughout the country, where there will be greater travel, administrative and salary costs to be met. Research that involves the use of ten focus groups will cost less than that which uses 60 focus groups. Observation that uses video equipment and high-specification software for recording and analysing the data will cost a lot more than that which uses observation schedules filled in by researchers using pens and clipboards.

For larger-scale social research the major expenses tend to revolve around the salaries of research workers, the costs of equipment and the costs of office accommodation. These can add up to a large sum, even for a fairly modest project employing two research workers over one year. Coupled with overheads (covering office accommodation, etc.), some travel costs, materials and the printing normally associated with survey research, it would not be surprising for funding estimates to be around £150,000 (at 2009 prices). If the research involves the purchase of equipment, the costs could rise still further.

Small-scale project research does not often involve the employment of assistants specifically to help with the research, and consequently tends to avoid many of the major costs. There are, however, a variety of other costs linked with research which still need to be taken into account. The following list contains items that are very likely to be used in order to conduct small-scale research – and each costs money.

- phone calls;
- Internet connection;
- computer equipment and consumables;
- specialist computer software (e.g. statistics package, qualitative data analysis software);
- services such as transcription or computer data preparation;
- photocopying;
- stationery (paper, envelopes, pens);
- postage;
- printing of questionnaires and/or reports;
- special equipment (e.g. voice recorder, transcription machine).
- inter-library loans for books or articles;
- travel to and from the research site;
- conference fees.

For the small-scale researcher some of these costs can be 'lost'. The researcher will be able to obtain the materials or services by means that do not require direct payment. Research that is conducted as part of an academic course or as part of action research within an organization might well 'lose' the costs of things like computer software, special inter-library loans and photocopying, where, effectively, the institution picks up the bill. A number of costs never get specifically itemized because they blend with facilities that are part of everyday costs at work and home (e.g. phone, computers, pens, paper). Strictly speaking, however, they remain the real costs of conducting research.

Time

Time estimation

Researchers need to make some reasonable estimate of how much time they are to spend on research over a given period of time. There is always a limit to the time a researcher is willing and able to devote to his or her investigation and this amount puts boundaries on the scale and scope of the research that is possible. In practice, this generally means arriving at a decision about the average number of hours a week that will be devoted to research work over a specified period of months or years. Full-time career researchers might plan on over 40 hours a week as a full working-week commitment. For part-time researchers, the limit needs to be set realistically to allow for other work, domestic and leisure commitments that need to be crammed into a busy life.

Time planning

Estimating the number of hours of a researcher's time that will be involved in a research project is difficult. Planning is made more difficult because the demands of doing research are not always predictable and the demands can come in waves rather than at a nice even pace. In practice, it is rarely possible to stick to a set number of hours per week. One thing, in particular, can create peak demands on the researcher's time: fieldwork and the collection of some kinds of empirical data. Unlike data collection via libraries, databases or the Internet, research that involves collecting data 'on site' and 'from people' inevitably requires an element of fitting in with the situation and adapting to other agendas. The opportunity to collect the data can be dictated by things that cannot be negotiated or arranged to fit in with the preferred schedule of the researcher. Data collection in work organizations and schools, as an example, cannot be scheduled for the evenings to fit in with the needs of someone doing research part-time. The people and the events simply will not be there. As a result, the collection of data might need to be planned as a special block of time that can be balanced out at some other stage with a relatively light workload per week.

Time planning is vital to the successful completion of a research project, and this involves not just the amount of time to be devoted to it but also the sequence of events and the time-span of each component. Without careful attention to this the research is likely to miss its deadline. There are certain elements of time planning which are fairly common to social research projects and the suggestion in Figure 3.1, though it might need adapting to meet specific circumstances, provides some guidance on the things that need to be considered. It is, however, a very idealized and sanitized version of what actually takes place in a research project.

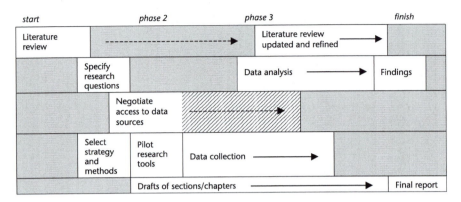

FIGURE 3.1 Time planning for small-scale research projects
Note: This scheduling does not depict the *volume* of work associated with the research; it deals with the *sequencing* of the work.

Example: Time planning for the data collection and analysis phases of research

The data collection and analysis phases of research can be quite complex in their own right and there is some value to planning the schedule of these in further detail. As Figure 3.2 indicates, where research uses multiple sources of data, care is needed to plan the collection and analysis phases for each. If, for example, the research wants to focus on the impact of a change in government policy on a particular organization, there might be five relevant sources of data. The government policy itself would warrant study. And then within the organization, evidence of the impact might be detected through the minutes and decisions of boards and committees, as well as in the experiences of senior management and of employees. The views of clients could also be added to the list of valuable sources of data. Each of the five data sources requires a degree of separate planning when it comes to data collection. There might also be a need to collect the data in an appropriate sequence to maximize the benefit gained from the separate strands. Bearing such points in mind, Figure 3.2 illustrates the kind of time planning that could be necessary for such an investigation.

1. *Government* *policies*	Identify key policies	Analyse key policies				Update and check on policies	
2. *Documents in* *the* *organization*	Identify relevant committee minutes and decisions	Content analysis of the documents					Update and check on organizational position
3. *Senior* *management*		Design and pilot an interview schedule	Conduct interviews	Transcribe and analyse interviews	Feedback and corroboration		
4. *Employees*			Design and pilot an interview schedule	Conduct interviews	Transcribe and analyse Interviews	Feedback and corroboration	
5. *Clients*				Design and pilot a questionnaire	Administer the questionnaire	Analyse the questionnaire results	

Data sources

FIGURE 3.2 Example of time planning for the data collection and analysis

Access to data

Data sources are a vital resource for successful research. Gaining access to documents, people, places and events is, indeed, a prerequisite for research, because a researcher who cannot get access to relevant sources of information can only engage in speculation on the subject. The blunt fact is that without access to relevant data, research as such is not possible.

The first necessity is for the researcher to 'make contact' with the sources he or she wishes to use. The researcher needs to be able to *see* documents, *talk to* people, *visit* places, *witness* events. But for the purposes of research, access means more than just 'making contact'. Essential though this is, it is only part of the meaning. In the context of social research, access also carries with it a notion of 'getting permission'.

The researcher who uses *documentary sources* of data – books, official reports, etc. – might not find the matter of access too much of a problem. Where things are published and in the public domain, getting permission to use the material will not generally be necessary (provided that the sources are explicitly acknowledged). With the use of documentary sources access is likely to have far more to do with identifying whether particular sources exist, where they might be located and how to get hold of them.

Undercover research, such as some types of participant observation, can sidestep the need to get permission. If researchers do undercover research in which their identity as a researcher and the purpose of their contact are kept secret, then there is clearly no way in which permission can be obtained, at least not from those being directly investigated. In a formal setting, such as an organization, permission might be obtained from someone in a senior position for the researcher to do the undercover work with some unsuspecting group lower down the organization, but to seek permission from those directly involved would inevitably expose the researcher's true role.

For many kinds of social research, though, access to the sources of information requires getting formal authorization. When researchers undertake surveys or case studies, when they conduct experiments, when they do fieldwork for ethnography or action research, getting permission is particularly important. When researchers choose these strategies they need to be aware that access to sources may have as much to do with getting the OK from those in authority as it does with finding suitable people, places or events. And here, the cooperation of key people can prove invaluable. Broadly, these people are known as 'gatekeepers'.

Gatekeepers are people who can grant permission and allow access. In formal settings, they exercise *institutional authority* to permit or deny access. In the world of education, for example, access to a school requires permission from the headteacher and probably from the local education authority as well. With authorization to research in a school having been obtained, access to the staff will need approval from the headteacher and access to the pupils will require the approval of teachers and, possibly, parents and school governors. Each level of contact requires the approval of someone with the authority to allow access to the people and events from which the data will come.

Link up with **ETHICS**

Access to people, settings and documents is increasingly dependent upon another kind of institutional authority – the *Ethics Committee*. Medical research is governed by powerful medical ethics committees and social research that deals with health issues or is conducted under the auspices of the health service will normally be vetted by such committees before it is allowed to proceed. It is a formal requirement that is strictly observed. Research conducted by staff or students of universities is also likely to require approval from a research ethics committee, and every care should be taken to ensure that such formal permission is obtained where necessary.

In informal settings, gatekeepers can take on a slightly different role. They can act as *personal guarantors* who vouch for the bona fide status of the researcher. They use their informal status to act as a broker, an intermediary who cements the contact by vouching that the researcher is someone who can be trusted. They can 'oil the wheels' in making contacts and gaining cooperation.

Seeking permission to conduct research is not necessarily a one-off thing.

With some types of research, in particular, exploratory research using qualitative methods, it is unlikely that the researcher could state at the outset of research the precise nature and extent of access that will be required. Access might be needed to new people, different places and unforeseen events as new lines of enquiry become incorporated in the research. Under such circumstances the access ought properly to be regarded as a *continual process* (Hammersley and Atkinson 1983; Burgess 1984). The matter of getting permission tends to become a routine and ongoing feature of the research process rather than a one-off affair.

The significant role of gatekeepers means that there are good reasons to consciously cultivate a good relationship with them. In view of their special position it is important that they are well disposed to the research and have trust in the researcher. Basically, both the research programme and the researcher as a person need to have credibility in the eyes of gatekeepers. With this in mind, it is important that potential gatekeepers should be approached in a way that is sensitive to the likely anxieties they might have about granting permission for the research to be conducted. Organizational leaders will probably be anxious not to expose themselves to criticism and will want to ensure that the interests of those for whom they have responsibility are not adversely affected by the research. They will want to feel safe about the research.

Cooperation by participants

A great deal of social research relies on information collected *directly* from people, on people, about people. The use of interviews and questionnaires, for instance, relies on informants supplying answers to questions asked by the researcher. Experiments and observation, likewise, are techniques that depend on people having their actions directly monitored by researchers. In such situations people allow themselves to be the subjects of research and seem willing to give their time and effort to help the investigation. This cooperation is a vital resource for social research; it should not be taken for granted.

The thoughtful researcher, recognizing this point, might then ponder the question: What motivates people to collaborate with social researchers? They might ask themselves why anyone should *willingly* participate in social research, why people should supply information to researchers or let themselves be observed. Well, to such questions there are four answers.

Obligation

Some of the data which social researchers use is collected and compiled by other people who have some statutory rights in terms of obliging people to supply the data. In the matters of the registration of births and deaths, the completion of income tax returns, etc. members of the public are under a legal duty to supply the information. Researchers, however, do not hold the power to oblige people to supply information. They are not like Customs and Excise or the police, who can oblige people to reveal certain types of information. Researchers can only *request* information.

Incentives

Under certain circumstances, people can be motivated to participate in research because there is some tangible reward on offer. Market research companies often offer people small amounts of cash or vouchers as some compensation for the time and effort respondents put into supplying completed questionnaires or attending focus group discussions. It is not payment as such because the amounts are not enough to make it worthwhile for its own sake. The money and vouchers, however, act as a token of thanks and a subtle way of motivating the respondents not to back out. With questionnaire surveys, another way of introducing an element of incentive is to enter all responses into a prize draw, offering the prospect for the lucky winner of some large prize such as a new car or a holiday.

Encouraging people to participate by offering them money can be controversial. Some experts would argue that paying respondents can compromise the research by causing biased responses. The belief is that paying people encourages them either to provide answers they believe are wanted by the researcher or to provide answers simply to complete the task and claim the reward rather than concentrating on giving accurate information. In contrast, there is also evidence that payments can increase response rates and, as Thompson (1996: 4) concludes, 'the dangers of making payments to respondents can be outweighed by the gains'. Things would seem to depend on the circumstances and the amount of payment offered.

For the small-scale researcher, however, the possibility of being able to offer monetary incentives are slim. The funding is unlikely to be available. There are, though, alternatives. Offering the participants something in return for their efforts can take the form of a promise to provide them with a copy of the final report. This might be considered an incentive simply because it will be nice for the participant to read the outcome of the investigation and to have a hard copy of the report to put on the shelf. On the other hand, a copy of the final report (or some other kind of feedback such as a presentation by the researchers about their conclusions) might be valued for the advice it might contain related to practical needs of the individuals or company that collaborated. Either way, something is given back in return by the researchers – something that might not fully compensate the participants for their efforts but which can, nonetheless, act as a tangible incentive.

Intrinsic rewards

The suppliers of information might have their own reasons for wishing to collaborate. It might be regarded as 'coming with the territory' as far as certain jobs are concerned – seen as a 'professional duty'. Alternatively, those who cooperate might simply find the experience rewarding. They might even have a particular interest in the success of the research and identify with the broader purpose of the research. If the research were in the area of health service provision, for example, the providers of the information might reasonably consider it in their own interest to supply full and accurate information as a means to improve their own treatment.

Trust and good will

Trust and good will are hidden resources that researchers use to improve their prospects of collecting valid information. This is because informants who trust the researcher and feel well disposed towards the aims of the investigation are more likely to supply information freely and openly without trying to hold back on certain areas through fear of how the information will be used. In essence, where trust and good will exist, the information collected by the researcher is more likely to provide full and accurate data. Without them, where information is supplied begrudgingly and with suspicion about the researcher's motives, the quality of the data will suffer and the research might well grind to a halt.

The importance of trust and good will for research has been recognized for a long time. However, in the twenty-first century there are signs that researchers will need to treat them as an ever more precious resource and will need to work harder than in the past to *establish* an atmosphere of trust and good will. As the 'information society' develops, people are likely to become increasingly tired and resentful of persistent requests for information about themselves and their lifestyles. The sheer volume of requests for information from all corners is likely to make people *'research weary'*, and therefore less likely to participate or collaborate with any spirit of enthusiasm. Indeed, the burden might make them less likely to collaborate at all.

Potential informants are also likely to become more *'research wary'* – suspicious about the motives of researchers and the way the information they supply will be used. There is likely to be a growing cynicism as the term 'research' gets hijacked by companies using it as a cover for selling things. The intrusive phone call at home on behalf of a 'market research' company that turns out to be a thinly disguised ploy to sell things like life insurance, double glazing or a time-share apartment in the Algarve will only serve to heighten the public's resistance to requests for information. Genuine researchers are likely to be faced with a culture of resistance to giving information – a backlash which places a value on privacy and which challenges the right of researchers to ask questions and investigate issues.

Tactics to combat resentment and distrust, then, will need to feature prominently in the minds of social researchers operating in the information society. In the first instance, potential participants will want to feel that they can trust the researcher to act in an honourable and professional manner. They will want to feel assured that their interests will not be harmed in any way through cooperation with the research. Guarantees about anonymity and the confidentiality of data are likely to help in this respect – reassuring people that participation will not lead to embarrassing exposés or the disclosure of information that could be commercially or politically damaging. And would-be participants might also want some reassurances that the research is worthwhile and relevant – something they can relate to as being 'for a good cause'. In all this, much will depend on the ability of researchers to be sensitive to the needs and wishes of those whose cooperation is sought.

Link up with **ETHICS**

Box 3.1 Feasibility	
The key issue	**Things to be considered**
Can the research be done properly with the resources that are available?	• Is there sufficient *time* for the design of the research, collection of data and analysis of results? • Will the available *resources* cover the costs of the research (e.g. travel, printing, etc.)? • Will it be possible and practical to gain *access* to necessary data (people, events, documents)?

Researcher's self as a resource

Physical and psychological danger

The researcher, as a person, is a resource that is easy to overlook when it comes to the process of undertaking research. Yet, like other resources involved in the collection and analysis of data, the researcher is a resource that needs to be used carefully. He or she has limits and real boundaries that cannot be stretched infinitely and, for this reason, the researcher needs to be conserved – protected and used to best advantage throughout the course of any research project.

Conserving the researcher, in one sense, means protecting him or her from danger. The personal dangers of doing research will not leap out as a major concern for the vast majority of those starting a research project. However, it is not a concern that can be dismissed as irrelevant. As Lee (1993, 1995) points out, social researchers often work on their own. They will travel alone and meet with people they have not met before. Interviews are often conducted in private, in one-to-one situations, and possibly deal with sensitive topics. As Craig et al. (2000: 1) argue, such situations 'involve close social interaction between people in a private setting ... [and] depending on the particular situation, there are various components of risk for the professionals involved:

- risk of physical threat or abuse;
- risk of psychological trauma or consequences, as a result of actual or threatened violence, or the nature of what is disclosed during the interaction;
- risk of being in a compromising situation, in which there might be accusations of improper behaviour;
- increased exposure to general risks of everyday life and social interaction: travel, infectious illness, accident.'

The safety of social researchers is a matter of growing concern. This does not necessarily reflect any increase in the chances of researchers being harmed in some way during the course of their work. What is driving it to the foreground is the fear of litigation by those who employ researchers. In the twenty-first century there is a legal obligation on employers to take reasonable steps to protect the health and safety of their employees. This means that potential risks can no longer simply be disregarded because they are quite unlikely to happen. They need to be taken into account and reasonable precautions need to be taken to safeguard researchers from the risks. The Social Research Association's *Code of Practice for the Safety of Social Researchers* argues that researcher safety should be a factor built into the design of the study, not tagged on as an afterthought (Social Research Association 2003).

Emotional involvement

As we saw in Chapter 2 on Relevance, a researcher's personal interest in the topic of research can be beneficial. However, it can also turn out to be dangerous if it starts to involve issues that the researcher finds it hard to cope with emotionally. Things like illnesses, addictions and divorces, for example, can act as a spur to research for those who have personal experience of the consequences. However, if the thrust of the investigation turns from wider issues towards personal reflection and introspection, the investigation might become too emotionally disturbing for the researcher to continue.

Another sense in which too much involvement can be harmful is in the way it can cause the investigation to dominate the researcher's life. Especially for those who do research part-time on top of other work/domestic responsibilities, the commitment to completing the investigation is likely to involve considerable pressure on time. This can prove hard enough to live with, but the problem can be compounded where the boundaries between the researcher-self and the everyday self begin to break down. Experienced researchers will be aware that the amount of time involved is not just a matter of the time actually devoted to conducting the research (fieldwork, library study, etc.) and to writing the report(s) of its findings. On top of 'doing' the research, there are the many occasions spent thinking about the research: sitting at traffic lights, lying in a bath, walking the dog. It can become an all-consuming passion or a dreadful burden – either way, impinging on other aspects of life and other people close to the researcher.

Researchers, then, need protecting; possibly from others but far more likely from themselves and their level of immersion in the project. Not enough attention is generally paid to this. Social research is very sensitive to protecting the interests of participants but, perhaps, equal attention should be paid to ensuring that researchers themselves are not harmed, physically or emotionally, by their experience of conducting research.

Box 3.2 Vital resources for social research

- *Money and facilities*: to conduct the data collection and analysis, and produce the necessary report.
- *Time*: amount of time required to conduct the research in terms of *working* hours and the *time-span* during which the research needs to be conducted.
- *Access to data*: the opportunity to gain access to sources, whether those be people, situations, events or documents.
- *Cooperation by participants*: good will and being prepared to sacrifice time to help to provide the data on which the research rests. Includes advisors, librarians, interviewees and those who fill in questionnaires.
- *Self*: The opportunity costs for the researcher (i.e. other things they could have spent their time on), the emotional costs and even the potential danger facing those who undertake social research.

Research quality and low budget research

Market research companies tell potential clients quite clearly that the quality and amount of information they receive, and the accuracy of that information, will depend on the amount of money the client can afford and how quickly the findings are needed. More money and more time will tend to buy better quality and more accurate information.

It is worth stressing, however, that there is no simple equation that says the more that is spent, and the longer the research takes, the better it must be. Or, vice versa, the quicker and cheaper the research is, the less dependable are its results. This is not necessarily the case. Good results can be obtained from low-cost research – sometimes achieving better results than far more expensive alternatives. Despite this, researchers who have more time or greater funding are generally able to exercise more choice over how they go about their work than those operating under tight budgets and short deadlines for completion. They will be expected, therefore, to produce research findings that can claim to be better in terms of things like their reliability, breadth of coverage or depth of investigation. Lower budget research, for its part, must operate with lower expectations.

There are two things that follow from this. First, the idea that lower budget, small-scale research needs to have lower expectations should not be taken as an excuse for producing poor quality research. What it *should* mean is that small-scale research needs to operate with lower expectations with respect to scale and scope of what it sets out to investigate. Researchers must tailor their ambitions to fit the amount of resources that are available. They must avoid hopelessly ambitious aims that cannot be achieved within the money and time-frame at their disposal. Second, small-scale researchers need to spell out to their audience the limitations imposed by the available time and money. They need to make the case that their research provides good 'value for money'. The resource limits, indeed, can be turned to advantage in the case of small-scale research by using the restricted resourcing as a means of establishing what it is reasonable – and what it is not reasonable – to expect as an outcome from the investigation. The limits on time and duration, rather than being seen as a measure of the research's inadequacy when stacked up against some vision of 'proper' or 'full' or 'perfect' research which might have been undertaken without restrictions of time or money in some perfect research world, should be presented as a routine factor affecting all social research and one that, in this instance, should be recognized as imposing certain specified limitations on the nature of the findings.

> **Key point**
>
> The quality of the research should be judged in relation to the resources available and the effectiveness with which those resources have been used to investigate the particular topic in question, not against some unrealistic notion of 'research with no constraints'.

Guidelines for good practice

An evaluation of possible approaches to the research should include consideration of the costs in terms of money, time and personal sacrifice

Decisions about the design and scale of a research project should be based on an estimation of the various resources that are available and the likely 'costs' associated with different strategies and methods. The research has to be *feasible*.

Decisions need to be made about the number of working hours that can be devoted to the activity of research and the period of time over which the research can be conducted

The researcher needs to address the crucial questions: Will there be enough time to conduct the research? Will the deadline permit an adequate period for the collection of data, the analysis of data and the writing of a report? Some basic time planning is essential in both respects, along with some attempt to calculate the likely number of hours work that will be involved.

A schedule of tasks should be produced covering the period of research

This will entail planning the main elements of the investigation and setting targets for the completion of a task in good time, bearing in mind that time is a resource that constrains social research just like money.

A clear statement needs to be made about the way the choice of research design reflects the constraints imposed by the available resources (and the way it should inform evaluations of the research)

Small-scale research projects do not need to feel too defensive about the fact that they have to operate on a low budget. However, what they do need to do is describe any particular *limitations* affecting the design and findings which the researcher feels ought to be brought to the attention of the reader.

Efforts should be made to foster good will and cooperation on the part of those controlling access to data

- *Try to cultivate contacts with the gatekeepers.* Whether these happen to be people with institutional authority or those with personal influence, they can prove to be especially valuable in terms of making the kind of openings on which research so often depends.
- *Be precise about the level and nature of commitment that is sought.* When seeking permission, the researcher should recognize that people will want to know what commitment they, and others involved, might be expected to make in terms of time and effort. The researcher should be prepared in advance to be as precise as is possible on such matters and this means there needs to be a clear vision of the time and effort needed by those whose collaboration is being sought.
- *Provide guarantees of confidentiality.* Those who grant permission will probably be anxious not to expose themselves to criticism and will want

to ensure that the interests of those for whom they have responsibility are not adversely affected by the research. They will want to feel safe about the research. The chances of getting permission for research, then, are generally enhanced when the researcher can offer guarantees about confidentiality.

- *Give something in return.* It is good practice for researchers to offer some kind of feedback, for instance, in the form of written reports on the findings. The offer can create the right kind of climate in which people are more likely to grant permission: (1) because they will get something out of it themselves; and (2) because, symbolically, it demonstrates an attitude of mutual respect; the researcher is not simply the taker, the researcher is also the giver.

The researcher, as an important resource in his/her own right, needs to be 'used' wisely

Good research ought to make provision for the protection of the researchers through precautions such as:

- *Incorporating 'safety' protocols into research design.* This means giving some formal recognition to the need to take safety issues seriously and adopting some routine procedures to reflect this. These might include, for example, things like keeping a log of all research-related visits and keeping someone informed about the destination, time of meeting and expected duration of the visit.
- *Retaining some personal space.* Researchers ought to be aware of the personal, psychological and emotional risks of allowing the research to become an obsession. There is a thin line between being fully committed to the research and finding that it invades nearly all aspects of life, leaving little personal space for a life beyond the project. This calls for a sense of proportion and conscious efforts to avoid becoming totally consumed by the research.

Further reading

Bell, J. (2005) *Doing Your Research Project: A Guide for First-time Researchers in Education, Health and Social Science*, 4th edn. Maidenhead: Open University Press, Chapter 5.

Blaxter, L., Hughes, C. and Tight, M. (2006) *How to Research*. Maidenhead: Open University Press, Chapter 5.

Cryer, P. (2006) *The Research Student's Guide to Success*, 3rd edn. Maidenhead: Open University Press, Chapters 8–10.

Lee, R. (1993) *Doing Research on Sensitive Topics*. London: Sage.

Levin, P. (2007) *Skilful Time Management*. Maidenhead: Open University Press.

Punch, M. (1986) *The Politics and Ethics of Fieldwork*. Beverly Hills, CA: Sage.

Checklist for FEASIBILITY

When considering the feasibility of the research you should feel confident about answering 'yes' to the following questions: ☑

1 Are there enough financial resources available to cover foreseeable expenses in relation to:
Travel? ☐
Materials (e.g. questionnaires)? ☐
Postage and phone calls? ☐
Data analysis? ☐
Report production? ☐

2 Has the scale of the research been based on an estimation of the working hours per week which can be devoted to the completion of the project? ☐

3 Can the overall project be completed within the time-span available? Will it meet the deadline? ☐

4 Is the scope of the research realistic in terms of the availability of, and access to, relevant sources of data (e.g. people, situations, documents)? ☐

5 If access to data relies on the good will of particular gatekeepers, have measures been taken to secure their agreement and continued cooperation? ☐

6 Are the kind of incentives that will encourage participation affordable within the funding available for the research? ☐

7 Have reasonable precautions been taken to safeguard the personal well-being of the researcher? ☐

II

APPROACH

4

ETHICS

Ethics refers to the system of moral principles by which individuals can judge their actions as right or wrong, good or bad – and social researchers are expected to conduct their research in an ethical manner. This means that researchers need to introduce a moral perspective to the way they design and conduct their investigations. When they think about what *ought* to be done and what ought not to be done, they need to do so not just in terms of what is likely to produce the best data but, distinct from this, they also need to consider what will be acceptable in the context of the values of the wider society in which the research is conducted.

Link up with **DESIGN**

The motivation for researchers to operate ethically should be a matter of professional integrity. It is part of the high standards that researchers might be expected to set for themselves. There are also practical reasons for operating in an ethical manner. As stated in the Social Research Association's (2003) *Ethical Guidelines*, 'The acceptability of social research depends increasingly on the willingness of social researchers to accord respect to their subjects and to treat them with consideration.' Research that does not do this will damage the reputation of social research. As was noted in Chapter 3 on Feasibility, without the good will and trust of the public large parts of social research will become starved of information. So much relies on the cooperation of participants that it is in social research's own self-interest to behave ethically.

Link up with **FEASIBILITY**

Moral and legal acceptability

Research of any kind takes place within a social context. This means that it must take account of the moral and legal climate of the time and the boundaries this places on the topics of investigation that are deemed acceptable and the nature of the methods of investigation it tolerates. *Social researchers have no status or privilege that puts them above the moral and legal codes that operate for the rest of the society*. They cannot break the law with impunity. Nor can they expect to avoid outrage and condemnation if their investigations openly contravene the public's ideas about decency and honourable conduct. Anyone considering research into sensitive or controversial areas, such as drug misuse, racism, pornography or corruption, would do well to appreciate this point. There is a clear obligation on researchers to stay within the law and to respect the cultural norms of the society within which the research is conducted.

Codes of ethics

There is no shortage of guidance when it comes to ethics. Professional associations whose members engage in research will almost always have a 'code of ethics' or 'code of conduct'. There are codes of ethics covering psychologists, sociologists, educationalists, market researchers, health researchers, etc. The codes vary a little, but it is easy to discern common themes within them and, later in the chapter, these will be outlined. Before we do so, however, there is an important point to make about the codes. They are *codes* of ethics – not *rules* of conduct. They do not constitute hard and fast rules of procedure for good social research. Nearly all writers on ethics in social research agree that it is not possible to provide a series of rules that should, or could, be applied to each and every instance of research because each new piece of research can give rise to its own special circumstances and these can call for different solutions.

The point is not that each principle should be *followed*, but that it should be taken into account and *considered*. Each principle provides a starting point, a baseline against which to compare the actual position adopted by the researcher. If circumstances arise where the researcher feels that he or she is not able to be bound by a specific principle, it becomes necessary to weigh the pros and cons of the situation and to arrive at a decision about whether it is legitimate to 'relax the rules' on this occasion. To do so does not automatically condemn the research as 'unethical', but it does warrant some explanation. *The principle should be acknowledged and any departure from it needs to be fully justified.*

There is another point that follows this. The burden of responsibility for the moral conduct of research remains squarely with the researcher. The codes of ethics do not provide a 'get out' clause where researchers can absolve themselves of any moral responsibility for their actions by simply saying 'I followed the rules'. Researchers do not follow the rules, they *interpret* the code and make decisions within the spirit of the code.

Ethics approval

Although responsibility for the ethical conduct of research rests with the researcher, it is becoming increasingly common for researchers to need to gain formal approval from a research ethics committee before they can embark on their research. The relevant committees are those that screen proposed pieces of research to check that they will accord with ethical principles for research. In some areas there are very strict protocols that require anyone planning to conduct research to submit a proposal to a research ethics committee for approval. In Britain, medical and health research is covered by local medical ethics committees that insist on scrutinizing all research proposals involving the use of people. Universities, likewise, normally make use of ethics committees to ensure that research conducted under their auspices conforms to the relevant principles. In the United States the committees are known as Institutional Review Boards (IRBs).

Researcher integrity

Most codes of ethics include reference to the need for researchers to act professionally in the pursuit of truth. Researchers should be committed to discovering and reporting things as faithfully and as honestly as possible, without allowing their investigations to be influenced by considerations other than what is the truth of the matter.

Link up with **OBJECTIVITY**

The need for this principle arises because findings from research can have consequences – political, commercial, personal – that can invite the possibility of corruption. There might be, for instance, pressure from sponsors of research to produce findings that are not critical or which actually support the sponsor's aims. After all, sponsors might well feel embarrassed or angry if the research they have paid for produces results that are damaging to them. The other side of the coin is that researchers might feel compromised, not wishing 'to bite the hand that feeds them'. Funding from drugs firms, the tobacco industry and the alcohol industry illustrates the potential dilemmas and awkwardness that could result from 'unsympathetic' findings. As Bulmer (1982) points out, sponsors can sometimes suppress the publication of findings if they find them unpalatable. They will not always do so, but there is the possibility – a possibility that cannot be ignored.

To counter any such suspicions, researchers are expected to be independent, objective and honest in the way they conduct and report the research. In the words of the Social Research Association's *Ethical Guidelines* (2003: 18):

> While social researchers operate within the value systems of their societies, they should attempt to uphold their professional integrity without fear or favour. They should also not engage or collude in selecting methods designed to produce misleading results, or in misrepresenting findings by commission or omission.

No misrepresentation or deception

As a general rule, social researchers are expected to be honest and open about who they are and what they are doing, and not rely on misrepresentation or deception as a means of getting the necessary information. In this sense, their professional integrity stretches beyond a responsibility to sponsors and the public to cover their dealings with research subjects and participants.

Without challenging this basic ethical principle, there are circumstances when researchers might find that some level of deception is necessary for the success of the research. A review of 1,000 psychological experiments in the USA concluded that some 75 per cent involved giving participants information that in some way or other served to mislead them (Menges 1973). Some observation studies need to incorporate deception by being secretive: if the people being researched knew they were being observed, they might refuse to cooperate or might cease to act as they normally would do, thus spoiling the research. Even with interviews and questionnaires there are sometimes good grounds for being less than 100 per cent truthful. The logic, here, is that if you tell the participant precisely what it is you are looking at, their response on that matter might be altered from normal.

Reflecting this problem, most codes of ethics incorporate some form of 'get out' clause, recognizing that, on occasion, total honesty might negate the possibility of conducting worthwhile research. These do not override the general premise that researchers should not engage in deception. They do, however, make allowance for some use of minor deception on occasion provided that:

- Such deception is treated very cautiously as an exception to the rule and as something which *warrants an explicit justification*.
- Where deception is used, there is a burden of responsibility on the researcher to ensure that after the research the participants are 'put in the picture' about the true nature of events. There needs to be a *debriefing* in which the researcher explains the real aims of the study to participants after their involvement in the study has been completed – thus leaving them fully informed about research after the event rather than before.

Protection of the interests of participants

Social researchers need to be sensitive to the likely impact of their work on those involved. Whether research is done *on* people or whether it is done *with* them, there is the possibility that their lives could be affected in some way through the fact of having participated. There is a duty on researchers, therefore, to work in a way that minimizes the prospect of their research having an adverse effect on those who are involved.

Key point
Participants should not be adversely affected as a consequence of engaging in the research.

Avoiding stress and discomfort

Research must not cause pain or distress to those being researched, and there is a duty on social researchers to think ahead and foresee any aspects of involvement with the research that could potentially cause mental stress or physical discomfort. Where appropriate, participants can be debriefed after their involvement to put their minds at rest about aspects of the research that might leave them worried. Of course, whether putting the research subjects in the picture about the purpose and design of the research afterwards is sufficient to purge any legacy of discomfort is another matter.

Avoiding undue intrusion

People have a right to privacy and social researchers need to be sensitive to the prospect that the research topic or methods might invade that privacy. The normal and routine aspects of people's lives deserve to be considered as valuable and researchers should not disrupt people's lives without regard for this.

Contact with people at home or work in connection with research ought to be made in a way that respects the privacy of these locations and avoids phone calls or personal visits that are ill-timed and a nuisance – invading territories of time and space in an unwelcome manner. Obviously the timing of calls is a key factor here. Most codes of ethics are fairly vague when it comes to specifying the boundaries to what is acceptable and what is 'undue' intrusion. Following the Market Research Society, however, calls made to domestic households between 9 a.m. on weekdays (10 a.m. on Sundays) and 8 p.m. on any evening might be considered acceptable, whereas outside these hours they might be criticized as intrusive.

Intrusion, of course, can concern the topic of the research as well as its timing. Questions about personal and possibly embarrassing subjects might have a justifiable place in an investigation, but the researcher would be expected to restrict these to the bare minimum necessary and certainly not include them unless they were absolutely vital. In times of grief or acute anxiety, it would be unethical for researchers to intrude on someone's personal life in the pursuit of data.

Confidentiality of data

Information that is given to social researchers during the course of their investigation should be treated as confidential. It should not be disclosed to anyone (other than co-researchers involved with the specific investigation) in any way that allows the information to be traced back to the individual who provided it. So, for example, it would be unethical to feed back views expressed during an interview with one person to her colleagues in subsequent interviews – unless, that is, some explicit agreement had been reached on the point. It is implicitly understood, unless formally agreed otherwise, that information coming from individuals is not 'leaked' to others. This could prove embarrassing and would constitute a breach of confidence.

There are, though, certain limitations to confidentiality. As was noted earlier in the chapter, researchers have no special status in law that privileges them when it comes to the information they collect. Researchers are not priests or physicians. If they are given certain information they might have a legal duty to disclose it, irrespective of any guarantees of confidentiality that might have been given at the start of the research. Those conducting research with children, in particular, need to be very wary on this point. This legal duty overrides other considerations about the ethical conduct of research and prior commitments to confidentiality. Information about being a victim of physical/sexual abuse, impending illegal activity, acts of self-harm, and so on might also cause the researcher to prioritize the disclosure of information ahead of research-based commitments about confidentiality.

Protection of identities: anonymity

It is normal good practice to avoid publishing reports of the research which allow individuals or organizations to be identified either by name or by role. Departures from this convention are certainly possible. However, the researcher needs to be absolutely sure that the relevant authorities have approved the use of real names and identities – and done so in writing.

To protect such identities, researchers tend to use *pseudonyms* for people and organizations. Here, though, researchers need to balance two potentially conflicting interests. They must publish details about their methods of data collection. This is fundamental to the notion of 'research' because, without such details, others in the research community would be unable to evaluate the work or do anything to check the validity of the findings. However, providing such details can run the risk of revealing the identities of those who contributed to the data. To get round the dilemma, researchers will often use pseudonyms, rather than the real names of places, people and organizations. Instead of an organization, such as a hospital, school or company, being given its real name, it is referred to by an alternative, fictitious name to mask its true identity. The alternatives can be chosen in two main ways. Either they can involve the replacement of a name with another name – generally something rather bland or generic like 'Central Hospital', 'Middletown School' or 'Acme Corporation' – or the researcher can use less inventive names. In writing about individuals, pseudonyms like 'consultant X', 'teacher Y' or 'director Z' can be used to replace the person's actual name.

Caution

The use of pseudonyms as a means for protecting anonymity can raise some awkward dilemmas for the researcher:

- Just changing a name might not be sufficient to protect the identities of people involved with the research. Insiders and the cognoscenti will delight in trying to solve the puzzle of who said what, and can be very good at managing to detect the identities of those involved. Disguising the identities might involve additional alterations to the details – such as changes to the information supplied about the role of the participant, and possibly their age and sex.
- The kinds of changes that might help retain anonymity might also compromise the analysis of the research. So, for example, the identity of a teacher in a school might be masked by attributing their input to someone from a different department and a different sex. However, the contribution of this participant might reflect personal experience as, say, a female teacher in a chemistry department. To attribute her words to a male teacher in a maths department might keep her identity secret, but it also destroys the integrity and significance of what was said. There are limits, then, to how far researchers can go to protect the identities of participants without jeopardizing the integrity of the data and the quality of the researcher's analysis.
- The better the identities of those involved are disguised, the more difficult it becomes to check the validity of the data. Other researchers are less able to compare the findings with similar instances since some of the details of the original have been deliberately altered or withheld. It is less likely than ever that a piece of research could be repeated to check its findings.

Security of the data

Where the research deals with information that relates to individuals there is a clear need to ensure that the records and data are kept secure. The researcher has a duty to make sure that the information that is collected cannot fall into the wrong hands or be used for any other purpose than that for which it was collected. At minimum this indicates the need for a 'lock and key' mentality as far as the data is concerned. With computerized data storage and retrieval, it calls for the use of passwords to protect against unauthorized access to the data. And this goes beyond just a matter of ethics. Most industrialized countries now have Data Protection Acts of some form which place a legal obligation on researchers:

- to take reasonable steps to keep the information secure;
- to ensure that the information is used only for the purposes for which it is collected.

Informed consent

After the Second World War, with its many abuses of human rights including the use of prisoners of war for medical research, it was felt that some internationally recognized statement on the rights of the individual in relation to (medical) research was needed. *The Nuremberg Code* of 1946 emerged to meet this need and Paragraph 1 of the code starts by stressing that informed consent is fundamental to the rights of any participant in research.

> The voluntary consent of the human subject is absolutely essential. This means that the person involved should have legal capacity to give consent, should be so situated as to be able to exercise free power of choice, without the intervention of any element of force, fraud, deceit, duress, over-reaching or any other ulterior form of constraint or coercion; and should have sufficient knowledge and comprehension of the elements of the subject matter involved as to enable him to make an understanding and enlightened decision.

Subsequently, the principle of *informed consent* has been embedded in numerous codes of ethics adopted by professional associations in the UK, the USA and elsewhere. These codes vary slightly according to the profession concerned and the country in which they operate but, as Homan (1991: 71) argues, the essence of the formulations is that:

- all pertinent aspects of what is to occur and what might occur are disclosed to the subject; } *informed*
- the subject should be able to comprehend this information;
- the subject is competent to make a rational and mature judgement; } *consent*
- the agreement to participate should be voluntary, and free from coercion and undue influence.

In some instances, researchers will find they need to be very formal in their requests for cooperation. In the sphere of health and medical research, for example, potential participants need to be provided with relevant information, in writing, about the research, their role in it and their right to withdraw at any time. Moreover, the consent needs to be obtained in writing. Participants are generally expected to sign a declaration that they have been provided with details of the proposed research, understand their involvement and are willing to cooperate.

There are other situations where the matter of getting informed consent is interpreted quite flexibly to meet the needs of the situation. In market research, as the prime example, the situations within which data are collected and the kind of information that is required often lead to a relatively relaxed interpretation of how much information needs to be provided, and what constitutes consent by the participant. The Market Research Society's *Code of Conduct* indicates that, when conducting surveys and interviews, it might be necessary to provide information only about the identity of the researcher and the organization for whom he or she works – with further information about the organization and the research being available if requested, possibly in the form of a leaflet.

The contrast largely reflects differences in the nature of the commitment required and the level of risks associated with agreeing to comply with the request for help. It is quite easy to see that a person who agrees to cooperate with health or medical research might be agreeing to become involved with an investigation that could involve tests and treatments which could have serious consequences, physically or psychologically. This is why researchers in this area need to be very cautious and precise when asking for consent. Market research, at the other end of the spectrum, might well involve a fairly minor commitment carrying very little by way of risk. Agreeing to answer a series of questions about lifestyles and shopping habits calls for less commitment and is unlikely to cause injury or distress. Market researchers, therefore, are not as inclined to want written consent and will consider themselves to be operating ethically provided the respondent agrees verbally to help with the research. In either case, though, there remains a belief in the underlying principle of informed consent: the amount of information and the formality of the consent merely differ in accord with the potential repercussions from agreeing to cooperate with the research.

There are, however, some kinds of social research that contravene this principle. The notion of *voluntary* participation embedded in the principle of informed consent does not operate when it comes to the biggest survey of all – the Census. There is a legal obligation to complete and return Census forms in the UK. Participation in the Census is not a matter of choice and, indeed, the penalty for not returning a completed form for the 2001 Census was a £2,000 fine. It has to be said that this example is very much the exception and, interestingly, despite the threat of a fine, a large number of households still did not complete the required forms.

Apart from this very unusual example, there are, as Punch (1986) argues, broadly two kinds of circumstances where the ethical principle of informed consent might not operate. The first is where it is not realistically possible to apply it. With certain kinds of observation studies there are clear practical constraints that mean it is not feasible to abide by the principle of informed consent. Researchers studying crowd behaviour at a football game, for example, could not hope to contact each one of the thousands of people present in order to ask their permission to be observed.

The second is where the quest for informed consent would seriously affect the validity of the data – such as with covert observational research. This strategy, typically found in ethnographies using participant observation, works by trying to see things as they normally occur without the disturbance of having a researcher's presence disrupting things. To seek informed consent would alert those being observed to the fact that they were 'under the microscope' and would probably entail disclosing the identity of the researcher, whose cover would be blown. In this case, an attempt to gain informed consent would effectively destroy the investigation. Codes of ethics generally take such circumstances into account and include a 'get out' clause in relation to the special needs of researchers undertaking covert research. In the fields of ethnography, market research and studies of social interaction, in particular, it is acknowledged that informed consent cannot usually be obtained. Significantly, though, researchers are generally reminded of the fact that such circumstances are special exemptions to the general rule and that, to compensate, additional care should be taken to respect the other rights of those being observed.

Link up with **ACCURACY**

Consent forms

To get *informed* consent the potential participant needs to be provided with written information to understand what the research is about and what type of commitment is called for (time, effort, nature of information, etc.). The request for consent from potential participants should be brief, probably contained on one sheet of paper, and it should cover:

- the purpose of study;
- the identity of the researcher and his or her sponsoring organization (if applicable);
- the basis on which the participant has been selected to take part;
- what the participation entails (e.g. being interviewed, taking part in an experiment);
- the time and effort needed by those whose collaboration is being sought;
- the purpose for which the data will be used (e.g. recommendations, reports, publications);
- the means for ensuring the security of data storage;
- the extent of anonymity and confidentiality that can be assured;

- the voluntary nature of participation, and the right to withdraw at any time;
- a signature and date to provide written consent (if applicable).

Adequate information

From the researcher's point of view, decisions need to be made about *how much information to supply*. Not enough information and the researcher can stand accused of not providing the basis for a fully 'informed' agreement. Too much information and the researcher can unintentionally contaminate the data by 'leading' the participant's responses. If participants know exactly what is being investigated, this might influence the replies they give. At a more practical level, too much information might deter participation. It could prove boring to would-be participants who have neither the time nor the desire to know about the finer points of the investigation. This would be a particular concern for those doing door-to-door surveys, telephone surveys, street interviews, etc. The aim must be to produce the most succinct statement possible, avoiding technical jargon, providing the potential participants with sufficient information about the person and organization conducting the research, what co-operation is required from participants, how the data will be used and the aims of research.

Consent from children and vulnerable members of society

From the point of view of researchers, it is important that the participants who agree to be involved with the research fully understand the implications of their agreement and have some reasonable perception of the repercussions of their consent. When research involves children or other 'vulnerable' members of society, this becomes a major concern. With anyone who is considered potentially vulnerable, the ethical principle to operate by is that consent is needed from another person, someone with direct, formal responsibility for the welfare of that person. Such consent is needed in addition to the assent of the child or vulnerable person. In the case of children, the additional consent will normally come from the parent or guardian of the child. Teachers in school, acting *in loco parentis*, might take on this role.

Power, authority and consent

Giving consent might seem a straightforward thing: a matter of 'yes' or 'no'. In practice, things are not so simple. The stipulation of *The Nuremberg Code* is that consent should be full, wholehearted and not begrudging. It should be entirely voluntary. In practice, however, an agreement to take part in research might be given as a result of *subtle means of persuasion* which, while they can hardly be considered as 'force, fraud, deceit or duress', do bring into question the degree to which the consent can be treated as completely voluntary.

In practical research this is frequently a very real concern for researchers who want to include relevant people in their study and might need to induce them to cooperate, but who also realize that the resulting cooperation might contain an element of coercion and 'arm-twisting' that could be seen as contravening the voluntary consent principle. To illustrate the point, research by Denscombe and Aubrook (1992) looked at the consent given by school pupils in connection with a large questionnaire survey of 14–16-year-olds in the East Midlands of England. The investigation into the research ethics was prompted by the very high response rates found for this and similar surveys that distribute questionnaires to pupils in schools. The high levels of agreement to participate could not be attributed to overt coercion. Measures were taken to ensure that participation was voluntary. The pupils were told by the researchers as they distributed the questionnaires, clearly and repeatedly, that they were under no obligation to complete the questionnaires, that their teachers would not see the completed questionnaires and that their responses would be treated in the strictest confidence. In the event, not one single pupil out of nearly 2,000 involved actually said 'no' to participation and very few spoiled their questionnaires by providing obviously silly answers. Research into *why* so many participated revealed that their participation owed a great deal to the organizational context in which the questionnaires were distributed – the school classroom during tutor group periods. They were willing to cooperate because it was during school time where the alternative to completing the questionnaire was not particularly enticing. To this extent, the consent was voluntary. Of course, had the request for participation occurred at the school gates as pupils went home at the end of the school day the alternatives would have been more attractive and the response rate decidedly lower.

The context affected the willingness to participate in another way as well. In the words of one of the girls who completed the questionnaire, 'It's just another piece of schoolwork' – it was no big deal. But this description hinted at something a little more sinister. Despite the efforts of the researchers to stress otherwise, the pupils obviously perceived the request as coming from adult/authority figures (equated with teachers), during school time, in the organizational context of the school. This meant that the request was easy to accede to since the task was seen as pretty routine and certainly not alarming or troublesome in any way. However, it also suggested that there might be subtle pressures on the pupils to 'obey' the request and fill in the questionnaires completely and correctly as they would other pieces of schoolwork. This worked fine for the research response rates, but was premised on consent that was given in an authority system (the school) where the pupils did not *feel* free to say 'no', despite being told that this was their right.

The degree to which people *feel* free to say 'no' to participation is important. Where the request occurs in organizations, there are power relations to be taken into account that can have a bearing on whether people give consent or not, and importantly the extent to which any consent given results from subtle pressure to obey. In work organizations this comes into play when subordinates are approached with a request for participation. If the boss is doing the research (for example, in action research) or has agreed to offer help (acting as a gatekeeper), the subordinates might not *feel* free to refuse to cooperate. To do so might be perceived as jeopardizing work relationships and adversely affecting job prospects in the future.

The difficulty of gaining consent that is completely voluntary has been acknowledged in some codes of ethics. The Social Research Association, for its part, suggests that for practical purposes researchers should at least gain 'adequate consent' from participants, appreciating the practical limitations of trying to operate via consent that is given with absolutely no persuasion or pressure at all.

> A subject's participation in a study may be based on reluctant acquiescence rather than on enthusiastic co-operation. In some cases, the social researcher may feel it is appropriate to encourage a sense of duty to participate in order to minimise volunteer bias. The boundary between tactical persuasion and duress is sometimes very fine and is probably easier to recognise than to stipulate. In any event, the most specific generic statement that can be made about *adequate consent* is that it falls short both of implied coercion and of full hearted participation.
>
> (Social Research Association 2003: 29)

Renewable consent and the right to withdraw

During the lifetime of a research project, the nature of the commitment sought from a participant can change and develop. This raises the question of whether the initial agreement to participate remains relevant and valid later on. In longer research projects, especially those with an emergent design and lengthy fieldwork, the answer might be that consent needs to be reviewed and renewed *en route* as the research moves forward and changes in terms of its demands on people.

The need to regain consent reminds the researcher that the participants are free to say 'no' at any stage of their involvement with the research. They can say 'no' at the beginning, but they are also free to withdraw their cooperation even once the research has started.

Key point
Participants are not obliged to go along with research even if they have initially agreed. They are *free to withdraw at any time* and should be aware of this.

Boundaries of consent

The idea that consent is a blanket agreement covering all subsequent involve-ment in the research has been questioned, and another area of concern relates to the *boundaries of consent*. Once people have agreed to participate with the research, they acknowledge that information they supply (or allow access to) can be used by the researcher as data. Legitimately, the researcher can make notes and records about the information for the specific purposes of the research. There is a question, though, about whether such consent is total or whether there are some implicit or explicit *limits to the consent*. Explicit limits are less of a problem in the sense that the consent is conditional and the details of what the researcher can use will have been sorted out in advance. In an organization, for example, a researcher might be granted access to some financial records but denied access to commercially sensitive documents. The researcher might get agreement to interview an executive but also have that agreement conditional upon not being tape recorded and having the identity of the organization kept secret in any written or verbal reports about the research. Such explicit limits are formally stated and provide the kind of routine boundaries within which researchers need to operate. Implicit limits are far more difficult to deal with. If a person agrees to be interviewed do they implicitly consent to having their views regarded as 'for the record' just during the time the tape recorder is running? Does it imply that the researcher may not use as data anything that is said before and after the tape recorder is switched on – things said 'off-the-cuff' on the walk from reception to the interviewee's office or comments made later over a cup of coffee? Such things can take the researcher into a grey area of uncertainty in which ethical decisions have to be made about the boundaries of the consent.

Box 4.1 Ethics	
The key issue	**Things to be considered**
Has consideration been given to the rights and interests of those affected by the research?	• How will the interests and the identities of participants be protected? • Will the research avoid any deception or misrepresentation in its dealings with the research subjects? • Is it possible to guarantee the confidentiality of the information given to the researcher? • What assurances can be provided about the integrity of the researchers and their use of an open and honest approach to the research?

Internet research

The use of the Internet for research purposes throws up some significant ethical issues. The principles of research ethics remain the same but, at a practical level, the Internet poses new challenges in terms of how to implement those principles. It also magnifies some of the dangers of the ethical minefield in the sense that any errors have the potential to take place on a global scale. A wrongly addressed email, for example, can have consequences vastly beyond that of a wrongly addressed envelope. Researchers and philosophers who have directed their attention to the nature of research ethics in Internet research have generally identified the following issues as particularly important.

Informed consent

The basic ethical principle is that those who participate in research should do so willingly and with knowledge of the nature of the research and its implications for them. This still operates for research on the Internet. However, from the researcher's point of view it is not always easy to get proof that the participant has agreed to participate in the research. Communication via the Internet does not supply the researcher with a personalized signature on a piece of paper. Fortunately, there are some reasonably simple and effective alternative ways of getting evidence of consent. These range from getting participants to post a hard copy consent form with their signature on it to the researcher via ordinary mail to getting participants to send a reply email in which they acknowledge that they understand the nature of the research and agree to participate in it. And, of course, there are the tick boxes on web-based forms that can be used to get some evidence that the participant has read and understands what the research involves. As with any research, these measures do not guarantee that the potential participant really has fully read and digested the information provided, but they do provide a reasonable and practical basis for informed consent sufficient for the purposes of most real-world social research.

Having said this, any Internet research involving *children or other 'vulnerable' groups* in society needs to be undertaken with particular caution when it comes to the issue of consent and, equally, the ethical requirement to protect the interests of the participants. Given the nature of identities on the Internet, it is not always possible for the researcher to be certain about who is participating and whether the participant's online identity matches their 'real-world' persona. In the specific context of research ethics, this poses some difficult questions for the researcher. 'How can I be sure the person is old enough to take part in the research?', 'How can I get the assent of a parent, guardian or other responsible adult?'

Privacy, intrusion and deception

Avoidance of undue intrusion is another basic principle of research ethics that throws up interesting challenges for the social researcher engaged in Internet research. These challenges generally arise as a consequence of the way that the Internet makes it relatively easy for researchers to join social groups using, for instance, chat-rooms, social networking sites, blogs, virtual worlds like 'Second Life' or Google groups. It is easier for them to engage in participant observation because the groups are virtual groups that do not depend on the physical presence of people. In a nutshell, it is easy to pretend to be someone else in order to fit in with the group and study their attitudes and beliefs. The danger here is that researchers can be tempted to 'snoop' on groups by pretending to be one of them without announcing to the group their real purpose for joining. Occasionally this can be defended in view of the nature of the group and the specific purposes of the research, such as in the research conducted by Glaser et al. (2002) who collected data from a chat room being used by white supremacists in the USA. They argued that racists appear to 'express their views rather freely (on the Internet), at least when they are interacting with those they perceive to be like-minded' (2002: 181) and that revealing the researchers' identity and purpose would have been likely to deter such openness. In this specific case, under these special circumstances, they were able to gain the approval of the ethics committee at their university on the grounds that:

- the deception was vital to the success of the research;
- there was little invasion of privacy or undue intrusion because the respondents' statements were made in a public forum and the respondents' identities were carefully protected.

Normally, however, researchers would be expected to reveal something about their research purpose to other members of the group and they would need to realize that *not* doing so might be interpreted as deception, as an invasion of privacy, and an undue intrusion into the life of the group.

Confidentiality

As with any research, reasonable precautions should be taken to avoid the disclosure of personal identities and sensitive information to third parties. And participants should be reassured on this point. However, with Internet research it is not possible to provide *absolute guarantees* that respondents' contributions will be private and never traced back to them. It needs to be acknowledged that ultimately – even with the use of encryption – governments and security agencies have the power and the ability to trace just about any kind of Internet communication should they wish to do so. This may not seem likely but, depending on the nature of the research, it needs to be recognized as a possibility. Researchers, therefore, should word statements about the confidentiality of data supplied via the Internet in a way that acknowledges the point.

Legislation

Data protection laws are important for research and, as with other research data, Internet data should be collected, stored and used in accord with relevant data protection legislation. There are, though, two aspects of legislation about which researchers who use the Internet should be especially alert.

- *copyright*: downloading text and images is simple, but the *use* of text and images needs to be in accord with copyright conventions and legislation concerned with things like trademarks and intellectual property rights. Special care needs to be taken to avoid plagiarism.
- *sensitive issues*: researchers hold no special position in the eyes of the law and need to exercise particular caution when investigating topics that are politically sensitive or which involve things like pornography or terrorism.

The situation is complicated somewhat by the fact that laws surrounding Internet use vary from country to country. Because the Internet has an international span this can give rise to questions about which country's laws to recognize. In the face of any uncertainty, researchers are best advised to make a clear statement about which country's legal jurisdiction is being applied so far as the research is concerned – normally the country in which the researcher is based.

Guidelines for good practice

There are practical reasons, as well as moral ones, for social researchers to respect the rights and interests of people who are involved in their research. The good will necessary for social research to continue in the future will get eroded unless social researchers operate with respect for those who supply data and those who grant access to data. It is vital, therefore, that social researchers operate according to high ethical standards and treat people and information in a way that, as far as is possible, avoids any damaging repercussions from collaboration with the research. There are a number of practical things that researchers can do to help in this respect.

Adopt an appropriate code of practice for research ethics

Good research needs to be conducted in accord with recognized ethical principles and it is important to indicate which code of research ethics has been adopted. Among relevant codes for social researchers there are those of the:

- Social Research Association
- British Sociological Association
- British Psychological Society
- Government Social Research (UK)

- British Educational Research Association
- Market Research Society
- Medical Research Council
- RESPECT (Professional and ethical codes for socio-economic research in the information age)

Each has a web-site at which the code of ethics or code of conduct can be viewed.

Ensure that approval from the relevant ethics committee is obtained (if necessary)

Researchers need to find out whether formal approval is needed from a research ethics committee (or other vetting body for the research). In particular, they should check with:

- the organizations for whom they work;
- any organization sponsoring the research or under whose auspices the research is to be conducted (e.g. a university);
- the authorities at any place where empirical research is to be conducted.

Acknowledge and justify any practice which deviates from the standard principles

It is worth emphasizing that research does not involve trying slavishly to adhere to 'rules' contained in the codes. It involves a range of decisions that ought to be guided by the spirit of codes. On some occasions, for good reason, researchers might need to deviate from the specific elements of the code. Departures from the standard ethical principles for social research ought to operate on three conditions:

- acknowledge the ethical principle in question;
- develop an explicit argument defending the specific violation of the principle;
- seek advice from experts about the advisability of proceeding.

Avoid, or minimize, any suspicion that the research might be compromised by commercial, political or personal interests

There are certain things researchers should do. They need to do the following:

- retain a certain level of independence and distance from the sponsoring body;
- be explicit about the source of any sponsorship;
- operate with professional integrity, respecting the 'truth' as their sole aim, and resisting the influence of any vested interests in the findings.

Provide a brief written statement to potential collaborators that outlines the nature of the research and the amount of commitment requested

If informed consent in writing has not been obtained, then there needs to be a justification for this (e.g. observations of people in public places, street surveys).

Take measures to safeguard the confidentiality of information and ensure the non-disclosure of identities of those participating in the research

The disclosure of identities of individuals or organizations should only occur if this has been formally agreed with those concerned. It is safest to get such agreement in writing.

Take special precautions when undertaking research with young people or other 'vulnerable' groups

Special care needs to be taken in the case of research involving vulnerable groups. Permission from someone with appropriate authority is needed according to most codes of conduct for research and this applies just as much to Internet research as it does to conventional data collection methods. Although it is difficult to be certain about the age of contacts on the Internet, researchers are still expected to do the following:

- use their best endeavours to identify any respondents who might be aged under 16;
- where appropriate, seek permission on behalf of young or vulnerable people;
- abide by relevant national laws relating to contact with children and vulnerable groups.

Further reading

Israel, M. and Hay, I. (2006) *Research Ethics for Social Scientists: Between Ethical Conduct and Regulatory Compliance*. London: Sage.

Kimmel, A.J. (2007) *Ethical Issues in Behavioral Research: Basic and Applied Perspectives*. Oxford: Blackwell.

Loue, S. (2000) *Textbook of Research Ethics: Theory and Practice*. New York: Kluwer Academic.

Oliver, P. (2003) *The Student's Guide to Research Ethics*. Maidenhead: Open University Press.

Checklist for ETHICS

When considering the ethics of the research you should feel confident about answering 'yes' to the following questions: ☑

1   Does the research abide by the laws and respect the cultural norms of the society within which the research is conducted? ☐

2   Has an appropriate code of research ethics been adopted and acknowledged? ☐

3   Has approval been obtained from the relevant Research Ethics Committee (or Institutional Review Board)? ☐

4   Will the data be collected via legal and legitimate means? ☐

5   Will the research be conducted with professional integrity (honest, objective, unbiased)? ☐

6   Will participants be supplied with sufficient information about the research? ☐
    If not, can this be justified in relation to the nature of the research? ☐

7   Will participants give their (written) consent to participation in the research? ☐
    If not, can this be justified in relation to the nature of the research? ☐

8   Will the research avoid any misrepresentation or deception? ☐
    If not, can this be justified in relation to the nature of the research? ☐

9   Have the interests of the research subjects been protected through:
    Avoiding stress and discomfort? ☐
    Maintaining the confidentiality of information? ☐
    Protecting their anonymity? ☐
    Avoiding undue intrusion? ☐

10 Have reasonable steps been taken to maintain the security of the data? ☐

5

OBJECTIVITY

Ground rule: **Researchers need to be open-minded and self-reflective**

Questions: Can the research really hope to be completely impartial and unbiased?

Aren't the findings inevitably biased by the researcher's prior attitudes and conceptions?

Answers: The research has been designed, conducted and reported in a genuine spirit of exploration.

Any vested interests, social values or aspects of the researcher's self-identity that might have a bearing on the impartiality of the research have been explicitly acknowledged.

For most purposes in social research, there is an assumption that objectivity is a good thing. It lies at the heart of what it means to engage in research and it is a crucial criterion for arriving at judgements about the credibility of findings. However, it is now generally accepted that social researchers can never be entirely objective. Because researchers inevitably see things in a way that is, to a greater or lesser extent, shaped by their culture, their socialization and the concepts they use to make sense of the world around them, they can never entirely stand outside things to see them from an objective vantage point.

This has prompted some investigators to regard any claims to objectivity as mere pretence. They argue that research findings will always reflect the person who produced them and the circumstances in which they were researched and, for this reason, research can never hope to provide an objective explanation of the thing being investigated.

Most researchers, it should be stressed, do not go down this route. They recognize that there are inherent limits to how far pure objectivity can be achieved, but still treat it as an ideal to which the researcher should aspire in terms of a reasonable level of detachment and a reasonable level of open-mindedness when it comes to the topic, the data and the findings from any particular piece of research.

Objectivity as detachment

The classic image of the researcher is that of a person who is dedicated to discovering the truth. Drawing heavily on the natural science model it conjures up images of the white-coated laboratory scientist working through the night with a passion to discover 'the formula' that will unlock the secrets of the universe. The researcher cares not a jot for the outside world, what time it is, what day or month. The researcher is unkempt – not caring about physical appearance and only eating and sleeping when nagged to do so by a faithful and supportive helper. Overstated as this might be, it embodies an enduring and powerful image about research activity – a *detachment from the world*.

The social sciences have not been immune to this powerful image, and great emphasis has been placed in traditional approaches within the social sciences on maintaining a position of detachment from the area of study. According to this ideal, good research should have nothing to do with power or money. It should have nothing to do with promoting vested interests. It should not set out with the purpose of changing the world, nor should it be undertaken for the personal benefit of the researcher (to make the researcher rich or famous). Research serves no master except the quest for knowledge itself.

Objectivity as open-mindedness

The notion of objectivity also carries with it the idea of being open-minded and, again, this owes a great deal to the natural science model of research. Science, as a form of knowledge and method of investigation, involves challenging traditional ways of thinking about the world. Superstition, sorcery, tradition and religion are seen as sources of knowledge about the working of the world which take the form of 'givens' – handed down from those with a special privileged insight. Science, by contrast, calls for a thoroughly different approach. It requires people to question things, to explore and to discover new forms of knowledge. It calls for an open-mindedness in the sense that research can throw up unexpected results and overturn long-held beliefs.

Those who engage in research, then, would not be expected to treat their existing beliefs and knowledge as immutable. Researchers will certainly need to use such knowledge as a starting point for new investigations and they might well be successful in building upon that existing knowledge. However, they need to be receptive to the possibility that new findings might cast doubt on such knowledge and that there might be a need to revise existing theories, or even replace them with entirely new explanations. In essence, *there has to be an openness to the possibility of being wrong.*

Box 5.1 Objectivity – the ideal

There are two notions related to the idea of objectivity that, traditionally, have been very influential on research. First, there is the idea of some external vantage point from which to gain a better view and, second, there is the idea of approaching matters in a fair and unbiased manner. Both facets of objectivity help social researchers to claim that their findings are better than those based on common sense or received wisdom.

Detached:
outside, separate from

Open-minded:
neutral, impartial, unbiased, fair, no vested interests

 Able to get a
clearer view

Bias

In practice, there are a number of things that can threaten the researcher's ability to take a detached and open-minded approach. Some of these things are quite subtle, such as the way that a researcher's background and culture might have a bearing on the choice of topic or interpretation of findings. Others are more blatant and involve the notion of bias. As Hammersley and Gomm (1997) argue, bias in social research has a number of dimensions. Behind them all, however, there lies the unpalatable prospect that, rather than being objective, researchers might be swayed by *vested interests* in the outcome of their investigation.

Sponsorship

When research is sponsored, the impartiality of its design and analysis can become something of an issue. There is the possibility that those who pay for the research might like to see their generosity rewarded by getting results from the research that work in their favour. Sponsors who have a vested interest in the outcome of the research might use their financial backing to exert some pressure on the researchers to arrive at 'appropriate' conclusions and, certainly, those who fund research are unlikely to react well if the results do not support their cause. If this happens, they might choose to withdraw their support.

Some sponsoring bodies, it should be recognized, do not have a strong stake in the findings of the research they fund. Sponsorship from national research councils and universities, for instance, is relatively free from pressures that might bias the findings. Their sponsorship will go some way towards enhancing the image of the research as 'objective' – distanced from any commercial or political pressures. However, there are other sources of funding for social research that can have a relatively strong and obvious interest in the findings of the research they fund. For example, the tobacco industry and the alcohol industry will have a commercial and political interest in the outcome of any social research they support dealing with people's consumption of cigarettes or beer. Charities and pressure groups, likewise, will have a vested interest in the findings of research they fund because they will want to use the findings to help their lobbying activities.

When research is sponsored, then, a number of questions arise concerning the objectivity of the findings and the amount of autonomy afforded to the researchers in relation to the design and analysis of the findings. When research is sponsored, it invites questions such as:

- How free was the researcher to choose the research questions?
- Has the research been designed in such a way that the results are very likely to support the interests of the sponsoring body?
- Are the researchers under pressure to interpret their results in a way that is favourable to the interests of the sponsoring body?
- What control, if any, did the sponsoring organization place on the disclosure of findings?

And, at a more speculative level, readers might be left to ponder questions such as:

- What is the likelihood of the sponsor continuing to fund research whose findings might put them in a bad light or jeopardize their future commercial success?
- Would the researchers be inclined to interpret their findings in a way that is sympathetic to the interests of the body that is paying for the research so that there is more likelihood of continued funding from that body for more research?

Caution

It is worth emphasizing that these are not allegations of corruption and unscientific practice. They do not imply that sponsorship automatically invalidates the objectivity of research. They are just reasonable questions that anyone evaluating the research findings might expect to ask in relation to the objectivity of the research.

Personal obligation

There is another way in which researchers can be affected by the sponsorship issue. In this case the sponsorship may not take the form of funding. The support for the research can take other forms which, though they might not involve money, still entail some degree of patronage and the sense of obligation that might well go hand in hand with this. Permission to conduct research in an organization – for instance, as part of an action research project or as part of a part-time degree course – could well require trust and good will on the part of the host organization, which the researcher might feel obligated to respect. Things can get tricky, however, if the trust and good will make the researcher reluctant to pursue certain avenues of enquiry which it is felt might jeopardize this, or if the findings are critical and it is felt that they might harm the interests of someone or some group who had been kind enough to facilitate the research. This kind of sponsorship can invoke a sense of *moral obligation* on the researcher that has the potential to militate against objectivity. And it does not occur just in organizational settings. Any research setting that creates a sense of commitment on the part of the researcher to those who enabled the research carries the same danger of generating a moral obligation which has the potential to detract from the objectivity of the research.

This does not mean that researchers should never feel a sense of moral obligation to those who enable the investigation to take place. Far from it. What it does mean is that they need to be sensitive to the way any such commitment or obligation might impact on their activity as a researcher and, if necessary, take this into account when considering the findings from the research.

Considering alternative explanations

Research that intentionally ignores theories or data which do not tally with the researcher's point of view will be open to the criticism of bias. To avoid this, researchers must 'take proper methodological precautions to avoid error, for example by assessing the relative validity of alternative interpretations' (Hammersley and Gomm 1997: 10). In effect, they should try to see things from the point of view of others. This can even mean giving consideration to views the researcher might find personally repugnant, offensive or outrageous if those views are being used by others in the field to explain a particular social phenomenon.

> [Research requires the kind of] self-discipline that enables a person to do such things as abandon wishful thinking, assimilate bad news, discard pleasing interpretations that cannot pass elementary tests of evidence and logic, and, most important of all, suspend or bracket one's own perceptions long enough to enter sympathetically into the alien and possibly repugnant perspectives of rival thinkers.
>
> (Haskell 1990: 132; cited by Harding 1992: 571)

Black researchers, accordingly, might need to give explicit consideration to theories about the nature of prejudice and discrimination which they regard as racist. Though such theories might be found to be personally offensive to the researcher, and though they may not be substantiated by the researcher's findings, if they have some currency in the field they cannot be ignored or summarily dismissed. Claims to objectivity will require the researcher to address such theories, consider their logic, and then present a rational argument against them.

> **Key point**
> Objectivity calls for the researcher to engage with the opposition. It does not allow researchers to ignore views they hold in contempt or theories they regard as inadequate.

Box 5.2 Objectivity	
The key issue	**Things to be considered**
Will the research produce fair and balanced findings?	• Will the personal values, beliefs and background of the researcher lead to biased findings? • Will the research be approached with an open mind about what the findings might show? • Has consideration been given to alternative and competing explanations, theories or ideas?

Taking sides

Objectivity can sometimes mean neutrality and, in the context of social research, this means *not taking sides*. To be objective means to be independent from the thing that is being studied, to be detached and to avoid getting embroiled in the rights and wrongs of the situation. According to this vision of the role of social research, the idea is to provide information and produce knowledge that others – the politicians and the policy-makers – can use to make decisions.

A value-free approach

If researchers are to operate in this fashion, their beliefs about what is right and what is wrong, what is good and what is bad cannot be allowed to interfere with the business of research. When it comes to conducting research, they will be advised to put such values to one side. They will be warned about the dangers of letting their values get in the way of objectivity and advised about the virtues of a *value-free* approach to the work.

Underlying such advice is the assumption that a clear distinction can be made between facts and values. At first glance this seems quite straightforward. Facts concern what actually exists (what *is*); values concern what should exist (what *ought*). Social researchers need to be clear that their task should be limited to matters of fact. If values are allowed to creep into the research, so the argument goes, then it paves the way for political rhetoric and ideology to be smuggled in under the guise of research. Social researchers need to avoid having their work 'contaminated' by such social values. In essence, the role of the researcher should be restricted to the discovery of what *is*, and not be engaged in promoting visions of what *ought* to be.

Link up with **POSITIVISM**

Partisan research

Although it continues to have a legacy in the thought of social researchers, the value-free position has been subject to criticism, not least from those who argue that it consigns social research to a politically conservative role. Objectivity through value-freedom means that social research should not promote visions of the world, not support certain ideas, not argue for change in any way. It should focus on 'what *is*'. As Gouldner (1962) famously argued, by preventing social research from taking sides, the value-free approach denies one of the key attributes of social science – its ability to move things forward by critically examining the status quo, pointing to its faults and suggesting ways in which things might be better. By denying the social research the right to 'take sides', research becomes a hand-maiden to the status quo and, inevitably, a conservative activity.

Reaction against the value-free approach has been most apparent in the case of 'partisan research'. A *partisan* approach abandons any 'pretence' at value-freedom or neutrality and openly takes sides, favouring the position of one side over another. Some *feminist research*, for example, is explicitly concerned with promoting the rights of women and makes no pretence to being neutral in terms of its approach. Its choice of topic, its research strategy and its analysis of results all reflect a clear commitment which, in this case, is the promotion of women's rights in a patriarchal society. Similarly, some *anti-racist research* adopts a partisan approach – again bringing to the investigation a self-acknowledged political stance underwritten by clear and explicit support for one particular group as opposed to others.

Because research that sets out to promote the interests of a particular group or individual – which seeks to *empower* them – does not claim to be impartial or neutral about the topic of enquiry, the notion of 'partisan research' has been challenged as an oxymoron – a figure of speech which combines *contradictory* terms so as to create a new notion. 'Research' (which is objective) is combined with 'partisan' (which is partial and biased). Hammersley (1993) picks up this point and offers some constructive suggestions about how it might be possible to conduct research that is partisan yet still carries with it some element of the objectivity that is associated with the notion of doing research. It is important, writes Hammersley, that though the research starts from a position of commitment on the part of the researcher (e.g. feminism), the partisan researcher still adopts a spirit of open-minded discovery. This is realistically possible because, as Sayer (2000: 59) argues,

> We demean ourselves if we imagine we can't possibly accept factual statements about circumstances we find unpalatable . . . While it is advisable to interrogate our research to see if we are not engaging in wishful thinking and to make sure it is capable of acknowledging possible circumstances of which we disapprove, our values need not be a problem.

Bearing these points in mind, we can draw the conclusion that a partisan approach need not contradict the aspirations of good research provided it retains:

- a willingness to be proven wrong;
- a willingness to acknowledge findings that are not desired or possibly not supportive of the aims of the research.

Key point
Partisan researchers need to match their commitment to a cause with an equally strong commitment to being open-minded about their findings.

Caution

The newcomer to research should realize that the use of a partisan approach runs against the grain of conventional wisdom and is quite controversial. It is, therefore, a risky stance to take for the newcomer or project researcher and one that will need careful defence in relation to the objectivity issue.

Relativism and postmodernism

For some researchers, the quest for objectivity is rejected on the grounds that it seeks the impossible. Researchers cannot strip themselves of their values. Such values will have been inculcated through family life, education, religion, the media and the community and be so deeply embedded that they cannot simply be taken off like a jacket and hung in a corner until it is convenient to put them on again. Our values are our skin, not our clothes. They cannot be changed at our convenience. It is inevitable that these values will shape researchers' choices of what is worth investigating and will have some bearing on how they perceive matters.

If social research cannot be value-free, this opens the possibility that objectivity itself is a delusion and one that social research would do well to jettison. After all, efforts to achieve objectivity are efforts to achieve the impossible. This kind of argument has been advanced in recent years by postmodernists and extreme relativists. Hammersley and Gomm (1997), critical of the stance, describe the position in these words:

> All accounts of the world reflect the social, ethnic, gendered, etc. position of the people who produced them. They are constructed on the basis of particular assumptions and purposes, and their truth or falsity can only be judged in terms of standards that are themselves social constructions, and therefore relative.
>
> (Hammersley and Gomm 1997: 5)

Taken to extremes, this can lead to a position in which any account of an event is taken to be as good (or bad) as any other. Each researcher produces an account of a social phenomenon which is unique to himself or herself and each account stands in its own right as a statement about that phenomenon – no better and no worse than others, just different. Taken further, the logic dictates that any person's explanation of a social phenomenon needs to be regarded as essentially a credible account that must be understood on its own grounds and not judged as better or worse than other accounts using criteria which are nothing more than conventions imposed to suit the interests of certain groups in society.

Link up with **PROOF**

Being explicit about values

The trouble is that if we follow the extreme relativist position to its logical conclusion, there is little basis for doing research at all, let alone trying to do 'good' research. This is why, even among those who recognize the problem of treating social reality as something that exists 'out there' as an external, objective and universal entity, there is a tendency to shy away from the full relativistic position. Rather than going down this road, most researchers and theorists prefer to take a stance that still involves the use of standards and criteria to judge the quality of investigations as being good or bad, better or worse, worthwhile or not (e.g. Lincoln and Guba 1985; Hammersley 1992; Silverman 1998; Seale 1999).

Link up with **PHILOSOPHY**

A far less controversial, less extreme, response to the criticisms of the value-free stance is one that recognizes the impracticality of social researchers ditching all their values but which retains some notion that the researcher's social values should not impinge on the research in an unwarranted manner. The logic of this position is that:

- All social research involves social values; ultimately this is inescapable.
- Those who claim to approach research from a value-free position are in fact either being naïve in not recognizing how their work is infused with values, or dishonest in trying to hide their value position behind a veneer of 'science'.
- Researchers need to be aware of the ways in which their values might have a bearing on the nature of the research being undertaken and should make efforts to design the research so that the possibility of findings which challenge those values are not precluded.
- Researchers need to acknowledge the values that underlie their research and make such values as explicit as they can to those who read the research findings. When this is done, the audience/readership can have a clearer vision of the enterprise and can judge the results/analysis from an informed position.

Reflexivity

There are a number of dimensions to the notion of reflexivity and its use in contemporary social science but what these various uses share is a belief that achieving a completely objective stance on the social world is not possible. And the key reason for this is that researchers are themselves part of the world they seek to study. 'Social science has to wrestle with the problem of human beings creating explanations about themselves and their society when they are part and parcel of that society' (Smith 1998: 7).

In the material sciences this kind of problem arises in the realms of nuclear physics. In the study of sub-atomic particles, the light that is used to observe the sub-atomic particles has sufficient mass relative to the minuscule particles to throw them off course when they collide. Since we cannot observe the tiny particles unless they 'collide' with a light particle, and because the collision knocks the tiny particle off course, we cannot observe the object without changing things. This kind of problem exists equally within the social sciences. Instead of the problem emerging from trying to measure particles with other particles, in the social sciences the problem comes from trying to study meanings with other meanings, language with other language, values with other values, people with other people. The means we have for constructing and interpreting our social world are the same as those for studying it. When we turn our attention to a particular phenomenon, the way we look at it, the sense we give to it, are part and parcel of the thing. And, for this reason, we cannot step outside our social world in order to gain an objective standpoint or standard measure that can act as an external referent point.

There is no simple solution to reflexivity that allows researchers to get around the problem it poses for objectivity. However, it is worth keeping the impact of reflexivity in perspective. Take the case of the natural scientist. The problem just described is real and significant as far as those working at the cutting edge of tiny particle physics is concerned. Yet it does not have much significance for many others who would use the laws of physics. Engineers and architects are not really troubled by it. They might know about it but it has no impact on their calculations – or on the success of those calculations. So it might be in the social sciences. Researchers should be aware that ultimately they are caught up in an eternal web of meanings and language from which there is no escape and which permits no absolute point of reference against which to plot measures of 'truth' of 'reality'. And they should understand that this is a real and significant issue when dealing with certain kinds of phenomena. But for much of the routine work undertaken by social researchers the point does not have an immediate and pressing impact. Studies of mortality rates, of educational success rates, of consumer preference, etc., which operate at a different level, can proceed relatively untroubled.

Seeing things from a different point of view

It is, then, impossible to approach things from a position of complete detachment. This would call for the researcher somehow to cease to be a social person with views of his or her own, with emotions and preferences, with a lifetime of experiences. However, rather than abandon any interest with the idea of detachment so far as objectivity is concerned, some social researchers have argued that it is better to treat detachment as a matter of degree, rather than an either/or situation. They have argued that some level of detachment is indeed possible and that when this is achieved specifically for the purposes of the research, it can provide a means to get a better view of the events and situations being investigated.

The stranger's viewpoint

While we may not be able to divorce ourselves from our past experiences or the social situation in which we live, we can *approach* the position of the detached observer by adopting the stance of the stranger (Schutz 1964). The stranger looks upon situations and events as an outsider who is faced at every turn with the task of making sense of what is happening. Customs and practices which are so normal that they do not warrant thinking about need to be worked out by the stranger. Instead of being blinded by the obvious, the stranger sees things with fresh eyes.

There is the potential for humour here. The entertainment industry has frequently relied on making fun out of the plight of the stranger. Either the humour revolves around situations where the stranger does not understand things and proceeds to commit errors of etiquette, fashion, etc. Or, of course, the viewpoint of the stranger has been used to expose some of the more ludicrous aspects of the host culture. Alien visitors to planet Earth, for example, are often used for this purpose in movies and TV shows where the visitors have the task of finding out how human societies work and are constantly puzzled by the customs and practices they observe. They see things afresh, unhindered by the values and prejudices the insider accumulates through living within the society. As strangers, they are able to view things in a way that is at once naïve and perceptive. The very naïvety of the outsider makes the significance of events and situations more apparent for them than it is for members of the society because, for the members, these events and situations are just too obvious and common to capture attention.

The film critic

Some social theorists, such as David Silverman, have used an analogy with the film critic as a means of explaining the kind of mind-set needed for the social researcher when it comes to the temporary suspension of common sense.

When we go to watch a film we would hope to become engrossed in the tale being told. As an audience we will feel emotions because we are willing and able to immerse ourselves in the characters and situations portrayed in the film. For the duration of the film, if it is a good one, we will become thoroughly *involved*.

After the film has finished and we are discussing it with others, there is every chance that we will shift in stance from the involvement of the film viewer to the stance of detachment associated with a film critic. In retrospect we might discuss the quality of the acting and the credibility of the plot. We might try to clarify the meaning of certain events portrayed in the film, or talk about the director's intentions. And, as we do so, we stand back from the experience of seeing the film to adopt a critic's stance. We begin to 'deconstruct' the film – analysing how it was put together and what strategies were used by the director and actors (and others, depending on how much of a film buff you are!) and to what effect.

The analogy rests on the fact that, as members of society, social researchers will be able and willing to operate as normal people doing routine things without constantly questioning the meaning and significance of everything they see and everything they do. They are immersed in the situation and their common sense allows them to relate to other people and predict the consequences of their actions. However, for the purposes of doing social research, they need to flip into the mind-set of the critic: standing back, distancing themselves from the action, questioning how things work, and – of course – being prepared to evaluate how well they work.

> ### Key point
> Social researchers need to suspend common-sense beliefs about the subject they choose to investigate and then question the obvious, taking nothing for granted.

Guidelines for good practice

The need to demonstrate some level of objectivity constitutes a ground rule for social research. Despite the recognition by most social researchers that it is difficult, if not ultimately impossible, to achieve in any pure or total form, it remains a core aim, with alternatives – things like bias and subjectivity – being seen as unacceptable so far as good research is concerned.

The recognition that something is unattainable does not imply that we should abandon efforts to move in that direction. An often cited analogy here is hygiene. The surgeon and the cook will know that it is impossible for them to work in situations that are entirely hygienic – totally sterile and free from germs. They will, none the less, make efforts to ensure that they work in environments that are as free from germs as is possible under the circumstances. The fact that totally sterile conditions are impossible does not cause them to abandon any attempt at hygiene. So it goes with objectivity. While it might be understood that researchers cannot ever be totally objective (by working without the influence of concepts, language or social values), good research should continue to strive towards objectivity *as far as is possible under the circumstances*.

These circumstances will depend on the nature of the investigation and its particular subject matter. The quest for objectivity will occupy the minds of some social researchers more than others. It is likely that researchers using qualitative data and the interpretation of meanings will be more concerned with reflexivity and the problems of values than those whose work analyses quantitative data such as birth statistics, mortality rates, election results and inflation rates. This is important to recognize. This point made, there are some broad themes of good practice that apply fairly generally and are worth considering for inclusion in relation to most kinds of investigation.

It is important to acknowledge any vested interests in the research or sources of sponsorship that could potentially compromise the objectivity of the findings

While sponsored research does not automatically reflect the vested interests of the funder, in the light of the potential influence it is good practice for researchers to be open about: (1) whether the research was conducted with support (financial or other); (2) the nature of any such sponsorship; and (3) the degree of autonomy the researchers had over the design and analysis of the research.

Researchers need to be very clear about their social values

They need to consider how these might influence the choice of topic to be researched, the analysis of the findings and the conclusions drawn from the research. They need to think about whether their own social values are blinkering their view of things.

The impact of the researcher's own background and personal experiences needs to be considered

Adding a *short biographical* note to the research can be very useful. This can explain any personal interest in the area of research and thus allow readers of the research report to gauge how the researcher's personal experiences might have impinged on the process of research or influenced the analysis and conclusions.

Researchers ought to question their own assumptions about what things mean and how they work

This might require researchers to suspend common sense temporarily and to stand back from what they 'know' as a normal person in society to look at things afresh, like a stranger.

Alternative explanations need to be considered

It is necessary to engage with the views held by others, even those whose beliefs or activities the researcher might regard as wrong. Good research does not ignore opposing ideas. It grapples with them, tries to fathom their logic, and then on this basis tries to show how and why the researcher's position is better.

Further reading

Alvesson, M. (2002) *Postmodernism and Social Research*. Buckingham: Open University Press.
Finlay, L. and Gough, B. (2003) *Reflexivity: A Practical Guide for Researchers in Health and Social Sciences*. Oxford: Blackwell.
Hammersley, M. (2000) *Taking Sides in Social Research: Essays on Partisanship and Bias*. London: Routledge.
Lincoln, Y. and Guba, E. (1985) *Naturalistic Enquiry*. Newbury Park, CA: Sage, Chapter 7.
Myrdal, G. (1969) *Objectivity in Social Research*. New York: Pantheon Books.
Rorty, R. (1991) *Objectivity, Relativism, and Truth:* Volume 1: *Philosophical Papers,* Cambridge: Cambridge University Press.

Checklist for OBJECTIVITY

When considering the objectivity of the research you should feel confident about answering 'yes' to the following questions: ✔

1   Has the research been designed, conducted and reported in a spirit of open-minded discovery? ☐

2   Has serious consideration been given to alternative explanations and the views of those the research might wish to contradict? ☐

3   If the research has been supported by a sponsor:
Has the sponsor been explicitly identified? ☐
Has consideration been given to the influence that sponsorship might have on the direction of the research and its findings? ☐

4   If there is an element of personal involvement or moral obligation that might affect objectivity on the part of the researcher, has this been explicitly acknowledged and discussed? ☐

5   Has consideration been given to the researcher's own background and the possibility that this might have a significant impact on the research? ☐

6   Where appropriate, has a biographical note been provided that gives an account of how the researcher's personal background or experiences influenced his/her involvement in the research? ☐

7   If the research has been undertaken with an explicit commitment to a moral or political point of view, has it been conducted with a willingness to find unexpected and possibly undesired results? ☐

© M. Denscombe, *Ground Rules for Social Research*. Open University Press.

III

DESIGN

6

DESIGN

Ground rule: **Research designs should be coherent and fit for purpose**

Questions: What is the overall plan for the project?

How do the components of the research link together?

How do you know the research design will work?

Answers: The research design provides an explicit link between the methods of data collection, the techniques of data analysis and the research problem being investigated.

The design draws on established good practice and has been evaluated in terms of reliability and validity.

The design is fit for purpose in relation to the aims of the research.

What is a research design?

A good research design does three things. First, it provides *a description of the various components of the investigation*. It specifies the general approach to the research that will be adopted – the strategy – and gives details about the methods of data collection and analysis that will be used.

Second, the research design *provides a rationale for the choice of research strategy in relation to the research questions*. It explains how the various methods of data collection and analysis link with the specific research questions being investigated and shows how they will produce data that are suitable for the kind of research questions being investigated. In this sense, the design must be 'fit for purpose'. The design of a new building serves as a good analogy for this point. The design of a new building will obviously take into account the specific purpose for which the building will be used. Factories, houses, offices and shopping malls will each be used for different purposes and, therefore, require different kinds of design. Within the broad types of building there will be a range of far more specific requirements that the design needs to meet. The design of a shopping mall, for example, will need to be tailored to suit the size and nature of the retail units that will occupy the building. The design must also satisfy relevant planning restrictions, environmental concerns and health and safety issues. And, of course, the size and structure of the building will be constrained by the geology of the land on which it will be built and the kind of foundations that can be used on such land. Such factors all need to be taken into consideration and brought together in the form of a design brief. The point of the analogy is that, just as it would be pointless to design a building without close reference to requirements of the design brief, so it makes no sense to produce a research design without having established a clear idea of the precise research questions that need to be addressed. The design must be 'fit for purpose'.

Link up with **PURPOSE**

Third, a research design *explains how the key components of a research project link together*. It explains the logic of the research process as it moves from one phase to the next, and it shows how the methods of data collection and analysis are consistent in terms of their general philosophy (see Figure 6.1).

> **Key point**
> A research design is a 'blueprint' plan for the research. It specifies what the key components look like, how they fit together, and how they will produce appropriate information to answer the research questions.

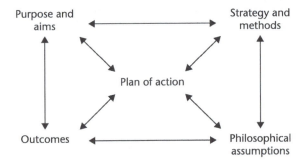

FIGURE 6.1 Research design: linking the parts together

Key decisions

At the beginning of any project, researchers need to make some key decisions about how they intend to approach the investigation of the topic. These decisions will have a fundamental impact on the research design (see Table 6.1).

Table 6.1 Key decisions about research design

	Alternative possibilities		
Time frame	Cross-sectional (snap-shot) e.g. survey		Longitudinal (movie) e.g. panel study, cohort study
Number	Depth (small number, specific) e.g. case study		Breadth (large number, general) e.g. survey
Environment	Controlled (in captivity) e.g. experiment, comparative research		Natural (in the wild) e.g. ethnography, case study, historical research
Data	Quantitative (numbers) measurement, statistics	Mixed methods	Qualitative (words and images) texts, interpretation, understanding,
Theory	Explanatory theory testing		Exploratory theory building

Time frame: cross-sectional or longitudinal (snap-shot or movie)

A key decision needs to be made about whether the research should be designed to record matters at a specific point in time or whether it should be designed to track the development of a phenomenon over a longer period of time. In reality, this decision will be affected by practical considerations such as the availability of resources and the deadlines for completion of the project but, in principle, there is a crucial decision to be made right at the start about whether the research should be 'cross-sectional' or 'longitudinal'. Cross-sectional research provides a 'snap-shot' of the situation at a particular point in time. This point in time need not necessarily be a specific date, time or instant. It could be a particular week or even a month. However, the aim is always to capture information about how things are/were at a pretty clearly defined moment rather than an attempt to follow changes and developments over a period of time. Opinion polls are a good example of cross-sectional research. They tell us about the public's opinion as it exists at a particular moment in time, for example, one month before a general election.

It is, of course, entirely possible to repeat such opinion polls at a series of later dates and, on the basis of the findings from the sequence of snap-shots, to track the changes that have occurred. If this is what the researcher has in mind, the design becomes longitudinal rather than cross-sectional. Its purpose is to trace changes and developments over a period of time – weeks, months, years – rather than focus on how things are/were at any given moment.

'*Cohort studies*' and '*panel studies*' are typical kinds of longitudinal designs. Cohort studies tend to be large-scale, long-term and expensive. Such studies focus on a particular cohort of people – identified according to some specific factor they have in common such as all being born on the same day, all being twins, all suffering the same disease. Members of the cohort are then contacted at regular intervals by the researchers to get updated information and to trace patterns and developments emerging in their lives. Based on this information, researchers can produce a detailed 'moving picture' based on developments over time. Panel studies follow a similar premise but are based on a representative sample of people or households who are surveyed to provide information on specific things such as the products they buy, the programmes they watch on TV or their views on political issues. Though sometimes smaller-scale than cohort studies, panel studies still tend to be large, expensive and beyond the resources of most small-scale research projects.

Number: breadth or depth of coverage (general or specific)

Researchers have the option to spread their net wide to capture a wide range of instances, or to focus their attention on a small number of examples of the thing they wish to study. Opting for a breadth of coverage has benefits in terms of the representativeness of the data and the ability to generalize from the findings. It is easier to include a representative cross-section of the population being studied when the research is based on large numbers of people, events or items. Opting for a depth of coverage, by contrast, allows researchers to obtain detailed data and to deal with the complex interrelationships that characterize many social phenomena. Resource constraints generally dictate that researchers need to decide whether to opt for either breadth or depth, but not both.

A design based on breadth is likely to be one that uses quantitative data. This is not a matter of principle so much as a matter of expediency. Basically, it is easier to store, code and analyse large volumes of data when it is in a numeric format. Analysing the data produced, for example, from a questionnaire *survey* of 1,000 people is easier where the data are quantitative (from fixed-choice items) than it is where the data come in the form of text responses to open-ended items.

Depth study designs, by contrast, are better able to make use of the rich content of qualitative data. *Case studies, ethnographies, phenomenology* and *grounded theory* approaches share the desire to probe deeply into a relatively restricted area of study and are best suited to making use of data in the form of interviews, documents and images where the number of items is likely to be relatively small.

Environment: controlled or natural (in captivity or in the wild)

Another key decision concerns the possibility and desirability of imposing 'controls' over the environment in which the research will take place. Researchers need to decide whether the design of the research is to be based on a highly controlled environment such as a laboratory or whether the purposes of research will be better met by studying events in their natural habitat. Again, in reality such decisions will take into account the feasibility of being able to exercise control over key variables but, in principle, there is a vital decision to be made about whether the environment for the research should be artificially created for the specific purposes of the research or whether it would be better to collect data in their natural context involving as little disruption to normality as possible.

The laboratory represents the most controlled environment for conducting research. Data collection is undertaken in circumstances that are created specifically for the purposes of the research and which are, in this sense, artificial rather than natural. This provides an environment in which researchers are best able to manipulate the relevant variables and establish the conditions in which it becomes possible to identify *causal* relationships between dependent and independent variables. In terms of design, these are sometimes referred to as 'causal research'.

Where circumstances do not permit the manipulation of variables sufficiently to meet the stringent criteria for causal research it is possible to retain some of the key principles of experimental research using designs such as 'field experiments', 'quasi experiments' and 'natural experiments'. These designs share with laboratory experiments the aim of observing the effect of a specific variable but, to varying degrees, they are restricted in their ability to apply the full range of controls that would be required under laboratory conditions. For example, researchers might be unable to comply with the need for the random allocation of participants to experimental and control groups. What these kinds of experimental designs do, however, is to make use of naturally occurring circumstances or arrangements which cannot be manipulated in order to *emulate* the conditions of an experiment. The designs make use of 'natural' events and circumstances to allow them to gauge the impact of specific variables. Some forms of *comparative research* work on this basis, making use of naturally occurring differences between societies as a means of observing the effect of specific factors.

The researcher might, on the other hand, decide that the purposes of the research are better served by looking at things 'holistically' rather than focusing on specific variables. Where this is the case, it is likely that conducting research in naturally-occurring situations will be regarded as preferable to the artificial environment of the laboratory. If researchers are interested in the complex values, norms and interrelationships of social life the decision might be taken to avoid any manipulation of variables and to avoid as far as possible any interruption of the natural habitat. They can opt to study the ecology of social life 'in the wild' rather than 'in the zoo'. *Case study* research and *ethnography* are examples of this approach. They require a design based on a naturally-occurring environment and researchers are generally concerned with getting 'the bigger picture' rather than focusing on specific variables. They want to see how the whole thing fits together (like an ecological system) rather than look at cause–effect relationships between specific, individual variables.

Data: quantitative, qualitative or mixed methods (measure or interpret)

The design of a research project will also depend crucially on the kind of data the researcher wishes to use. One option is to use quantitative data. Such data lend themselves to various forms of statistical calculations and are useful for detecting patterns of activity that allow researchers to forecast the likelihood of future events. So, if the research question is best answered using frequency counts, measurements, proportions or probabilities then quantitative data are appropriate. To illustrate the point, insurance companies will find the use of quantitative data the best way of finding out what premiums to charge to their customers. Presuming their objective is to adjust their premiums for different types of customer according to the likelihood of a claim, their purpose will be served by calculating the number of claims associated with the age and sex of the driver, the kind of vehicle involved and the area of residence, and then make accurate predictions about the risk of claims coming from specific types of driver. The higher the risk, the higher the premium.

Qualitative data would not prove very useful for such a task. However, if the purpose of the research was to find out how to reduce the likelihood of claims from high risk groups – for example, young males – then qualitative data would be a better option. An insight into the attitudes, motivations and behaviour of such groups could be what is required and this might be better achieved using qualitative data. Words and images, rather than numbers, might help the researcher to interpret the situation and to gain a depth understanding of the group's norms, values and perceptions of risk.

A third option is to have a research design which uses both quantitative and qualitative data – *mixed methods*. Recognizing that quantitative and qualitative data each have their respective strengths and weaknesses depending on what the research is trying to achieve, there is an increasing tendency to incorporate both kinds of data within a single research project.

Theory: exploratory or explanatory (theory building or theory testing)

The choice of design must be appropriate for the kind of research question that is being investigated and, as de Vaus (2001) argues, there are broadly two types of question that social researchers ask:

- What is going on? (exploratory research, descriptive research)
- Why is it happening? (explanatory research).

Where researchers set out to study an area on which there is not a well-developed body of theory they might choose an exploratory research design or a 'descriptive' design. Such designs are based on the need to map out a new area, to provide descriptive material about the contents of the area and, literally, to explore the new area. Sometimes there is a need for the design to be exploratory simply because there has been relatively little work done on the area previously. There is little to work on, and there is a lack of theory on which to build. However, there are also circumstances where researchers prefer to adopt an exploratory research design irrespective of the volume of existing research. Particularly with some kinds of qualitative enquiry, researchers can choose to take a fresh look at things and be keen to avoid having their vision of events 'clouded' by the cumulative theories and wisdom of previous researchers. *Grounded theory* approaches are a good example of this. So is phenomenological research. The research designs in such approaches are founded on the principle of keeping existing theories at arm's length to prevent them shaping the way the researcher understands what he/she is seeing. The design of the research should enable the discovery of new theory or the provision of fresh, unblinkered descriptions; the design is not intended to test existing theory.

Explanatory research designs are driven primarily by the wish to know why things are like they are, rather than what things look like. They look for the causes of things, and are most developed in connection with experiments. Explanatory research tends to build on a large volume of evidence from previous studies and a well-established body of theory. Research questions will often take the form of hypotheses and researchers are looking to test theories by checking the occurrence of events that have been predicted using existing theories. Rather than developing theories afresh (theory generation), the emphasis is on checking and developing existing theories (theory testing).

Evaluating research designs

A good research design provides a blueprint for research activity. It provides details of what is to be done and shows how the various parts fit together. But, how do we know that it works? Why should we believe that the design will actually achieve its intended goal? To answer such questions there needs to be some *evaluation* of the design which assesses its viability and which provides a degree of confidence that use of the design will lead to the production of accurate and relevant data.

Validity and reliability

Validity and reliability are the concepts that are generally regarded as the cornerstones for evaluating social research designs.

- *Validity refers to the quality of the data*. The data need to be precise enough for the purposes of the research and they need to be sufficiently detailed. The data need to be accurate and record things correctly. And, importantly, the data also need to be based on the right thing. Researchers need to have asked the right questions and got answers to questions that really hit the target as far as the research question is concerned. They need to be sure that the indicators they use accurately reflect the concept they are investigating.
- *Reliability refers to the quality of the methods*. Researchers need to feel sure that the methods they use will be consistent and not provide fluctuating measures. They need to know that any difference in results found when using the methods represents a real difference in the property that is being measured rather than a rogue 'mis-reading' produced by an unreliable instrument.

The concepts of validity and reliability originate from the use of quantitative research within a positivist philosophy, but have been adapted for use with qualitative research within an interpretivist philosophy as well. When using quantitative research there are a variety of statistical tests and procedures that can be employed to check on validity and reliability. When using qualitative research, there are alternative steps that can be taken which serve a similar purpose (Lincoln and Guba 1985: Maxwell 2005; Marshall and Rossman 2006; Yin 2008; Creswell 2009). Further details of the types of checks on validity and reliability can be found in Chapter 8 which deals with the issue of accuracy in social research. At this point, however, the vital point to recognize is that good research designs normally involve some self-evaluation process which justifies the design in terms of the reliability of the methods used and the validity of data produced by the research.

Pilot studies

With manufactured products, the design process will involve a series of meticulous tests, trials and development to ensure that the eventual design produces something that fits together nicely and works well. The process can take a long time and consume a lot of resources because the eventual design has to work perfectly. The equivalent process in social research involves the use of *pilot studies*. Pilot studies are small-scale trial runs that researchers can use as a means of checking how well their proposed research design works. If things go wrong during the pilot study, it is not a tragedy. The idea is to learn from what happens and to iron out any problems that might be encountered so that when the full-scale 'real' research begins, everything runs smoothly. For this reason, the use of pilot studies would generally be regarded as beneficial for the research design and a good thing. However, in practice, social research designs are rarely tested and refined to anywhere near the extent of product designs before being put into practice (Middleton et al. 2006). The main reason for this is to do with the resources and scale of research. Whereas large-scale social investigations will be able to use some form of pilot study in advance of the main study, small-scale research is less likely to make use of a full pilot study. In practice, the pressure to complete research within a given time frame, especially when working on a limited budget, means that it is often a matter of getting things 'right first time'.

Drawing on established good practice: adapting existing designs

The pressure on small-scale researchers to get things 'right first time' does not mean, though, that they need to start from scratch whenever they produce a research design. There is, of course, a mass of accumulated wisdom and experience on which to draw. Parts of the design might well have been subjected to considerable pre-testing. For example, some questionnaires, tests and interview schedules might have been validated extensively to confirm that they work well. This is the case particularly within the discipline of psychology where researchers can make use of an array of well-established research instruments as part of their design. And social researchers can also make use of standard types of design (experiments, surveys, etc.) as a guide to the basic pattern for their design. Experimental designs and survey designs, in particular, can make use of models which have been tried and tested on many occasions in previous projects. Validated components and existing models, indeed, can provide a solid foundation on which to build a research design and good social research is normally expected to have its roots in some clearly identified foundation such as these.

Having made this point, it should also be appreciated that social researchers are rarely able to pick a design 'off the shelf' that will entirely suit their purpose with respect to a new research project. Research design, almost inevitably, calls for the creative adaption of an existing model and its application to the particular circumstances of the new research project.

Key point

Good research design involves coupling:

- best practice and wisdom from established models of research, with
- good insight and imagination about how this might apply to the unique circumstances of the new research project.

Limitations

All research designs have their limitations. Good research recognizes its own methodological limitations and provides an explicit account of them. The discussion of limitations demonstrates the researcher's awareness of the boundaries to what can, and what cannot, be concluded on the basis of the findings and it also serves as a warning to readers not to draw unwarranted conclusions from the findings.

There are two related aspects to this facet of research design. First, there are limitations which specify the potential weaknesses of the methodology. This is effectively a self-evaluation that shows the researcher himself/herself is fully aware of the pros and cons associated with the approach that has been used. It is important to appreciate that the researcher should not destroy the credibility of the research by identifying *fundamental* problems with the design. The point is to fend off potential criticism by openly acknowledging that, although the design is fit for purpose, it is not perfect. Partly, such limitations can stem from an inherent feature of the design. For example, a case study approach will almost inevitably run up against the question of how far generalizations can be based on findings from one or a few cases. This does not invalidate the use of the case study approach, but it is an 'issue' that should be acknowledged as a methodological limitation. Partly, limitations can stem from practical matters. For example, certain sources of data may not be available that would have been beneficial for the investigation. Or, perhaps a survey might face limitations in terms of its response rate and geographical coverage.

Second, there are 'delimitations' which concern the scope of the research. In effect, these specify what is included and what is excluded from the study. The topic and research questions, in themselves, will serve as delimiters by focusing the research on specific aspects of a broader, general issue. The delimitations might also involve things like a focus on selected variables or particular groups of people. Delimitations establish boundaries around what

Box 6.1 Design	
The key issue	**Things to be considered**
What is the overall plan and logic behind the research?	• Does the choice of research design correspond with the kind of research questions being investigated? • Have the various components of the research been described with sufficient detail and clarity? • Are the distinct parts of the research linked in a logical and explicit fashion? • On what basis can we be confident that the research design will work?

the research is trying to do and to what is included (and excluded) from the study.

Link up with **ACCOUNTABILITY**

Qualitative research designs

Research designs for qualitative research are not generally as detailed and fully mapped out at the start of research as they are with quantitative research. This owes something to the way such research does not lend itself to the degree of control over factors that characterizes designs associated with quantitative research, for example, experimental designs. It is also because qualitative research is more associated with exploratory research in which there needs to be a degree of flexibility and potential for development built into the design. It would be a mistake, however, to think that qualitative research does not need careful planning. This is a point stressed by many key writers on qualitative research who are critical of any assumption that qualitative research can be conducted without a research design (e.g. Miles and Huberman 1994; Maxwell 2005; Marshall and Rossman 2006). According to de Vaus: 'The need to attend to issues of research design (. . .) applies equally to "qualitative" researchers as to "quantitative" researchers. It applies regardless of the particular methods that are used to collect data' (de Vaus 2001: xvi).

There are, however, some important differences between qualitative and quantitative research designs that need to be recognized. First, there is the matter of *flexibility and adaptability*. It is more normal for qualitative research to adapt and change as the research progresses. The success of qualitative research, indeed, can often depend on its ability to react to developing circumstances. Qualitative research designs, as a result, tend to have a built-in flexibility that allows them to be responsive to emerging circumstances. As Marshall and Rossman (2006: 52) emphasize:

> The researcher should demonstrate to the reader that she reserves the right to make modifications in the original design as the research evolves: building flexibility into the design is crucial. The researcher does so by (a) demonstrating the appropriateness of and the logic of qualitative methods for the particular research question, and (b) devising a (design) that includes many of the elements of traditional models. At the same time she reserves the right to change the implementation plan during data collection.

Second, there is the matter *specific detail*. Qualitative research, especially when it is exploratory in nature, might rely on the use of an *emergent* design. This means that, at the outset of the investigation, the researcher is not likely to have a firm schedule for the completion of data collection and is not likely to know exactly who or how many people/instances are to be included in the sample. The research is a voyage of discovery. It would be wrong, however, to infer that such research can be started without having given some thought to the scope and scale of the investigation. There are boundaries to research which dictate how long it can take and what resources it can consume.

Link up with **FEASIBILITY**

Qualitative research, just like quantitative research, needs to be designed with a view to meeting the restrictions imposed by time and money and, with this in mind, even an emergent research design needs to include some estimation of the likely numbers and the likely schedule for the research. The emergent nature of the research will mean that it may not be possible to specify exactly who or exactly how many people might be involved, nor exactly where or exactly when the data will be collected. But the reality is that the research will need to be completed by a certain date and that there will only be a certain amount of resources available to undertake the research. Bearing these resource constraints in mind, the research design should include a calculation of reasonable target figures – even though it is recognized that these might well need to be revised as the research project evolves.

Descriptions of the research design

Link up with **ACCOUNTABILITY**

Good research requires a clear and explicit account of the research design. In the first instance this calls for a description of the *strategy* that is adopted for the investigation and the *philosophy* underlying the research. However, as we have seen, research designs also concern the way the various components of the overall project fit together – their logic and rationale. So, although descriptions of research designs will tend to focus on the strategy and the philosophy of the research, their links with other parts of the research should not be overlooked. In particular, the account of the research design should always keep an eye on the way in which the design is connected to the purpose and the outcomes of the enquiry (see Figure 6.2).

Purpose and aims		What is the research trying to achieve?	e.g. exploratory research, explanatory research
DESIGN	**Strategy**	Which approach will best meet the aims of the research?	e.g. survey, case study, experiment, qualitative data, quantitative data, mixed methods
	Philosophy	What are the underlying assumptions?	e.g. epistemology, ontology
Methods		Who/what will be included in the study?	e.g. population, sampling technique, sample size
		How will the data be collected?	e.g. questionnaires, interviews, focus groups
Analysis		How will the data be interpreted?	e.g. statistical techniques, coding of qualitative data
Evaluation		What confidence can we have in the findings?	e.g. checks on validity and reliability
Ethics		How will people's rights be protected?	e.g. protection of confidentiality and anonymity
Outcomes		What will be the end-products of the project?	e.g. practical guidelines, advances in knowledge, developments of theory

How will the outcomes of the project address the initial purpose for the research?

FIGURE 6.2 Research design and the process of enquiry

The amount of detail researchers might be expected to provide will depend on the context in which they are writing about the design. On some occasions, the description needs to be quite detailed. Where, for example, research designs are described as part of a research thesis, a dissertation or a book, it is to be expected that researchers will devote a substantial amount of space to the description and justification of the design. This will take place initially in the Abstract and the Introduction, and then it will receive detailed attention in the Methods section before being returned to more briefly in the context of the Conclusions to the study.

On other occasions, researchers need to capture the essence of the design very succinctly. Where, for example, the design is described in the context of a research proposal or a journal article, there are normally quite strict word limits. This means that researchers can do little more than provide an *outline* that highlights the key aspects of the design. In such contexts they cannot indulge in some essay-like justification for the choice of approach: there is little scope for wasted words, flowery language or any material that is not directly relevant to the design.

When researchers are obliged to work within such word constraints their description of the design can benefit from the use of *precise technical terms*. This is particularly the case within disciplines that favour quantitative methods and the disciplines allied to science and medicine where researchers are often required to provide details of the research design in a rigid format in very few words. But, actually, the use of precise technical terms has enormous value in relation to descriptions of any research design whatever the context and whatever the constraints on space. A well-chosen word or two can communicate masses of information to an audience who share an understanding of what the term signifies and what the ramifications of its use might be. Good accounts of research design, then, capture the essence of the design through the use of technical terms such as:

- embedded case study design;
- pre-test/post-test nonequivalent groups quasi-experiment;
- single panel design with replacement;
- interview survey using a quota sample based on demographics for the population being studied.

Guidelines for good practice

The design should be fit for purpose

Any research design must be 'fit for purpose'. 'Fit for purpose' means that the kind of research that is undertaken meets the needs of the research question. The choice of research strategy, the selection of data collection methods and the kinds of data analysis undertaken must all be appropriate in the sense that the findings they produce will be of a kind that is likely to be valuable for answering the research question.

There should be a logical connection between the various elements of the research design

'Logical' means that the decisions made with respect to the strategy, methods and analysis are both coherent and consistent. As Green and Browne (2005: 32) put the point, 'A research design is more than just the data collection methods used (such as interviews or questionnaires) – it refers to the *logic* of how these data will be collected.' The research design needs to be based on some explicit rationale that justifies the use of the various components in terms of how they connect with one another.

Research designs should be 'made to measure' and, also, make use of established good practice

Research designs are generally tailored to meet the needs of each specific project because, to an extent, each research project is unique. Designs, therefore, need to be 'made to measure'. Although previous designs can be used, almost inevitably they will need to be *adapted* to fit the particular circumstances of the research. Having made this point, researchers do not need to develop their designs from scratch. There are a variety of established types of research design that can be used as the starting point. From the researcher's point of view the task is: (1) to identify a relevant and useful type of design (from established alternatives); and (2) to *adapt* this to fit the needs of the proposed investigation.

Some form of evaluation should be applied to research designs (checks on validity and reliability)

Before using any particular design, researchers should subject it to scrutiny in terms of its viability and in terms of the likelihood that it will produce accurate and relevant data. The manner in which this is done will vary depending on the nature of the design, and can include the use of pilot studies, checks on reliability and validity, and comparisons with designs successfully used in other studies. In whatever way chosen, though, researchers are expected to engage in some evaluation of the design and to provide support for the belief that the research design is likely to work well.

The design should be ready from the start

The design for research should be in place before the empirical investigation begins – and this can apply to even 'emergent' designs such as those involved with grounded theory. This applies to both quantitative and qualitative research.

There should be a clear and explicit description of the research design

In most cases, the design needs to be expressed succinctly because research proposals and research reports are generally constrained by tight word limits. Careful thought, therefore, needs to be given to the precise terms that will describe the key components of the research design bearing in mind the backgrounds of those who might be assessing the quality of the design. This is a (rare) occasion when technical terms and jargon can play a very positive role – and they should be used to good effect in the context of any research design.

Further reading

Creswell, J.W. (2009) *Research Design: Qualitative, Quantitative, and Mixed Methods Approaches*, 3rd edn. Thousand Oaks, CA: Sage.

Denscombe, M. (2007) *The Good Research Guide: For Small-scale Social Research Projects*, 3rd edn. Buckingham: Open University Press, Chapters 1–8.

De Vaus, D.A. (2001) *Research Design in Social Research*. London: Sage.

Marshall, C. and Rossman, G.B. (2006) *Designing Qualitative Research*, 4th edn. London: Sage.

Yin, R.K. (2008) *Case Study Research: Design and Methods*, 4th edn. Thousand Oaks, CA: Sage.

Checklist for DESIGN

When considering the design of the research you should feel confident about answering 'yes' to the following questions: ☑

1   Have clear decisions been made about whether the
    research should be:
    Based on a cross-sectional or longitudinal time frame? ☐
    Geared to breadth or depth of coverage? ☐
    Conducted in a controlled or a natural environment? ☐
    Producing quantitative or qualitative data (or both)? ☐
    Aimed at theory building or theory testing? ☐

2   Does the choice of research design meet the needs of the
    research questions being investigated? ☐

3   Has a clear and explicit description of the research
    design been provided? ☐

4   Have details been provided of the:
    Population/sample being studied? ☐
    Procedure for selecting this group of people, events or things? ☐
    Methods for collecting data? ☐
    Techniques for analysing the data? ☐

5   Does the research design explain:
    The overall plan and logic behind the research? ☐
    How the key components of a research project link together? ☐
    The underlying philosophical assumptions (including ethics)? ☐
    The feasibility in terms of the resources and access to data? ☐

6   Does this description of the design specify:
    How far it is based on existing designs and established good
    practice? ☐
    How it adapts existing designs and is 'made to measure'? ☐

7   Has some self-evaluation of the design been undertaken
    (e.g. in terms of reliability and validity, use of a pilot study,
    recognition of limitations)? ☐

8   If using a qualitative research design, has sufficient
    flexibility been built into the design to allow it to be responsive to
    emerging circumstances? ☐

© M. Denscombe, *Ground Rules for Social Research*. Open University Press.

7

PHILOSOPHY

Ground rule:	**Research should be aware of its underlying philosophical foundations**
Questions:	What ideas and assumptions underlie the approach to the research?
	How are these ideas and assumptions reflected in the nature of the research questions and the kind of methodology used for the research?
Answer:	Accounts of the research demonstrate an awareness of the underlying philosophical assumptions of the approach and, where appropriate, acknowledge their implications for the nature of the knowledge produced by the research.

The philosophical foundations of research have been discussed at length and in detail by researchers, philosophers and social theorists over a long period to time. This reflects the importance that is attached to getting a clear and precise picture of what the foundations are and how they manifest themselves in the nature of social research. There is, however, no consensus of opinion resulting from these discussions – and the debates rumble on. As a result, newcomers and seasoned researchers alike are faced with the prospect of working in a 'contested' terrain where they need to make choices and where those choices are likely to need defending against criticism from those who advocate a different approach. The project researcher will soon come to realize that 'you cannot please all of the people all of the time'.

The debates on the philosophical foundations of research can be complex, sophisticated and intellectually challenging. The language in which the issues are expressed is often dense and difficult to understand and, to make life still more complicated, many of the concepts and terms used by protagonists in the debate seem to mean different things to different people. Bearing these points in mind, the purpose of this chapter is to help project researchers to do the following:

- grasp the fundamental issues relating to the debates;
- understand how to address these issues in the context of small-scale research projects;
- appreciate the importance of philosophical foundations in relation to the nature of social research.

Why are philosophical foundations important?

There are three reasons that social researchers need to have some basic understanding of the philosophy that underlies the design and implementation of their research. The first of these is because philosophical assumptions constitute the *foundations* for research in the way that:

- they underpin the perspective that is adopted on the research topic;
- they shape the nature of the investigation, its methods and the questions that are asked;
- they specify what type of things qualify as worthwhile evidence;
- they point to the kind of conclusions that can, and cannot, be drawn on the basis of the investigation.

The second reason is because there are *alternative types* of philosophical assumptions which support different positions with regard to the nature of social research. Basically, it is possible to approach the social world from different perspectives and to see things differently depending upon the philosophical position that is taken. The alternative perspectives are not only different, they are generally depicted as incompatible as well. Researchers are therefore expected to be aware of their philosophical assumptions because they need to know where they stand in relation to the alternatives on offer, and how the positions differ.

The third reason is that the different types are generally regarded as *competing* alternatives, with advocates of one philosophical position being critical of the alternatives and contending that their own approach is best. When battle lines are drawn between the advocates of these competing alternatives, researchers need to know where they stand and whose side they are on.

Box 7.1 Philosophy	
The key issue	**Things to be considered**
What are the implications of the research philosophy for the investigation?	• What assumptions underlie the choice of topic as something important to study? • How does the choice of research methodology align with a particular vision of social reality? • On what basis are the data considered to be valid and worthwhile evidence? • In what ways does the research philosophy place boundaries around the kind of conclusions that can be drawn?

Understanding the social world: ontology and epistemology

There are three concepts which researchers need to understand because they lie at the heart of the discussions and controversies surrounding research philosophies. These are 'ontology', 'epistemology' and 'paradigm'. There are other important philosophical issues, but these are the ones that it is vital for project researchers to be aware of. The concepts of ontology and epistemology will be outlined at this point by way of introduction to the subsequent discussion of the main philosophical positions in contemporary social research (positivism, interpretivism, critical realism and pragmatism) (see Figure 7.1). The concept of a research paradigm will be dealt with separately later in the chapter in the context of quantitative, qualitative and mixed methods approaches to social research.

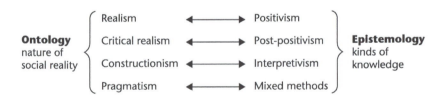

FIGURE 7.1 A simplified model of basic social research philosophies

Ontology refers the nature of social phenomena and the beliefs that researchers hold about the nature of social reality. Debates between social researchers on this point have been deep, complicated and sometimes abrasive but at the heart of the debates surrounding the matter of ontology there are two basic positions:

- '*Realists*' regard the social world as something that exists 'out there' – an objective reality that exists independently of whether any particular individual believes in it or approves of it. The social world, like the natural world, is seen as having properties that can be measured, and as having structures and relationships that are fairly consistent and stable.
- '*Constructionists*' regard the social world as a creation of the human mind – a reality that is constructed through people's perceptions and reinforced by their interactions with other people. Social reality is seen as something that is constantly being produced and re-produced; something that exists only as long as people persist in creating it through their everyday actions, words and beliefs. The constructionist vision of social reality acknowledges the possibility that the nature of the social world might vary between different cultures and different groups and, unlike realists, they see the social world as comprised of *multiple realities* rather than a single objective social reality. The quest for some ultimate, definitive account of social phenomena, it follows, is misguided and impossible. Instead, researchers should focus their attention on explaining how different groups construct their social realities and on describing what those realities entail.

Epistemology refers to the ways that humans create their knowledge about the social world and involves philosophical debates about the bases on which we can claim to have knowledge of social reality. Epistemology, then, is not concerned with what social reality actually 'is' so much as the logic behind our ability to acquire our knowledge of what it is. There are two fundamental positions on this and, not surprisingly, these link quite closely with the realist and constructionist positions in relation to ontology:

- '*Positivism*' centres on the idea of using scientific methods to gain knowledge, and it regards the observation and measurement of the properties of objects as crucial to the way we find out about social reality. This, of course, fits neatly with a realist ontology in which social reality is regarded as something which exists 'out there' with properties that lend themselves to being objectively measured. It also fits with the quantitative research paradigm – as discussed later in the chapter – where, again, there is great value placed on the processes of observation and measurement in the process of building knowledge.
- '*Interpretivism*', by contrast, regards our knowledge of the social world as something that relies on human capacities to literally 'make sense' of a reality which, of itself, has no inherent properties, no order, no structure. The knowledge we have about reality is something that is produced, rather than being discovered. Only through *interpreting* the world do we come to know anything about it. This epistemological position tallies with the constructionist ontology.

Key point

Good researchers should be aware of the philosophical assumptions underlying their approach and how these are reflected in the choice of topic to research and the methods used to study it. They should also be sensitive to the limitations resulting from the underlying ontology and epistemology of their research approach.

Positivism

Because science has been extremely successful in explaining the causes of things in the natural world, there is an obvious temptation to copy the natural science method as a recipe for understanding, and possibly even controlling, social phenomena. And this, indeed, is what has happened under the guise of an approach to social research called 'positivism'. Recognizing the success of science in the natural world, the aim has been to replicate this success by transposing the research methods used by natural scientists on to studies of the social world.

The term positivism has come to mean slightly different things to different people and sometimes there is disagreement about which elements can rightly be subsumed under the notion (Burrell and Gibson 1979; Halfpenny 1982; Smith 1998; Blaikie 2007). The positivist position, however, generally adheres to the following *ontological assumptions* concerning the nature of social reality:

- There are patterns and regularities, causes and consequences, in the social world just as there are in the natural world. There is an order to events in the social world which lends itself to discovery and analysis just as there is order in the natural world.
- The patterns and regularities in the social world exist quite independently of whether they are recognized by people. Positivism presumes that there is an objective reality 'out there' waiting to be discovered. Researchers do not create the patterns and regularities of social life – they discover them.

Positivism is also based on the following *epistemological assumptions* about how best to generate knowledge about social reality:

- Scientific research methods are best for studying the reality of social life. They represent a gold standard that should be used as far as possible for all instances of research.
- Empirical observation is crucial in the sense that theories and explanations can have no credibility unless they can be corroborated through observation of events in the world.

- Social research should make use of reliable tools and techniques that provide accurate measures of the social phenomenon being studied. These research tools must not impinge on the thing being measured, not disturb it and not alter it in the process of data collection.

Link up with **ACCURACY**

- Researchers should be objective. They are expected to retain a detached, impartial position in relation to the thing being studied and not to let personal feelings or social values influence the questions pursued, the results reported or the analysis of the findings.

Link up with **OBJECTIVITY**

> *Key point*
> Positivism is an approach to social research that seeks to apply the natural science model of research to investigations of social phenomena and explanations of the social world.

Interpretivism

Interpretivism is an umbrella term for a range of approaches that reject some of the basic premises of positivism. As with the term positivism, there are points on which experts disagree and there are terms that are sometimes used to mean different things by different people. Some writers, for example, use the term *constructivism* instead of interpretivism. This hints at the dangers of trying to cover a diverse range of approaches and terminologies in a straightforward way. Having made this point, the term 'interpretivism' itself tends to be used extensively by social researchers and in common use conveys the notion of a broad philosophical position that represents an alternative to positivism. It is generally regarded as making the following *ontological assumptions* about the nature of social reality:

- *Social reality is subjective*. It is constructed and interpreted by people – rather than something that exists objectively 'out there'. From the interpretivists' point of view the social world does not have the tangible, material qualities that allow it to be measured, touched or observed in some literal way. It is a *social* creation, constructed in the minds of people and reinforced through their interactions with each other. It is a reality that only exists through the way people believe in it, relate to it and interpret it. And for this reason, interpretivists tend to focus their attention on the way people make sense of the world and how they create their social world through their actions and interpretations of the world. Whereas positivism focuses on the way that social reality exists externally to people, acting as a constraining force on values and behaviour, interpretivist approaches stress the way that people shape society.

- *Humans react to the knowledge that they are being studied.* Humans have self-awareness in a sense that makes them very different from the materials studied by the natural sciences. When humans become aware that they are the focus of attention for research, there is the very real possibility that they will act differently from normal. They might possibly become self-conscious or alter their behaviour to take account of the purposes of the research. The process of collecting the data, in this sense, can alter the thing being studied – distort it and alter its natural state. Now, while this can be a problem for natural scientists too – for example, in relation to subatomic physics – the extent of the problem tends to be far greater for social research than natural science research, and it hinges on the point that the subjects of the investigation have self-awareness and the ability to react to being studied in a way that natural matter does not. Chemicals do not get embarrassed by researchers delving into their inner workings. People might.

There are also some basic *epistemological assumptions* associated with the notion of interpretivism and its understanding of the nature of social reality:

- *Humans react to the knowledge produced by being studied.* Social research faces the difficulty that the knowledge it produces can feed back into the situation and interfere with, even confound, the explanations or predictions that were initially made from the investigation. Across the various disciplines within the social sciences there is the ever-present possibility that research can produce a feedback loop which complicates matters in a way that the natural sciences do not have to contend with. If, for example, research leads to predictions about high inflation rates in the economy, there is the prospect that this information might be used to change the course of events so that the prediction does not come true. Those with influence, those with responsibility, those with vested interests, might react to the knowledge and actively take steps to ensure that the prediction does *not* become a reality.
- *Objective knowledge is not possible.* Positivism has come under fire from those who contend that it is more or less impossible for social researchers to be objective and that social research is always going to be influenced by the values and expectations of those undertaking the research. Social researchers are part and parcel of the world they want to investigate. This means they cannot stand outside things to get an objective viewpoint. The implication of this is that observations and explanations of the social world

are inevitably coloured by *expectations and predispositions* that are brought to the research and by the *language* which mediates what is known through observation.

- *Social research cannot explain things in terms of grand theories or universal truths.* Interpretivists argue that, because explanations are inevitably influenced by researchers' expectations and conceptions of the social world, researchers cannot claim that their research is objective. '*Postmodernists*', in particular, have taken this scepticism about objectivity to a logical extreme and used it as a central plank of criticisms levelled at conventional forms of social research. Their position has been that we should abandon all pretence at objectivity and appreciate instead that there are a number of alternative versions of reality and truth – alternative '*discourses*'. Perhaps more significantly, they argue that there is no logical ground for seeing any one version of reality as superior to others. In this respect, postmodernism offers a thoroughgoing challenge to the whole notion of scientific methodology and the quest for theories that explain universals about nature or society. Indeed, it is hostile to the adoption of a 'scientific' approach to research because it contends that this perpetuates a myth from the age of the Enlightenment that there is the possibility of discovering universal laws of nature that apply in all circumstances and everywhere. The search for grand theories, argue postmodernists, is futile. For postmodernists, social reality is a shifting and contradictory thing that only lends itself to short-lived, small-scale and partial accounts by researchers.

There are three repercussions of adopting the interpretivist position that can prove uncomfortable for many social researchers. First, there is a *relativism* associated with interpretivism that challenges the idea that the researcher's explanation can be taken to be the right one – true and correct. Without being able to claim an objective position in relation to the thing they are studying, interpretivists' accounts are always open to the possibility that another researcher might see things differently and produce a different account. There is scope for alternative and competing explanations, each of which can claim validity. And, taken to its logical extreme, this can invite the argument that 'anything goes' and that findings from social research are no better (and no worse) in terms of their standing than knowledge produced by other means and from within other discourses. But even without going down the extreme route, the point is that interpretivism can be seen as undermining the status of the researcher as the expert and 'the one with all the answers'.

Second, there is a degree of *uncertainty* contained within interpretivist explanations of the social world that can be uncomfortable for researchers. The interpretivists' concern with 'subjectivity', with 'understandings', with 'agency' and the way people construct their social world, introduces complexities that involve elements of uncertainty. There is even the possibility of contradictions and internal inconsistencies arising as part of the explanations that interpretivists produce. This does not sit comfortably with the scientific search for universal laws or certainty about how things work. To caricature things a little, interpretivists' explanations are likely to be messy rather than nice and neat; they might be open-ended rather than complete.

Third, interpretivist research can *appear to lack rigour*. It ought to be stressed at this point that good interpretivist research actually calls for an approach that is very systematic and rigorous in its approach. However, because it tends not to involve statistical analysis and because it allows for an emergent research design (in which the research questions and the research sample take shape during the course of the research itself rather than being specified in advance), it might *appear* as though the research lacks rigour. Unfortunately, such an impression has been made more likely by the way these aspects of interpretive research have been hijacked and abused by people doing sloppy research. For those who do not like statistics, interpretive research might seem to be the easy option. For those who do not prepare for research properly, an emergent design allows them to justify making things up as they go along.

There is no doubt that interpretivism has been influential on thinking in social research. It has prompted researchers to reconsider the grounds on which they can claim to be objective and, in general, it has caused social researchers to be more careful, more modest, more tentative about their claims to have produced theories about the social world. Certainly, good social researchers in the twenty-first century are sensitive to the reflexivity of social knowledge. The fact is that very few social researchers would now adhere to the classic positivist view that the methodology of the natural sciences can be applied to the social world without qualifying their position in some way that took on board the problems linked to objectivity, etc. What the interpretivist critique has not done, however, is to persuade all social researchers to abandon all vestiges of positivism. Far from it. Despite the impact of the interpretivist critique, the repercussions in terms of relativism, uncertainty and rigour have meant that many social researchers, some would argue, the majority, have preferred to adopt an approach that constitutes some modified form of positivism (e.g. 'post-positivism', 'critical realism') that incorporates significant parts of interpretivist critique in relation to objectivity and the use of scientific methods.

Critical realism

Critical realism has emerged as a popular alternative to positivism and interpretivism. It has proved attractive to many social researchers who have concluded that neither positivism nor interpretivism, on their own, could provide a satisfactory philosophy for research. It is, however, a *'post-positivist'* research philosophy. It is a development from positivism and, although it incorporates certain elements of the interpretivist critique, it has more affinity with positivism than with interpretivism. The philosophical development of critical realism owes much to the work of Roy Bhaskar (1975, 1979, 1986) and, in discussions of critical realism, he is generally regarded as the originator of the approach.

What critical realism has done is to transform positivism by taking the certainty and the absoluteness out of the approach. It has abandoned an exclusive preference for scientific methods as the only worthwhile means to discover how the social world works and accepted that there are inevitable limits to how far social researchers can discover the 'true reality' of the social world in which they live (Layder 1990; Pawson and Tilley 1997; Sayer 2000; Pawson 2006). Critical realism calls for the social researcher to be more cautious about their claims and to treat their theories more as tentative propositions than perfect and complete explanations of how things work. In essence, critical realism has taken the 'positive' out of 'positivism'.

There are four main *ontological assumptions* underlying critical realism. The first of these appears to align with positivism but the other three develop and refine the vision of social reality.

- *Reality exists independently of any individual's experience or interpretation of it.* The critical realist approach believes that both the social and the physical worlds have a *real* existence. They exist independent of any individual's knowledge of them.
- *Reality is not always observable.* In the realms of social reality this is illustrated by phenomena such as social class, mental health and personal motivation. These are not the kind of things whose existence can be detected through the senses of sight, touch, smell or sound. They cannot be directly observed, and nor can they be directly measured. From the critical realist position, though, they are nonetheless very real. They exist whether or not you or I decide to believe in them, and they can have an influence on our lives whether or not we wish this to be the case.
- *The impact of reality is not always predictable.* The critical realist position is that something is 'real' if it has an effect. This is close to the pragmatist position (see below), but critical realists go on to make the point that an effect is something that will 'probably' occur not something that will definitely occur. Social reality does not exist through a simple cause–effect relationship where every time a cause is present, an effect will happen. To illustrate the point, consider the relationship between social class and educational achievement. Critical realists argue that social class is real and this is demonstrated by its impact (effect) on educational achievement. Those from a working-class background achieve fewer educational qualifications than those from a middle-class background. Class has a causal effect on achievement. But this does not mean that each and every person from a working-class background gains fewer qualifications. What it means is that their chances of gaining qualifications are less. The effect occurs in terms of probability – not certainty.

- *Social reality is complex and not necessarily revealed by things that can be measured and observed.* A reality can exist, but it may not always be observable. As with the example of social class and educational achievement, the cause (social class) may not be evident in each and every individual instance of educational achievement (effect). It is an underlying and sometimes hidden cause that has a *potential* impact, not a definite impact. To complicate matters, in the social world there can be *multiple causes* of things, and their effects can intertwine and not be observable on all occasions. This means that researchers should not rely on what they can observe at the surface level as providing them with all the information they need to know in order to arrive at conclusions (theories) about the phenomenon. On this point, critical realism clearly moves away from positivism and empiricism by casting doubt on the idea that the careful recording and measurement of observable traits can provide the necessary clues for understanding social reality. What can be observed 'on the surface' needs to be interpreted, not taken at face value, and this requires the construction of theories about what is going on hidden beneath the surface. The theories can then be tested against how well they explain observed events and can be compared and evaluated in terms of their adequacy in explaining events. In principle, the theories can even be shown to be wrong.

Coupled with this vision of social reality, critical realism is characterized by two main epistemological assumptions:

- *We can only 'know' the real world via theories.* There is no direct way of representing social reality. It is always seen through theories that social researchers produce to explain the realities. And these theories should not be treated as neutral; they can shape the appearance of reality. The theories are regarded as attempts to understand and predict the reality that can achieve this to a better or worse degree but never a perfect fashion. There is always the possibility that they might contain errors and that they can be improved. Indeed, the possibility of 'getting it wrong' is very important for the critical realist approach. This possibility not only motivates researchers to strive constantly for better theories but it also confirms the existence of social realities as something separate from the theories through which they are understood. If a theory can 'get it wrong', then the social reality must have effects which are to some extent independent from the theory.
- *Research methods are 'theory-laden'.* As the previous points indicate, for critical realism the role of theory is deeply embedded in the understanding of social reality. It permeates research activity and, as Sayer (1992: 46) has noted, 'theory is increasingly recognized as affecting observation itself, so the latter is said to be "theory-laden" '. This means that the methods that are used to collect data should not be considered as neutral tools. If we scratch beneath the surface, we can see that they are actually infused with

assumptions. This is why, from the critical realist point of view, theory and methods are tightly connected.

In practice, critical realism invites the researcher to investigate social phenomena in terms of their causes and effects. This sits comfortably with positivism's agenda and allows social researchers to produce findings which have a scientific feel to them. Critical realism does not rule out the use of methods associated with the natural sciences and, although there is some debate among critical realists about the virtue of such methods, overall it is accepted that they can be useful in the social researcher's quest for knowledge.

The major break with positivism comes in the role of theory and interpretation. Critical realist researchers do not 'collect facts' and 'discover theories' in the sense that positivist researchers might see their role. Instead, facts are interpreted and theories produced in a way that recognizes the interpretivists' tenet that it is impossible for researchers to understand the world in an entirely objective, neutral way. The researcher's influence is far more open than with positivism, with the researcher's values and beliefs becoming an active consideration in terms of the way social realities are explained. Critical realism, however, avoids the relativism that is associated with some extreme versions of interpretivism. Crucially on this point, critical realism's vision of social reality ensures that social science is not forced into a position where there are as many realities as there are individuals, and where varied accounts of the realities are all equally valid.

Although social phenomena cannot exist independently of actors or subjects, they usually do exist independently of the particular individual who is studying them. Social scientists and historians produce interpretations of objects, but they do not generally produce the objects themselves.

(Sayer 1992: 49)

Box 7.2 Why 'critical' realism?

There are two ways in which the approach adopts a 'critical' position. The first is outward-looking in the sense that it takes a critical stance in relation to the objects in society that it studies. It is committed to a vision of social science as something whose purpose is to suggest alternatives and promote change rather than restrict itself to explanations of how things are at present. The second is inward-looking – in the sense of being self-critical. It regards its own attempts to explain the world as always open to challenge. Its theories are not absolute, once and for all time explanations of reality.

Pragmatism

Pragmatism judges approaches to research in terms of 'the practical outcomes of their use'. It is sceptical about the philosophical debates between positivism, interpretivism and critical realism, and regards these debates as rather unproductive. Instead, pragmatism takes the *research problem* as its starting point and it gauges the value of any particular approach or method primarily in terms of how well the outcomes work in practice.

Pragmatism has been in widespread use among social researchers for a long time although in published discussions of research philosophy it has not been as prominent as positivism, interpretivism or critical realism. Partly, this is because it is an approach more readily associated with practitioners undertaking applied research who, for better or worse, have tended to focus on the practical usefulness of their findings rather than its underlying philosophy. And partly it reflects the fact that, in practice, empirical social researchers have not been obsessed with the purity of their ontological or epistemological positions (Bryman 2006, 2007). Although the 'theory' might say that positivism and interpretivism are incompatible in terms of their basic beliefs about social reality, in practice, social researchers have tended to pick and choose from the array of methods at their disposal – using questionnaires when they serve the purpose, relying on observation when it produces suitable data, conducting experiments where they are possible and analysing official records if these contain the information that is needed. They have focused on getting the best from the tools that are available, recognizing that no single approach is perfect.

The roots of pragmatism are to be found in the writings of Charles Sanders Peirce in the late nineteenth and early twentieth century (Peirce et al. 1931). His 'pragmatic maxim' was that the quest for truth and reality requires thinking based on *testable* concepts, and that such concepts can only be expressed and checked in relation to the 'practical outcomes of their use'. Pragmatism has changed and developed since then, and has been evident in the work of symbolic interactionists such as Dewey, Mead, Blumer and Goffman, in the grounded theory of Glaser and Strauss, and the ethnomethodology, conversational analysis and discourse analysis of people such as Garfinkel, Cicourel and Foucault (Guignon 1991; Rorty 1991; Cherryholmes 1992; Maxcy 2003).

It is in relation to the Mixed Method approach, however, that pragmatism has received particular attention in recent years (see, for example, Maxcy 2003; Johnson and Onwuegbuzie 2004; Morgan 2007). Indeed, pragmatism has come to be regarded as the philosophical partner for the Mixed Method approach, providing a set of assumptions about knowledge and enquiry that suit the use of different methods and different research strategies within individual investigations.

Caution

There is an important distinction to be drawn between the everyday meaning of pragmatism and its philosophical meaning. In common usage the term pragmatism not only means 'what works', it also carries with it a sense of expediency and lack of principle. To be 'pragmatic' means to take some course of action because it works but, implicitly, it conveys the idea of doing so purely as a means to an end and without being guided by relevant principles or moral codes. There is the danger, here, that the pragmatist approach to research is associated with this common-sense understanding of the word and thus becomes regarded as an approach in which 'anything goes'. It should be stressed that this is not the philosophical meaning of pragmatism and it is not a meaning that should be associated with it in relation to social research.

When it comes to the *ontological assumptions* underlying pragmatism it needs to be recognized that consistency with a specific philosophical position is not the key issue; it is the practical usefulness of the outcomes that is the crucial thing. Bearing this point in mind, for pragmatism:

- Social reality can be treated as being 'out there' and external to individuals and, at the same time, social reality can be regarded as something that is socially constructed and 'in the mind'. The vision of social reality that the researcher uses depends on which is likely to prove more useful.

In terms of *epistemological assumptions*, pragmatism tends to revolve around the following core ideas:

- There is no single approach to research that is the indisputably the best. What is best will tend to depend on the specific question being investigated and the kind of knowledge that is required.
- Knowledge is based on practical outcomes and 'what works'. The key criterion for judging knowledge is how useful it is perceived to be and how well it works when applied to some practical problem.
- Knowledge is provisional. What we understand as truth today may not be seen as such in the future. Knowledge is seen as a product of our times. It can never be absolute or perfect because it is inevitably a product of the historical era and the cultural context within which it is produced. The quest for absolute 'Truth' is consequently seen as hopeless cause.
- The traditional dualism between quantitative and qualitative research is regarded as not helpful. Good research should focus on the possibilities of integrating quantitative and qualitative approaches rather than keeping them separate.
- Research should test what works through empirical enquiry.

Pragmatists consider the research question to be more important than either the method they use or the worldview that is supposed to underlie the method. Most good researchers prefer addressing their research questions with any methodological tool available.

(Tashakkori and Teddlie 1998: 21)

Pragmatism, then, is a philosophy that allows researchers to be eclectic in their choice of methods. It allows them to mix methods and mix strategies because it judges research in terms of how well it addresses practical problems rather than how consistent it is with any particular ontological or epistemological stance. For those conducting applied research, whose aim is to produce solutions to specific problems, this has an immediate appeal. It also fits neatly with the requirements of much small-scale research to the extent that it helps researchers to avoid worrying persistently about how far their methods accord with a specific ontology or epistemology. However, it is important not see pragmatism as an approach that entirely side-steps the need for researchers to engage with matters of ontology or epistemology. Although it stresses that social research should not be shackled by its philosophy, it also calls on researchers to avoid any naïve assumptions regarding the knowledge produced by their research. The choice of research problems, the choice of methods and the meanings attributed to the findings all reflect the context within which they occur, and good research based on pragmatism needs to be constantly aware of this. It needs to be reflexive.

Research paradigms

A research paradigm refers to a pattern or model for research. Clearly, this involves a philosophy of research. However, the notion of a research paradigm has come to include more than this. As well as a philosophy, it tends to include:

- reference to the *practices* of research;
- *preference* for one set of beliefs and practices as better than others; and
- identification of particular *research questions* as more worthwhile than others.

The philosophy, practices and preferences of a paradigm are encapsulated in a variety of ways – a point emphasized by Thomas Kuhn (1970) in his *The Structure of Scientific Revolutions* which is generally regarded as the core work in relation to research paradigms. In Kuhn's discussion of research paradigms he argued that they could operate via:

1 *an exemplar*: a key piece of research which could be held as a shining example of how things should be done. Researchers should 'follow the example' in terms of how they approach their research.
2 *a community*: a group of researchers with a shared sense of which problems are the most important to investigate and what research methods qualify as 'good practice'. The community exists through networks and collaboration, and can operate at a number of levels – from a community based on a whole discipline to a community based on a small core of expert researchers working at the cutting edge of new ideas.
3 *an ideology*: a higher level belief system which concerns questions about the nature of reality and fundamental issues about the knowability of this reality – about ontology and epistemology. These set parameters for the type of questions that are worth investigation and the kind of research methods that are acceptable.

In recent years, social researchers have focused almost exclusively on just one of those forms: the ideological version of paradigms as 'epistemological stances'. And most emphasis has gone on the competing models of research captured in the notions of 'quantitative' and 'qualitative' research. Indeed, the distinction between these two paradigms has become embedded in social research. Each term provides a short-hand way of capturing a set of ideas that are intertwined and which hang together with some sort of consistency. They provide a signpost which is easily recognized by social researchers as indicating the broad nature of the research in question and kind of assumptions and practices to be associated with it. Quantitative and qualitative research, however, not only provide a convenient means for distinguishing between alternative paradigms of research, they have also come to represent two opposing camps with beliefs and practices that are incompatible and funda-mentally opposed.

 Caution

The distinction between quantitative and qualitative research is far from watertight. In theory and in practice there is no ultimate dividing line and it needs to be recognized that, although the terms are useful for conveying a general sense of the research approach, the boundaries are not always clear or sustainable.

Quantitative research

The quantitative research paradigm involves a basic belief in the need for data in the form of numbers. This leads to a preference for the study of things that lend themselves to being measured and having numerical values assigned to them. For this reason, quantitative research is generally linked with a realist ontology and a positivistic epistemology because these operate on the idea that social phenomena have an existence that is 'out there' and available in a way that allows the researcher to use methods to measure them. Its focus on the measurement of external realities also gives this paradigm a tendency to focus on 'the way that the world shapes people', emphasizing the ways in which human activity is determined by realities whose existence is beyond the control of any particular individual. It emphasizes 'structure'.

Armed with numerical data, quantitative researchers can assume the aura of 'scientific research'. This has proved very attractive for some social researchers. It has allowed them to present themselves and their work as having high status and credibility – aligned with social standing of research in fields such as physics, medicine and engineering. This is because the use of numeric data has some key attributes and expectations that tally with the notion of science. Specifically numeric data lend themselves to:

- *precision*: measurements consist of exact amounts not vague proportions;
- *statistical analysis*: data can be subjected to analysis using mathematical principles;
- *rigour*: research design and data collection tools can be tested and validated;
- *repeatability*: research procedures can be checked and results verified;
- *comparison*: findings can be compared 'like for like' with those from other research;
- *objectivity and value neutrality*: reliance on standardized procedures and mathematical principles minimizes any personal influence on the part of researchers.

Critics argue that, in fact, quantitative research is not as objective and value neutral as it would like to think. Data do not 'speak for themselves' and close inspection of the processes of data collection and analysis actually reveals that value judgements and interpretations are routinely smuggled in by researchers in order to make sense of the data. A second criticism is that a reliance on things that can be measured means that the non-occurrence of events will be systematically overlooked in terms of becoming research data. As critical realism argues, underlying causes may not always become manifest and occur in a measurable fashion. And a third criticism of quantitative research is that it almost inevitably focuses on the measurement of distinct and discrete components (variables) of an overall situation which means that it fails to give a holistic vision of the bigger picture and also decontextualizes the small parts upon which it focuses.

Qualitative research

Contrasting with the quantitative paradigm, qualitative research is primarily concerned with 'the way in which people shape the world'. It emphasizes the ways in which human activity creates meaning and generates the social order that characterizes the world in which we live – what is termed 'human agency'. And not surprisingly, therefore, the paradigm favours a constructionist ontology and an interpretivist epistemology.

The qualitative research paradigm involves a preference for data in the form of words, text and images. These kinds of data are used on the premise that they are better suited than numbers to gaining a depth understanding of the subtleties and complexities of the social world. The meanings conveyed through words, texts and images allow the researcher to probe the intricate and sometimes messy nature of the social world and to achieve the primary goal of qualitative research – an *understanding* of social phenomena. This understanding is not the same thing that quantitative researchers are trying to achieve through the discovery of cause and effect relationships which can *explain* how the social world works. Distinct from this, qualitative researchers generally aim to get an understanding based on some insight into the meanings which people give to phenomena, seeing it from their point of view. In this sense, qualitative researchers have a research agenda broadly in line with Max Weber's notion of 'verstehen' and are interested in things such as:

- *motives*: what reasoning is used by people to justify their decisions to act in particular ways?
- *constructions of reality*: how do social interaction and the use of language work? And how do they produce the everyday world in which people live?
- *perceptions*: what sense do people make of specific things or events? What does their understanding involve?
- *experiences of life*: what is it like, from the person's point of view, to live through particular events?

In the first instance, qualitative research sets out to *describe*, rather than analyse, these motives, constructions, perceptions and experiences. The descriptions need to be sufficiently detailed to provide an accurate portrayal of the many aspects of the phenomenon being studied. They need to be so-called 'thick descriptions' which deal with the complex and multifaceted nature of the phenomenon in a way that allows readers to gain a revealing insight into the particular situation.

Within the paradigm of qualitative research, there are some approaches which favour the production of 'pure' *descriptions*. This means descriptions that are untainted by the researcher's values and predispositions. Researchers are encouraged to 'bracket off' the prejudices they might have resulting from their past experiences and existing knowledge in order to see and describe the situation 'as it really is'. Mostly, however, qualitative researchers recognize the implausibility of achieving such a detachment from personal beliefs and knowledge and take the position, instead, that researchers should acknowledge the impact of their own values and be open about their own biography and the way this could affect their account of the situation. There is an appeal for *researcher self-awareness* and a recognition of the potential effect of the researchers' 'self' on the findings that emerge from the investigation.

At one level, this can involve matters of *objectivity*. There could be some bias resulting from the opinions and values held by the researcher and the way in which this could colour the account of the situation provided by the researcher. Acknowledging this possibility, the researcher needs to be open and explicit about such values, and thus allow the reader to arrive at his/her own judgement about the quality of the research findings, taking into account this potential source of bias.

At another level, the matter of researcher involvement involves the issue of *reflexivity*. Basically, this arises because researchers are part of the social world they wish to study, and their ways of interpreting their own world – their concepts, theories and the language they use – are not completely separate from those they use for research purposes to describe and understand particular situations. This makes the prospects of a 'pure' description unlikely because researchers will always need to view the situation in a way that relies to a greater or lesser extent on their own background assumptions. They can never entirely step outside their existing knowledge to see things 'first hand' from the point of view of those involved in the situation. The best they can do is to offer a 'second-order' account which provides a researcher's analysis of a 'first-order' reality.

Critics of the qualitative paradigm argue that its reliance on data in the form of words, texts and images means that it forfeits the possibility of some rigorous and objective form of analysis (i.e. using mathematics and statistics). The analysis must always rely on the individual interpretation of the researcher rather than some universal system of analysis. This leads on to the criticism that there is little way of comparing and evaluating the findings that come from different pieces of research which, in turn, opens up the possibility of *relativism*. Qualitative researchers, it should be stressed, can take steps to overcome many aspects of this but there is still a residual criticism that the findings of each piece of qualitative research stands on its own merit, that it is difficult to compare, contrast or combine such findings, and that the findings ultimately reflect the individual researcher's approach to the investigation.

Mixed methods research

Mixed methods research has developed rapidly in recent years and has evolved to the point where it is increasingly regarded as a third research paradigm (Tashakkori and Teddlie 1998, 2003; Creswell and Plano Clark 2007; Johnson et al. 2007; Creswell 2009). The distinctive feature of this paradigm is its belief that the choice of research questions and research methods should not be judged by how well they fit with the ontology or epistemology of the quantitative paradigm (positivism) or the qualitative paradigm (interpretivism). The decision should be based on how *useful* the methods are for addressing a particular question, issue or problem that is being investigated.

For those who adopt the mixed methods approach, the crucial consideration is how well the research tools *work* rather than how well they fit within a specific research philosophy.

The defining characteristics of the mixed methods approach are its use of:

- quantitative (QUAN) and qualitative (QUAL) methods within the same research project. This can provide a fuller description and/or more complete explanation of the phenomenon being studied by providing more than one perspective on it.
- a research design that clearly specifies the sequencing and priority that is given to the QUAN and QUAL elements of data collection and analysis;
- an explicit account of the manner in which the QUAN and QUAL aspects of the research relate to each other, with heightened emphasis on the manner in which *triangulation* is used;
- pragmatism as the philosophical underpinning for the research. Although the case for combining quantitative and qualitative research has been advanced from a critical realist perspective (see, for example, Bryman 1988; Layder 1998), the mixed methods paradigm is generally associated with pragmatism.

Mixed methods research, then, involves something more than the use of quantitative and qualitative approaches within the same project. It emphasizes the need to explain why the alternative approaches are beneficial and how the alternatives are to be brought together. It calls on the researcher to provide a clear rationale for the combination of the alternative methods and strategies and to explain how data from one approach link with data from the other.

Guidelines for good practice

Researchers should be aware of the philosophical assumptions underlying their approach to research

All research methods and strategies are based on assumptions about the nature of social reality (ontology) and the ways in which it is possible to gain knowledge about this reality (epistemology). These philosophical assumptions have implications for what can be investigated and what can be concluded on the basis of the research.

The philosophical position adopted by the research should be clear and explicit

The amount of information provided will depend on the purpose of the research and who will be reading the research report. Research students who present a thesis for the award of PhD and Master's degree students whose dissertations involve empirical social research should normally include some discussion of their research philosophy and demonstrate as awareness of the philosophical assumptions upon which the research is based.

Link up with **ACCOUNTABILITY**

The choice of research philosophy should be justified

It can be justified in terms of its benefits, especially when compared with alternative approaches. The benefits are likely to related to nature of:

- the *research questions* being tackled;
- the kind of *data* that are required;
- the type of things that qualify as worthwhile *evidence*;
- the *purpose* for which the findings will used.

Link up with **DESIGN**

There needs to be consistency between the various components of the research in terms of their philosophical positions

The philosophy underpinning the research design should be echoed in the methods of data collection and techniques for data analysis. It is bad practice to couple a research design based on interpretivism with data collection methods based on positivism or to mis-match other components in such a way. However, it is quite appropriate to use a mixed methods approach provided that the research philosophy can accommodate the use of components that operate on different premises. This is where pragmatism, or possibly critical realism, would provide the necessary philosophical foundation.

The kind of conclusions drawn from the research should accord with the philosophical premises of research methodology

The researcher should be clear about the kind of *conclusions* that can, and cannot, be drawn on the basis of the investigation. There are inherent limits to what can be concluded on the basis of a positivist approach just as there are with an interpretivist approach. And though the use of a pragmatist or critical realist approach might hope to address some of the limitations, the kind of conclusions that can be drawn on the basis of a piece of research will always reflect the underlying philosophy of the methodology. Good research recognizes this point and seeks to identify the limits to what can be said, and what cannot be said, on the basis of the evidence arising from the research.

Link up with **PROOF**

Further reading

Babbie, E. (2004) *The Practice of Social Research*, 10th edn. London: Thomson/ Wadsworth, Chapter 2.

Crotty, M. (2003) *The Foundations of Social Research: Meaning and Perspective in the Research Process*, 2nd edn. London: Sage, Chapters 1–5.

Dyson, S. and Brown, B. (2006) *Social Theory and Applied Health Research*. Maidenhead: Open University Press, Chapters 2–4.

Grix, J. (2004) *The Foundations of Research*. Basingstoke: Palgrave Macmillan, Chapters 4–6.

Kalof, L., Dan, A. and Dietz, T. (2008) *Essentials of Social Research*. Maidenhead: Open University Press, Chapters 1 and 2.

May, T. (2001) *Social Research: Issues, Methods and Process*, 3rd edn. Buckingham: Open University Press, Chapter 1.

Sayer, A. (2000) *Realism and Social Science*. Thousand Oaks, CA: Sage.

Smith, M.J. (1998) *Social Science in Question*. London: Sage/Open University, Chapter 5.

Checklist for PHILOSOPHY

When considering the philosophy of the research you should feel confident about answering 'yes' to the following questions: ☑

1   Has the research philosophy been discussed in terms of its epistemology (e.g. positivism, interpretivism, post-positivism, pragmatism)? ☐

2   Has the research philosophy been discussed in terms of its ontology (e.g. realism, critical realism, constructionism)? ☐

3   Has the approach to the research been linked with a research paradigm (e.g. quantitative research, qualitative research, mixed methods)? ☐

4   Does the underlying philosophy of the research match the project's:
Aims? ☐
Research questions? ☐
Design? ☐
Methods? ☐
Analysis? ☐
Conclusions? ☐

5   Have the implications of the underlying philosophy been acknowledged in relation to:
The kind of data collected? ☐
The type of data analysis used? ☐

6   Have the depth and detail of discussion about research philosophy been tailored to meet the particular requirements of the readership (e.g examiners, funders, the general public)? ☐

© M. Denscombe, *Ground Rules for Social Research*. Open University Press.

IV

METHODS

8

ACCURACY

<table>
<tr><td colspan="2">Ground rule: Research should produce valid data using reliable methods</td></tr>
<tr><td>Questions:</td><td>Has the research asked the right questions?</td></tr>
<tr><td></td><td>Are the data sufficiently precise and detailed?</td></tr>
<tr><td></td><td>Do the data depict the 'reality' of the situation?</td></tr>
<tr><td></td><td>Are the procedures used for data collection likely to distort the findings?</td></tr>
<tr><td>Answers:</td><td>The accuracy of the data has been checked using appropriate tests of validity.</td></tr>
<tr><td></td><td>The impact of the research process on the data obtained has been assessed using suitable measures of reliability.</td></tr>
<tr><td></td><td>Reasonable steps have been taken to avoid the use of any naïve, simplistic or erroneous indicators of the 'underlying truth'.</td></tr>
</table>

The idea that good research should be accurate is one that has an immediate appeal. After all, what value is research if it turns out to be *in*accurate? The vast majority of people who undertake research, who read the findings and who judge the quality of the work will operate on the assumption that research aims to be accurate. It is a core belief about research and a criterion that helps to establish research findings as better and more worthwhile than common sense, speculation or casual kinds of investigation. It is not surprising, then, that social researchers tend to devote considerable attention both to achieving accuracy in the design and execution of their enquiries and, almost as important, to assuring readers of reports on their research that what they are reading is indeed accurate.

Accuracy: the basic concerns

In essence, social researchers are faced with two broad questions when it comes to accuracy. The first question is 'Are the data valid?' This concerns the need for a precise focus on the right target and involves:

- *the appropriateness of the questions*. Is the researcher asking the right questions?
- *the precision and detail of data*. Are the findings exact enough for the purpose of the investigation?
- *the truth of the information gathered*. How do you know if the informants have given honest answers? How do you know that those being observed behaved normally?

The second question is 'Are the methods reliable?' This concerns the need to ensure that data are not artificially affected by the method used to gather them and the key issues here are:

- *the normality of the setting*. Has the process of doing the research disrupted the 'normal state of affairs' in the thing being investigated?
- *the neutrality and consistency of the research tools*. What confidence can we have that the research tools did not influence the results and produce erratic findings that vary each time the tool is used?

Obviously, different styles of social research will place different emphasis on the relative importance of each question and, indeed, there might be a need to rephrase the questions slightly to fit them with the specific mode of research being conducted. For example, a person conducting library-based research using literary sources might feel that their research is unlikely to be affected by concerns about disrupting the normal state of affairs, and thus treat other aspects of accuracy – such as whether their findings are precise and detailed enough – as more important. Quite right. Similarly, a researcher using observation techniques might well need to consider the issue of disrupting the normality of the situation as a higher priority. But the principles behind the questions are ones that most social researchers will want to consider in relation to their own particular interests, perhaps prioritizing some over others, perhaps adapting the questions to their specific kind of investigation. *Rarely would good social research wholly disregard the basic concerns outlined above.*

Box 8.1 Accuracy	
The key issue	**Things to be considered**
Are the data valid and precise enough for the purposes of good research?	• Has the investigation focused on the most vital issues and revealing indicators? • Are the data sufficiently precise and detailed? • Do the data and findings reflect the 'reality' of the situation rather than the context in which the data were collected or the methods used to collect them?

Validity and reliability

The matter of accuracy is often linked to the notions of validity and reliability – notions that carry a lot of weight as far as social research is concerned. As Carmines and Zeller (1979: 15) make the point: '[R]eliability and especially validity are words that have a definite positive connotation. For anything to be characterized as reliable and valid is to be described in positive terms . . . If it is reliable and valid, then it has gone a long way toward gaining scientific acceptance.' Unfortunately, as Hammersley (1987) has demonstrated, the terms 'validity' and 'reliability' have not been used in a completely consistent fashion in the literature on research methodology and, bearing this point in mind, the following distinction between the two provides a useful starting point.

> *Validity* concerns the accuracy of the questions asked, the data collected and the explanations offered. Generally it relates to the *data* and the *analysis* used in the research. It refers to the quality of data and explanations and the confidence we might have that they accord with what is true or what is real.

Claims to validity involve some demonstration that the researcher's data and his or her analysis are firmly rooted in the realms of things that are relevant, genuine and real: they act to reassure the reader that the research is not based on poor data and erroneous interpretations. Such claims, of course, are seen as vital by most researchers because they provide the basis on which researchers can argue that their findings are better than common sense or casual investigations. However, since claims to validity inevitably involve some connection between research activity and what is 'true', 'real' and 'accurate', it is quantitative researchers and those adopting a positivistic epistemological position who have placed most emphasis on matters of validity. As we shall see, though, the large majority of qualitative researchers and those who are not positivists still take an interest in defending their work in terms of its validity. In line with their different epistemological stance they have adapted the criteria some-what, but not rejected entirely the importance of staking claims to have produced an investigation that can be judged in some senses according to how far it matches what is 'real'.

> *Reliability* relates to the methods of data collection and the concern that they should be consistent and not distort the findings. Generally it entails an evaluation of the *methods* and techniques used to collect the data. It refers to the ability of a research process to provide results that do not vary from occasion to occasion and that do not vary according to the particular persons undertaking the research.

The importance of such reliability is fairly obvious. Researchers need to feel confident that the results they obtain are not being affected by a research instrument that throws up different results each time it is used. They want reassurance that their results reflect differences in the thing being measured, not vagaries of the research process, the methods or the tools employed. The research process, for this reason, needs to be assessed for consistency. To gauge this researchers apply the logic that:

- if other factors are not interfering;
- and nothing has changed;
- then the research should yield the same results.

Developing from this, methods can be seen as 'reliable' when, *all things being equal*, they produce very similar findings when used:

- in different settings, or
- by different researchers, or
- with the same people at different times, or
- with separate groups of similar people at the same time.

Asking the right questions

> The issue here is whether or not the investigation is focused accurately on things that will genuinely illuminate the matter under investigation.

The task of 'asking the right question' occurs for the researcher in two principal ways. First, the researcher needs to be sure that he or she is asking an appropriate question in terms of knowledge that already exists. There is no point in asking questions that have already been answered by previous research. Nor is there much value in asking questions that are naïve, ill-informed or unimportant. In the first instance, then, asking the right question involves making sure that the question is on target as far as what needs to be known and what is already known about the topic the researcher wishes to investigate. This, of course, is where the literature review comes in.

Link up with **RELEVANCE**

Second, asking the right question means using indicators that best reflect the concept the researcher wishes to study. Researchers are often interested in ideas, attitudes, perceptions, experiences, feelings and emotions – things that do not lend themselves to *direct* measurement. On such occasions, unless the researcher also happens to be a mind reader, it is necessary to rely on *in*direct indicators of the thing that is being investigated. For example, to study 'racial prejudice', it becomes necessary to rely on things like statements by people or instances of behaviour that serve as an indicator of the thing being investigated. Because racial prejudice itself has neither mass nor volume, because it has no colour, speed or direction, the only way to study it is to measure its outcomes, its effects, its side-products, things that:

- are deemed to be associated with it;
- lend themselves to being directly measured.

Asking the right question, in this instance, means the researcher needs to be confident that the indicators chosen are directly linked to the concept, and that there are no other, better, manifestations of the concept that could be used.

The accuracy of the research in terms of whether it is asking the right questions and using the right indicators relates to its *content validity*. Initially this can involve checking with the views of those who might reasonably be expected to be knowledgeable about the topic. The researcher might seek corroboration for the use of specific questions or indicators by checking them out with relevant people to see if they are acceptable 'at face value'. This method is sometimes known as *face validity* for this reason. Next, the questions and indicators might be further justified by establishing that they are in accord with *expert opinion*. This may mean sending a request to the top ten experts in the area to get their comments on the proposed questions or indicators. More likely, the views of the community of research experts will be gleaned through a review of the existing literature.

The right question, however, is not simply the question that others see as appropriate; it also needs to be appropriate within its own frame of reference as part of a coherent, consistent and logical explanation. This is known as *construct validity*. Construct validity relies on comparing the results from two or more indicators of the concept. If the pattern they reveal is in line with the theory, then there is support for the idea that the indicator is valid. So, if weight is regarded as one indicator of fitness and stamina is another, the validity of weight as an indicator can be judged by the extent to which it correlates with stamina (taking into account the factors of age, sex, height, etc.).

The precision and detail of data

Data need to be sufficiently precise and detailed in terms of the specific purposes of the research.

This aspect of the issue of accuracy highlights the fact that it is not only necessary to be measuring the right thing in research, it is also necessary to do so with sufficient detail and precision to make the results of some value. This relates to both qualitative and quantitative data. It is as important for precise and detailed data to be held about interviews and focus group discussions as it is for observational results from a laboratory experiment.

Depending on the nature of the study, researchers can use a variety of 'tools' to help them achieve detailed and precise measures. Observation schedules will allow a researcher to work on precise numbers (occurrences of a particular event). Questionnaires, likewise, have the potential to supply researchers with exact figures (responses to questions). Fieldwork notes provide an exact record of when and where events happened. Tape-recorded interviews contain details of the precise words spoken by an interviewee. Each, in its own way, helps the social researcher to achieve the desired standard of 'exactness'.

The truth of information gathered

The use of inaccurate information is of little value for research, and this poses the question: 'How do you know that the data collected are based on information that is true?'

Researchers need to feel as confident as is reasonably possible that their data are an accurate reflection of some underlying 'truth'. They will want to feel that their data reflect things that are genuine, authentic and real, rather than fantasy, mistakes or lies.

A crucial means of checking this aspect of accuracy is to *compare the findings with external benchmarks*. Such comparisons concern the *criterion validity* of the research. The criteria for gauging the validity of the data are markers that act as standards or 'given facts' with which the data might be expected to correspond. Similar studies, for example, offer themselves as benchmarks against which the new research can be compared. In effect, results from tried and trusted research instruments can act as the baseline for evaluating findings from the new research. This is referred to as *concurrent validity*. Obviously, the 'benchmark' research itself needs to be reputable, established, designed for the same purpose, administered to similar people and dealing with similar concepts.

Another kind of criterion validity uses future events and conditions as the external benchmark, assessing validity in terms of the predictions made by research. This *predictive validity* assesses the quality of data (and explanations) in terms of how well the emerging events or conditions confirm the expectations of the research. This is clearly a form of validity that is more at home in the natural and physical sciences, where cause and effect are easier to establish and where controls are easier to put in place. In the social sciences it is not often feasible to use such a stringent measure because so many variables come into play.

The accuracy and precision of data can be assessed by comparing them with findings on the same topic produced using different research methods, produced by other researchers or based on alternative theories/approaches. This is known as *triangulation*. Triangulation provides social researchers with a means of assessing the quality of data by coming at the same thing from a different angle. It allows them to gauge the validity of the data in relation to alternative positions. The alternative positions, we should note, do not necessarily constitute 'known facts'. Triangulation, then, is not exactly like criterion validity because it uses alternative positions, rather than external benchmarks, as the basis for claims about the validity of the data.

Another check on this aspect of validity, and one frequently adopted by qualitative researchers who are uncomfortable with the positivistic connotations of the concurrent and predictive validity, is one where the accuracy and precision of data can be checked out by providing the kind of information that allows *verification*. Now, it might seem that there are some kinds of data, in particular qualitative data, that do not really lend themselves to independent verification; for example, eye witness accounts of events or descriptions of interactions between people. However, there is frequently scope for incorporating confirmable data along with such accounts in a way that enhances the validity of that data. Qualitative data as well as quantitative data benefit from corroborating information that can be checked out by other researchers; things like dates, times and numbers, records and evidence such as tape recordings. Such information, factual and quantitative though it might be, serves a purpose for all research by allowing the possibility of verifying the data and findings (Lincoln and Guba 1985; Seale 1999).

Link up with **ACCOUNTABILITY**

If the research instrument takes the form of a questionnaire, an assessment of the honesty can be made on the basis of *check questions*, where researchers *know* what the answer should be. This can involve ploys like asking the same question twice, but in a different way and in a different part of the questionnaire. If the answers differ, it challenges the belief that the responses are honest. Alternatively, the level of honesty can be checked by incorporating reference to fictitious things and seeing whether people's answers include these things. For example, a questionnaire about drug use among young people might ask about the extent of use of a drug whose name is entirely made up. Careful attention will be paid to the answers to this question to see if respondents say they have used the drug. To the extent that respondents say they have used the fictitious drug, they can be seen to be answering wrongly or dishonestly. The check question, then, provides a useful indicator of the level of truthfulness and the level of 'fantasy/boasting/bravado' among respondents.

An alternative possibility for confirming the validity of the data is to *check the findings with informed people*. This can take the form of *member validation*, which is used principally in connection with findings from qualitative research. There are a variety of approaches to member validation (Bloor 1997; Silverman 2005) but, in essence, it is a method of assessing the accuracy and precision of findings by checking the extent to which they 'ring true' and are 'credible' to those whose ideas, attitudes or culture are being researched. So, for example, on the basis of many interviews with young people a researcher might be drawn to the conclusion that they hold a particular view on using soft drugs, in which case the validity of the (interview) data can be checked with the young people themselves by asking them (at some subsequent point) if it is a fair representation of their views.

The validity of the qualitative data can be addressed by checking how far the data are *grounded* on 'facts'. As Miles and Huberman (1994) indicate, grounded research involves a process in which initial conclusions are verified (or not) as the research progresses. Through the 'constant comparative method' it involves a continuous process of comparison between the empirical data and the emerging theoretical explanation. The ideas and data are checked out, and this can mean comparing them with extreme cases or negative cases – cases that are most likely to 'falsify' the emerging theory. The accuracy is thus under constant scrutiny and review in relation to the empirical evidence that is collected.

 Caution

To minimize the prospect of getting answers that are not true, the social researcher needs to be aware of the principal causes of 'wrong' answers. Bearing these in mind, it is then possible to take suitable precautions. Such precautions, it is worth stressing, will not *guarantee* that the researcher gets honest answers – but they do help the researcher to avoid conducting research in a way that unintentionally invites respondents to give false answers.

The normality of the setting

> Research that is intrusive and disrupts normality is likely to produce distorted results. The issue for the researcher, then, is whether the actual process of doing the research influences the nature of the results obtained.

Observational studies and studies of behaviour which rely on laboratory experiments both face a similar problem with regard to the accuracy of their data. Both face the possibility that their data can be distorted as a consequence of having been collected in situations that are 'not natural'.

With experimental studies conducted in laboratories, participants provide the data in settings that are intentionally removed from natural situations in everyday life. The advantage of laboratories, of course, is that they allow the researcher to control variables that are connected with the thing being studied. The price to pay, however, is that the participants are put in a context that is far removed from their everyday life. This may, or may not, be significant depending on the kind of thing that is being studied. But to illustrate the potential problem faced by researchers, the example of research on risk-taking behaviour makes the point. Many studies of people's willingness to take risks are conducted under laboratory conditions where the nature of the risk being considered and the responses of the participants can be controlled and measured accurately. Researchers can introduce variations to the risk factor and monitor changes in responses precisely and effectively – which is fine. However, the limitation to such studies is that the data they collect are based on a kind of 'false reality'. The findings from the laboratory experiments might not be a good reflection of what actually happens in the real world, where people's risk decisions involve real dangers, real costs, real losses and decisions that really matter. There is the matter of the *ecological validity* to be considered. Some things that are measured by social scientists are especially sensitive to the context in which they are produced. Certain actions and certain attitudes arise in response to particular settings, particular times and particular social interactions – so much so that they can become *context-specific* actions or attitudes which are not easily transposed to other circumstances at other times.

Link up with **DESIGN**

With observational studies, social researchers need to be aware that people act differently as a direct consequence of their awareness of being studied. They might be embarrassed by the attention they are receiving. They might feel flattered. They might feel threatened. Whatever, there is the very real prospect that they will cease to act 'normally'. This is known as the 'halo' effect. 'Normal' activity is temporarily adjusted to take into account the person who is doing the observation and the ways in which the data might be used. When conducting this style of research, therefore, social researchers need to make efforts to minimize the extent to which their presence in the location where the observations take place is likely to be perceived as breaking the normality of the setting. They will want to 'fade into the background' as far as is possible, present themselves in a non-threatening light, and spend time on site so that the participants in the situation can get used to being observed. But, though researchers using observational techniques can do things to reduce the potentially disruptive effect of their presence, what they should not do is ignore the issue or pretend that there was no problem as far as the research was concerned.

The neutrality and consistency of the research tools

Do the findings genuinely reflect the situation rather than the means of data collection itself?

In some respects this concern echoes the previous point about the way that the process of conducting the research can, itself, have an impact on the situation and thereby distort the findings that are obtained. In this case, however, the concern is focused on the potential impact of the research tools themselves. The worry for the social researcher is that the data collected are not a picture of the 'truth' or the 'reality' of the situation as much as a picture of the truth or reality *plus the impact of the research method.*

Researchers need to feel confident that their findings have not been distorted in some way by the methods and techniques used to collect the data. They want to be confident that their questionnaire, their observation schedule, their experiment, etc. is:

- *neutral*, in the sense that it does not bias the results obtained using the particular data collection technique;
- *consistent*, producing the same results from the same situation when used on different occasions or by different people.

For quantitative researchers, the research tools tend to be things like questionnaires and observation schedules. Their concern is that the use of such a tool might produce variable results – results which differ not as a result of real differences in the thing being investigated but due to a failing in the research tool which causes it to give inconsistent readings. They wish to ensure, as far as possible, that their means of data collection are reliable.

The consistency and neutrality of the methods can be checked by comparing the results obtained from uses of the research tool with results obtained from the same method when used on other occasions. The most common form of this is the *test–retest* check. The test–retest approach to reliability operates on the assumption that, all things being equal, a research method should produce consistent results each time it is used. To check this the researcher needs to administer the same instrument to the same group of people on a later date with the expectation that the same results should be produced on the second test as on the first. In principle, this might seem straightforward. In practice, however, there are some limitations to the viability of the test–retest approach. The time-span between test and retest is crucial if 'all things are to be equal'. Too short a time and respondents may recall their earlier answers. Too long a time and there could be genuine changes in attitudes and circumstances that would change the results. Locating exactly the same cohort of people to take part in the retest is, in practice, very difficult. And the test–retest method takes considerable resourcing.

Using the same principle as the test–retest method, alternative groups of similar people can be used for the purposes of comparison, with the retest effectively occurring simultaneously with the test. To the extent that the groups are similar and to the extent that there are no other factors affecting the results, the data produced by the groups should be very similar.

The consistency and neutrality of the methods can also be checked by comparing the results obtained from uses of the research tool with results obtained from research using very similar methods to investigate a similar topic. This is known as the *alternative form* or *parallel form* method. As a means of checking reliability, this hinges on the existence of research which is truly 'parallel' and against which a genuinely useful comparison can be made.

A third way of checking to make sure the methods are not distorting the results is by looking for a high level of internal consistency within the data produced. This check on reliability commonly uses the *split-half method* or looks for *inter-item consistency*. With the split-half method of assessing reliability, the items of the research instrument are separated into two sets, with the results of each half then being correlated to see how closely they match. Patterns of results that are to be found in one half of the items should be equally evident in the other half. If they don't match closely, the chances are that the research instrument itself may not be reliable. Of course, extreme caution needs to be exercised to avoid splitting along lines which might be expected to involve predictable and real differences. On most occasions the researcher would be ill-advised, for example, to split the data in terms of factors like age and sex, where there might well be genuine differences in the profile of the data collected. Inter-item consistency checks reliability in terms of the way responses to individual questions or items exhibit a pattern of consistency. Specific questions or items might be expected to produce results which fit a pattern that is consistent with other items geared to the same concept, or they might be expected to match the overall result. Inter-item consistency is generally applied in the case of questionnaire responses which include a series of individual questions or items relating to the same concept.

Observation studies can make use of *inter-observer reliability*. The simple premise of this is that any two observers who see the same situation or event should record data about it that are identical. Two researchers using an observation schedule, it follows, should produce data that are exactly the same – presuming that they saw the same thing and, crucially, that the schedule is a reliable research instrument. In practice, the amount of correlation between what any two researchers will record may be something less than perfect, but the extent to which such observations of the same situation or event produce the same data provides a useful and straightforward indicator of the reliability of the method.

Qualitative researchers share this concern for consistency but, in their case, there is an interesting twist to the situation. In qualitative research, the researcher tends to assume much greater significance as an instrument of data collection and, in the case of methods like participant observation, can be regarded as a research tool in their own right. Consistency, in this instance, requires that the same person would find the same things in a very similar situation and, more challengingly, that another participant observer would record the same events and emotions if investigating the same situation. These things are hard to achieve, and even harder to prove in terms of evidence that might persuade the reader of the research.

To the extent that the researcher is part and parcel of the data collection process, the consistency and neutrality of the methods require what Miles and Huberman (1994: 278) call 'relative neutrality' on the part of the researcher. Within the bounds of what is possible, the qualitative researcher needs to be self-aware enough to retain some objectivity in relation to the situation within which he or she is working. It has been suggested that to help this, researchers should try to use 'low inference indicators' (LeCompte and Goetz 1982; Seale 1999) – things that explain the situation with a minimum amount of inter-pretation on the part of the researcher and the readers of research. The more the explanation calls for intricate insights and detailed insider knowledge, the more it opens the way for bias to creep into the analysis.

Link up with **OBJECTIVITY**

Box 8.2 Example: the concepts of validity and reliability

Scales provide an appropriate tool for measuring weight. However, for the results to have any credibility with other researchers, the research instrument needs to be both valid and reliable. We need to be reasonably sure that the scales are consistent and do not provide fluctuating readings which have nothing to do with the actual weights of the individuals involved. (How many of us have bathroom scales that tell us one weight, then, after we have stepped off and back on again, tell us a different weight? Not a very reliable research instrument.) When researchers provide information about the *reliability* of a research instrument, what they are doing is assuring us that the instrument itself (the scales in this example) had no influence on variations in the results (the weights recorded for each individual). In terms of the example, people of the same weight would produce the same measure of weight on the scales. Equally, a person whose real weight had not changed would record the same measure on each occasion he or she was weighed.

It is, however, no good producing results which are reliable but wrong; the data need to be reliable *and right*. Only if they are right can the data be deemed *valid*. To make sure the results are right, the researcher needs to establish some objective baseline against which to calibrate his or her findings and by which to provide reassurance that the research instrument is supplying results that are *consistent with other standardized measures*. Clearly, in the example of the scales, it is vital that a measurement of 67 kilograms using the researcher's scales accords exactly with what everyone else expects as the standard for 67 kilograms. It does not matter whether the measure is in kilograms or pounds as long as the measurement accords with a standard that others can use.

Second, the measurement has to be accurate in the sense that a reading of 67 kilograms on the researcher's scales matches exactly a reading of 67 kilograms on other researchers' scales.

Third, the unit of measurement has to be *precise* enough – that is, detailed enough – to provide meaningful results. Actually, a measurement in terms of kilograms or pounds might prove far too broad for the purposes of research on human body weight. That level of precision might be quite adequate for railway engineers concerned with the weight of rolling stock and the strength of bridges, but will provide insufficient detail for the person concerned with body weight, diet and fitness. Precision will need to go to grams or ounces for this purpose.

Accuracy, truth and reality: a cautionary note

The notions of accuracy and validity would seem to suggest that research findings ought to reflect things as they actually exist in reality. Research needs to produce results that are right in the sense that things have been recorded as having a value which is the same as their 'real' value. When the research uses quantitative data and adopts a more or less explicitly positivistic notion of reality as an objective state of affairs 'out there', things are relatively straightforward because researchers can identify an objective referent point against which to compare results and calibrate their measures. However, developments in the social sciences in recent years have challenged the notion of an objective 'truth' or 'reality' that exists *out there* to be discovered, and many social researchers do not buy in to the idea that there is a single, undisputed, objective referent point (truth, reality) against which accuracy can be measured. For many social researchers, in particular interpretivists, reality is better understood as a social construction. For them, the *reflexive* nature of the social world and our knowledge of it mean that external, objective referent points become difficult, if not impossible, to identify.

Link up with **PHILOSOPHY**

A small minority use this as the basis for abandoning any concern with validity and reliability. More commonly, though, qualitative researchers prefer to retain some engagement with the issues of validity and reliability rather than ignore them, arguing that there are no good grounds for qualitative research to excuse itself from the criteria for good research that apply to other social science approaches (Kirk and Miller 1986; Hammersley 1992; Silverman 1998, 2006; Seale 1999, 2007). Hence qualitative researchers like Lincoln and Guba (1985), Miles and Huberman (1994) and Marshall and Rossman (2006) suggest some ways in which the conventional positivistic/scientific canons of validity and reliability can be rephrased, remodelled and reworked – *not* abandoned – to provide a set of criteria which accord with the nature of qualitative research.

Guidelines for good practice

The need for accuracy provides a basic platform for designing, conducting and evaluating social research. Accuracy is a guiding principle that should remain at the forefront of the researcher's mind throughout the whole process of investigation.

There should be an explicit account of the steps that were taken to ensure accuracy

Accounts of the research should explain what efforts were made to achieve accuracy. Different styles of research and different situations will call for different ways of justifying the research in terms of its accuracy. Whatever the procedure, however, readers of the research will wish to know how the researcher sought to achieve accuracy because only when they are in possession of such information will they be able to arrive at a judgement about the quality of the research and what credibility can be given to the findings.

The choice of questions or indicators needs to be justified

The choice of questions or indicators used in the research needs to be justified by establishing a convincing case that the researcher has looked at the right things – issues, questions and indicators that are recognized as appropriate by 'experts' and that are part of a logical and coherent set of ideas. In this context it can be useful to refer to:

- content validity;
- face validity;
- construct validity.

Claims to accuracy should be supported by comparison with external benchmarks

Such benchmarks might be regarded as objective referent points, or they might be regarded as recognized standards. They might even be just alternative positions. Whatever, claims about accuracy can make use of such external benchmarks as a way of demonstrating how the data and findings compare with what is already known. In their different ways, both quantitative and qualitative research can use this as a way of justifying the accuracy of the research – establishing that it is on target and using data that are sufficiently precise and detailed. Some concepts of relevance here are:

- criterion validity;
- concurrent validity;
- predictive validity;
- triangulation;
- verification;
- member validation.

The data need to be suitably precise and detailed

The various tools available to social researchers should be used to produce data and findings that contain enough precision and detail to allow for meaningful analysis and comparisons. Amounts, dates, locations, etc. need to be recorded and, where appropriate, included in accounts of the research to allow readers to evaluate its methods and findings. Vague statements like 'many' or 'often' should be avoided where possible in favour of precise measures. This relates to qualitative as much as quantitative research. It is good practice to include facts and figures about the sources of data (e.g. 54 interviews were conducted over a six-month period in 2009, producing 47 hours of recorded discussion with 14 managers and 40 shopfloor workers), even where there is a preference to adopt an interpretive approach.

Factors affecting the truth of responses need to be considered

There are no cast-iron guarantees for the social researcher concerning the honesty of the responses from those who provide information. However, good research practice can reduce the possibility of inaccurate or untruthful responses:

- *Do not ask those types of question which invite 'wrong' answers.* Avoid questions that are too complicated or too long, that are too demanding in terms of memory and recall or that cover sensitive topics without due caution.
- *Be aware of the circumstances in which the questions are asked.* Is it likely that the climate will encourage the respondent to provide full, open and honest answers? Or is the climate a threatening one that will lead respondents to tailor their responses to avoid getting themselves in trouble?
- *Take account of the interaction effect.* The personal identities (e.g. age, sex, ethnicity) of the researcher and respondents might affect the openness and honesty of responses depending on the nature of the topics being investigated.

Checks should be made on the consistency of the methods

The accuracy of data depends on the consistency of the particular method that has been used. Qualitative research in which the researcher is an integral component of the data gathering exercise relies on efforts by the researcher to minimize the dependency of the findings on himself or herself as an individual. Research based on quantitative data, for its part, can employ certain techniques to support claims about the reliability of the methods. Among such techniques are:

- test–retest;
- alternative form;
- split-half;
- inter-observer reliability.

The impact of the research process on the normality of the situation might warrant consideration if it affects the accuracy of the findings

Certain approaches to social research will intentionally disrupt 'normality'. Most obviously, laboratory experiments involve the imposition of controls that are designed to create an artificial situation in which the impact of key variables can be studied. Observational studies, however, operate on a different logic and rely on collecting data in situations which are normal in the sense that the act of doing the research does not create a new situation and cause things to happen in a way that they would not do under normal circumstances. The very presence of the researcher in a particular setting can be disruptive.

The degree to which the findings are 'context specific' should be taken into consideration

Because things do not happen in a 'social vacuum', we need to ask to what extent the explanation is *sensitive* to the setting, time and circumstances in which the research was undertaken and the way these might have affected the findings. To what extent does the analysis of the data take account of the influence of factors in the environment? Have the findings been linked to the social environment in which they occurred? Has the research avoided taking things out of context? Such concerns involve ecological validity.

The limitations to accuracy need to be discussed

Good research will normally stake a claim to being accurate, but it should also be aware of the implications of the term, especially the way it draws on notions of truth and reality. Social researchers need to be conscious of the limitations they face in trying to establish claims to accuracy, particularly when using qualitative data and conducting research into things like attitudes, meanings and opinions. Qualitative researchers need to avoid naïve assumptions about the way accuracy can be associated with notions of truth or reality, and be particularly sensitive to the issues involved when it comes to the validity and reliability of their research. Where the possibility of finding firm, objective benchmarks of truth or reality is rejected, researchers need to acknowledge that the validity and reliability of the research have to be *inferred* (using suitable techniques), not proved by reference to objective criteria.

Further reading

Carmines, E. and Zeller, R. (1979) *Reliability and Validity*. Beverly Hills, CA: Sage.
Cook, T.D. and Campbell, D.T. (1979) *Quasi-experimentation: Design and Analysis Issues for Field Settings*. Chicago: Rand McNally, Chapter 2.

Cryer, P. (2006) *The Research Student's Guide to Success*, 3rd edn. Maidenhead: Open University Press, Chapter 8.

Denscombe, M. (2007) *The Good Research Guide: For Small-scale Social Research Projects*, 3rd edn. Buckingham: Open University Press, Chapter 14.

Dyson, S. and Brown, B. (2006) *Social Theory and Applied Health Research*. Maidenhead: Open University Press, Chapters 7 and 10.

Firebaugh, G. (2008) *Seven Rules for Social Research*. Princeton, NJ: Princeton University Press, Chapter 3.

Lincoln, Y.S. and Guba, E.G. (1985). *Naturalistic Inquiry*. Newbury Park, CA: Sage.

Checklist for ACCURACY

When considering the accuracy of the research you should feel confident about answering 'yes' to the following questions: ☑

1   Are the questions or indicators the most relevant and most revealing in terms of the topic of the research? ☐

2   Has the accuracy of the research been gauged in relation to:
Established benchmarks? ☐
Similar studies? ☐
Other existing knowledge? ☐

3   Is there sufficient detail and precision to the data? ☐

4   Are the climate and circumstances of the research likely to encourage honest, full and accurate answers? ☐

5   Did the data collection process avoid any disruption to the normality of the situation which might have had a significant impact on the data and findings? ☐

6   Has the interaction effect been taken into consideration in terms of its likely impact on the data? ☐

7   Are the research methods reliable in terms of their consistency when used:
On different occasions? ☐
With different participants? ☐
In comparable settings? ☐

8   Does the research avoid making any naïve or simplistic connections between accuracy and notions of 'truth' and 'reality'? ☐

© M. Denscombe, *Ground Rules for Social Research*. Open University Press.

9

ACCOUNTABILITY

Ground rule:	**Research should include an explicit description and justification of the methodology**
Questions:	Why should we believe the research results?
	Why should we trust the researcher?
Answers:	The research has been reported in sufficient detail to allow checks on the authenticity of the research and the validity of the data.
	The methods of data collection and analysis have been described in a way that allows people to make informed judgements about the quality of the findings.

Readers of research can be a diverse audience. They can include fellow researchers, policy-makers, students and members of the public. As such, they might bring to bear a widely varying degree of expertise in the area of the research and a different set of interests in what the researcher has to say. What they will share, though, is a common thought: *Why should I believe the findings of this research?*

This is a reasonable question to ask and one that researchers need to take seriously. They should not operate on the assumption that those who read the research will take the findings at face value. Indeed, they will be far better off operating on the assumption that people will *not* believe the research unless and until they can be persuaded that the knowledge arising from it is better than what they already know. Research-based knowledge, after all, lays claims to being better than common sense, different from gut reaction and more believable than the outcomes of casual bits of investigation. The researcher cannot rely on assertions along the lines of 'This is what I found' or 'I am the expert and therefore you should accept what I say.' Research cannot rely on some act of faith that the researcher is telling the truth and has conducted the investigation in a proper manner. Nor can it rely on some deference to the researcher as 'the expert', whose word on the matter should be accepted simply on the basis of his or her status as an 'expert'. It needs to *convince* the readers that its research strategy, methods of data collection and mode of analysis are reasonable and that they can be expected to produce findings that are better than anything based on common sense.

To convince readers about the credibility of the research it is vital that reports of the research contain sufficient information for readers to make the necessary judgements. Specifically, in order for readers to evaluate the research, they need to be supplied with an *account* of the research that incorporates:

- an explicit description of the methods of data collection and analysis;
- a justification for the choice of approach (in preference to possible alternatives).

Without these, readers have no way of deciding whether the research has been conducted in accord with 'good practice' or whether it has been poorly designed and conducted. And, in the absence of such an account, astute readers are likely to maintain a scepticism about the findings – to be hesitant about accepting the findings without being in possession of the facts they need to evaluate the research.

Box 9.1 Accountability	
The key issue	**Things to be considered**
Is the research credible and trustworthy?	• Is there an *explicit account* of how the data were collected? • Have key decisions about the research strategy, methods and analysis been *justified*? • Is there sufficient detail provided to allow an *evaluation* of the conclusions drawn on the basis of the research?

Checking up on the research

One important way in which an account helps to establish the credibility of the research is by allowing the reader to check on its procedures and findings. It provides:

- the means to check that the research actually took place (*authenticity*);
- the means to replicate research and to check its findings (*verification*);
- the means to check the logic for decisions made by the researcher (*audit*).

Authenticity

Perhaps the first and most fundamental questions that a reader might ask are: *'Did the research actually take place?'* and *'Are the data genuine?'* It is all too possible for people to claim to have conducted research but not actually done so at all. The sceptical reader of the research will justifiably want some reassurance at the outset that the results are the product of a genuine investigation and that the findings are not fabricated.

To address this issue, researchers should make careful and detailed records of the process of the research, the decisions taken and the data collected. Particularly, the researcher should be at pains to store the data collected. The existence of such data, in the form of voice recordings, questionnaires, laboratory observation notes, etc., acts as *a permanent record* of the events of the research. In a practical way, such research records stand as proof that the research took place, proof which at least in principle could be checked by other people at a later stage to confirm that the research genuinely took place.

Verification

Having established that the research and its data are genuine, the next question readers might ask in relation to the credibility of the research is: *'How can we check the findings?'* For some research traditions, the more positivistic ones, the point of providing a detailed account of the research process owes much to the idea of verifying the results of the research by being able to repeat the research. The idea of repeating an experiment to check its findings epitomizes this. Before we accept the conclusions and add them to our stock of knowledge, it is assumed that the research will be checked by other researchers who will replicate the research. To do this, of course, other researchers will need to adopt the same procedures and this is why it is vital that the original research contains a detailed 'map' of what was done, how it was done and why it was done. Following the same 'map' of the research, other researchers should find the same results from their research.

Most social researchers, however, struggle with the idea of literally replicating a piece of research. Qualitative researchers, in particular, are not comfortable with such a prospect because they tend to place high value on retaining the naturalness of the setting and generally seek to avoid imposing controls on the situation in the way that an experimental approach would do. They recognize that in reality it is difficult, if not impossible, to recreate the exact conditions that existed at the time of the original investigation and, as a consequence, they rarely pursue the idea of replicating research in a literal sense. Instead, they treat idea of replication more as a guiding principle (Miles and Huberman 1994). The need to supply information about the research process, from this perspective, rests on the premise that the reader of research should be supplied with sufficient information about the research so that *in principle* they could reproduce it – even though it is recognized in practice that any attempt to do so will face substantial, probably insurmountable, difficulties. What is important is that the readers could *imagine* what the research would look like if it was repeated elsewhere on some other occasion, and could then use their judgement about the extent to which the findings might be the same.

Audit

The term 'audit' literally refers to an examination of accounts by someone with expertise and authority to judge the accuracy and honesty of those accounts and, of course, is generally associated with the financial accounts of companies. However, Lincoln and Guba (1985) proposed a form of auditing for use with research which they argued was a more practical way of checking the reliability of (qualitative) research than trying to replicate it. They argued that the use of an *audit trail* could act as a proxy for repeatability.

Lincoln and Guba's vision of auditing research involved outside experts actually viewing material during the process of research. Almost like inspectors, they could look at the data and examine the way the researchers were analysing the material in order to assess the quality of the procedures and to verify that data were genuine. An audit, in this sense, is something that takes place during the time of the investigation and involves 'hands-on' inspection by other expert researchers. In practice, however, when researchers refer to an 'audit trail' they generally have in mind a less intrusive process of accounting based on:

- a *self-evaluation* by the researcher, rather than having other researchers inspect the procedures;
- a *summative evaluation* that takes place at the end of the research, rather than being a formative evaluation occurring during the process of the research;
- *records about the researcher's decisions* taken with regard to the data which, in principle, could be made available to other researchers so that they could see the researcher's rationale for particular decisions taken at specific stages of the research. Qualitative data analysis software (such as NVivo) can prove useful to the researcher in this respect.

> **Key point**
> 'An "audit trail" can be defined as 'the provision of a fully reflexive account of procedures and methods, showing to readers in as much detail as possible the lines of inquiry that have led to particular conclusions. This enables readers imaginatively to "replicate" studies, and also helps to ensure that claims are supported by adequate evidence' (Seale 1999: 157–8).

Self-evaluation in the research account

The inclusion of self-evaluation as part of accountability reflects developments in the realms of auditing and evaluation more generally. The researcher is expected to recognize the strengths and weaknesses of his or her own research and to convey some overall *self*-evaluation of the work to the readers. Self-evaluation helps to establish the credibility of the research through statements that:

- support the choice of strategy, methods and analysis as appropriate (*justification*);
- recognize the boundaries to what can be concluded from the research (*limitations*).

Justification

The need to provide a justification arises because social research is rarely, if ever, a matter of simple 'right' or 'wrong' when it comes to the choice of strategy, methods or analysis. With many disciplines and competing epistemologies (positivism/interpretivism), the credibility of social research tends to rely on arguing a case in support of the decisions made – a case which rests on whether the choice is *reasonable* rather than 'right'. To be deemed 'right' there would need to be a general consensus among social researchers about the merits of particular approaches, a consensus that does not (yet) exist. What social researchers can do, however, is establish a case supporting their selection of strategy, methods and analysis. They can do this by showing that the approach is:

- *fit for purpose* (produces findings directly linked to the research questions). Claims to credibility are based on judgements about the *suitability* of the strategy, methods and analysis in relation to the particular research question. This means that what might be deemed good practice in relation to one kind of research project might not be deemed appropriate for the investigation of some different question or problem.

Link up with **DESIGN**

- *logically organized* (is consistent within its own frame of reference). It is to be expected that, whatever the approach, there is a coherence and consistency to the perspective that is adopted.
- *better than the alternative approaches*. Rather than attempting to argue

that the choices were absolutely the 'right' ones, the justification takes the form of arguing that the approach that was adopted was better than – or no worse than – other possibilities. There are, perhaps, three main criteria that come into play when it comes to claims that the research is justified relative to alternatives. First, there are time and resource constraints that need to be taken into consideration. A short time-span and small budget might justify an approach as the best available, whereas under other circumstances it would not be. Second, there is the matter of the feasibility of the approach. The use of brief questionnaires in preference to semi-structured interviews, for instance, might be justified not in terms of any inherent advantages to the method itself but in terms of the circumstances of the research, in which the time and location render the use of semi-structured interviews not possible. Third, the research questions themselves will have a strong bearing on how the research is undertaken. Where the questions concern matters such as emotions, feelings, attitudes and relationships, it might invite the use of in-depth case studies with qualitative data. By contrast, research questions concerned with objective facts (e.g. income, car ownership) might be better tackled using a survey and the collection of quantitative data. It depends on the questions being asked.

Limitations (good research recognizes its own limitations)

There is no such thing as perfect research because every investigation involves some kind of compromise. The researcher is obliged to confront the reality of limited resources and less than perfect research tools, and eventually strike some kind of balance which involves a trade between competing demands and priorities. In the end, therefore, every piece of research has its limitations. Good research does not try to deny such limitations or sweep them under the carpet. Rather than denying any limitations, it gives due consideration to what can be, and importantly what cannot be, concluded on the basis of the specific approach adopted for the piece of research. Acknowledging limitations is not a sign of weakness or failure.

When outlining limitations, the researcher can include a variety of factors that might be felt to have impinged on the findings and that the researcher feels should be brought to the attention of the reader so that the reader is not misled in any way. There tend to be three main types of factors involved:

- *Resources*. Time, facilities and money provide limiting factors on all research. Where they have a particular bearing on the nature of what was undertaken and/or the outcomes from the research, then they might deserve to be discussed as a 'limitation'. So, for example, a tight deadline might be cited as a factor affecting the research that the reader ought to bear in mind when evaluating the end-product of the investigation.

Link up with **FEASIBILITY**

- *Underlying assumptions.* When discussing the limitations, the researcher needs to appreciate that there will be inherent limitations due to the nature of the theories and assumptions that underpin the research. At a fairly practical level this might translate into the recognition of the relative merits of quantitative and qualitative data in terms of shedding light on different types of research question. The best advice here is to 'know the enemy'. Positivists should be aware of the criticisms levelled at their position by interpretivists just as interpretivists should be conversant with the criticisms that positivists make of their position.

Link up with **PHILOSOPHY**

- *Research design.* Limitations that arise from the *design of the study* – its strategies, methods and analysis – include the following:
  - the *scope* of the research (the research questions): what was included among the questions and, importantly, were there relevant issues that could not be covered by this research?
  - the *breadth* of coverage (the sample, access): did the research approach allow the inclusion of sufficient numbers and categories of data to justify generalizations from the findings?
  - the *depth* of the research (validity): were the findings significantly affected by factors inherent in the approach which limited how far the research could deal with the complexities and subtleties of the situation?
  - the *objectivity* of the research (researcher self-interest, social values): were there aspects of the research design that might compromise the impartiality or honesty of the investigators or the data they used?

Link up with **DESIGN**

 Caution

When considering limitations, researchers should not embark on a whole-sale destruction of the worth of their own work. The point of the exercise is to acknowledge the boundaries to what can justifiably be concluded from the research with the important assumption that, whatever the limitations, on balance, the chosen approach provided more useful kinds of findings than would have been obtained from using some other approach to the research question. If, upon reflection, the limitations to the research start to challenge such an assumption then, clearly, doubts will arise about the overall worth of the research and its contribution to knowledge.

Writing an account of research

The amount of detail that is provided in an account of research will depend on the nature of the report. There is far more scope to describe and explain the intricacies of the methods in the context of a PhD thesis, for instance, than there would be in a short article for a popular journal or a report for a commercial organization. What is certain, though, is that in the vast majority of cases researchers will not be allowed the space to provide an account of their research methodology which covers all aspects of what was done. This means that they will need to do the following:

- prioritize what they report and concentrate on what they regard as the most significant features of their procedures;
- present as much detail as possible bearing in mind the space available for dealing with methodological issues.

It is not just the available space that affects the amount of detail that can be included. The account of the research will also need to be tailored to suit the expectations of the readers and the varying levels of expertise they might bring to their reading of the report. Certain details might be considered a necessity in the context of a report geared to one audience, but not for a different audience, where the decision might be made to omit the particular points in order to make space for other aspects of the research which are judged to be of more interest and relevance. When you are writing about the research, in other words, *it is important for the expectations of the readership to be considered.*

The manner in which the research is reported might also be shaped by certain formal conventions that define the information to be included, the order in which it is placed and the headings under which it is presented. There are, for instance, conventions applied by journal editors that specify the layout of the report and specify the kind of information that must be reported about the methodology. The science and medical journals are most prescriptive on this but even when it comes to research dissertations or reports for popular journals, *the nature of the report needs to correspond to any relevant regulations or requirements.* Whatever the context, it is usually expected that reports of research are presented in fairly formal language, using the third person, and adopting a standard referencing style to cite the sources used for the work.

Accounts of research tend to be shaped by another convention as well – the need to present the research process as a neat, logical sequence of events. This owes much to an image of good research which sees it as thoroughly planned, meticulously implemented and systematically analysed. This vision includes the idea that research is basically a sequence of logical steps that lead from the identification of a valuable research question through to the conclusions and recommendations at the end.

Reports of the research which reflect this sequence have the benefit that, from the reader's point of view, they follow a familiar path and are therefore easier to understand. Equally, they portray the research as successfully implementing a pre-planned and logical path – a path associated with rigorous methodology. In practice, however, social research can be a complex process that is hard to describe in such a straightforward way. In reality, it rarely occurs in a nice, neat order and, even though meticulous planning can help to avoid many potential pitfalls, things do not always go according to plan. When *reporting* the research, however, researchers are generally expected to adopt a narrative in which the research is packaged and presented in line with some

---

Box 9.2 Writing an account of research

An account of research calls for the researcher to be:

- *factual*: keeping a research diary, coupled with the careful maintenance of records and data, helps to ensure factual accuracy to what is reported.
- *succinct*: the account needs to communicate effectively with the readership of the report. It needs to be 'to the point' and as brief as possible bearing in mind the audience to whom it is addressed.
- *selective*: there are invariably word limits to what can be written. These are often very severe word limits that are formally stipulated, for instance, within the context of research degrees, journal articles or executive reports. Necessarily this can force the researcher to miss out what he or she might regard as relevant information about the research process. Within the constraints of word limits, the researcher has to identify the most important features and try to supply the most vital bits of information that a discerning readership might be expected to demand.
- *conventional*: there are conventions to do with the account of the research which can provide markers for its structure and style. The degree of flexibility afforded to the researcher in this respect varies depending on the context of the account (e.g. research thesis, journal article) and the discipline from which the research originates.
- *retrospective*: accounts of methodology generally constitute a version of events that is produced after the completion of the project. They involve a reconstruction of events. This reconstruction almost inevitably glosses over many of the complex aspects of doing research, presenting things in the kind of ordered and sequential format that will be quickly intelligible to the readers.

logical and sequential vision of research. This is a challenge that is all the more evident in the case of those styles of social research that need to be rather flexible in their approach and do not fit into the rigidly planned and executed vision of the research process. Grounded research, exploratory research and qualitative research, for example, can involve styles of investigation where the process of research involves a journey of discovery in which it is neither possible nor desirable to know in advance the exact details of how the research will unfold. Under such circumstances it is almost inevitable that researchers will need to engage in some simplification of events to avoid confusing readers with the sheer complexity of the real-world research process.

Bearing these points in mind, it becomes apparent that producing an account of research methodology involves more than simply recounting in a literal fashion the details of what was done. It calls for something more creative – editing skills and writing skills. This is an important point to appreciate because it alerts us to the fact that *accounts of research are constructions more than literal descriptions. They are an edited version of what took place.* They are crafted by the researcher to take account of the constraints of space, the expectations of the readership and the relevant reporting conventions.

 Caution

Although researchers need to present a 'selective' account of what took place, this should never be used as an opportunity to miss out those things the researcher might feel would put the research 'in a bad light'. It should be stressed that *there is no place in good research for an account that deliberately misrepresents what happened or misleads the reader about the truth.* That is unacceptable practice.

Box 9.3 Example of an account of research

The following example is not presented as a 'perfect' example of an account of research methods, but it does illustrate many of the points raised earlier in the chapter in relation to the information that needs to be included, and it shows a style of doing this within the constraints of a journal article. The methods chapter of a dissertation, obviously, would provide a context calling for more detail and more discussion.

Description, evaluation and justification of the data collection and analysis	Items in the account
A review of the literature has shown that there is a need to investigate the meaning that smoking holds for young people. There is a need to understand how they view smoking and what significance it holds in terms of their	Research questions derived from the literature review

Description, evaluation and justification of the data collection and analysis	Items in the account
perceptions of themselves. And there is a need to link the findings to the social context within which young people find themselves at the start of the new millennium. This article addresses these research needs by listening to the voices of young people and hearing what they have to say on the matter.	
The data used in this article came from research in the East Midlands of England conducted between January 2008 and June 2009. There were two phases to the research, the first of which was a questionnaire survey targeting young people aged 15–16 years. This was conducted between January and April 2008. The survey was based on 12 schools in Leicestershire and Rutland selected to be representative in terms of their catchment areas (social class, ethnic composition, urban/suburban/rural).	Time and place Survey strategy Representativeness
Questionnaires were given out during tutor group sessions and PSE lessons, at which time students were told the background to the research and reminded that they were under no obligation to complete the questionnaire. The groups were mixed ability and mixed sex. Students were assured that their responses would be treated in the strictest confidence and that the questionnaires were anonymous. Completed questionnaires were put immediately into envelopes and sealed prior to analysis by the researchers.	Questionnaire method Access Selection Consent Confidentiality
From the 1,679 young people who took part in the survey, 1,648 usable questionnaires were returned. These comprised 46.4 per cent males and 53.6 per cent females. There were two main ethnic groups represented in the survey; Whites (71.2 per cent) and South Asians (24.6 per cent). The young people who responded to the questionnaire survey reflected a pattern of smoking which largely matched the national picture for the age group, with nearly one in three being occasional or regular smokers, and with girls being more likely to be smokers than boys.	Response rate Sample numbers Data details Representativeness
The second phase of the research consisted of focus group discussions. They were tape recorded and generally lasted for about one hour. Sessions were started with a preordained routine that emphasized the voluntary basis of their participation, provided information about the purpose of the study and gave reassurances about anonymity and confidentiality in relation to the data arising from the discussions. The structured beginning to the focus groups also involved the presentation of certain data arising from the survey part of the research.	Focus group methods Access Consent Confidentiality

Description, evaluation and justification of the data collection and analysis	Items in the account
The *focus group discussions* were conducted with 123 young people aged 15–16 years (20 groups of four to seven people). Two focus groups took place in each school, except for one school that declined to be involved in this phase of the research and two others where only one focus group proved to be possible. The focus groups did not necessarily comprise a representative sample of the young people.	Sample size Selection Sampling Representativeness
The participants were not selected at random, nor were they selected on known attributes of the whole population. Added to this, the anonymity of the survey questionnaire meant that specific respondents could not be followed up. Selection of the young people was consequently based on (a) getting a range of the available attitudes and experiences (smokers/non-smokers, drinkers/non-drinkers) and (b) making sure that key groups were represented (gender, ethnic groups).	Limitations
Collaborating teachers were asked to select young people they knew to meet the requirements in terms of smoking and drinking and whom they felt were likely to 'have something to say'. These people also needed to express a willingness to participate; an ungrudging willingness to participate was considered essential on ethical grounds.	Identification and selection
This pragmatic basis for the selection of focus group and interview participants, however, inevitably had an impact on the representativeness of the participants. For one thing, they might be expected to be young people who were more confident and opinionated than the 'average'. The quiet, shy ones were likely to be under-represented. Also, of course, those absent from school on the day could not be included in this phase of the research.	Limitations
Transcripts of the tape recorded focus group discussions were analysed through an iterative process of reviewing and returning to the words of the young people. The extracts used in this article were selected to illustrate specific themes.	Analysis
Though some information about the speakers is provided, the data are inevitably decontextualized to some extent when presented within the constraints of an academic article, and it should be recognized, therefore, that the extracts support the argument as illustrations drawn from the empirical data rather than objective evidential proof of the point at hand.	Limitations
The use of a mixed-methodology approach produced both quantitative and qualitative data. The questionnaire survey involved a substantial number of young people. It covered a range of topics related to the research questions as well as providing data on key factors like the sex,	Justification

Description, evaluation and justification of the data collection and analysis	Items in the account
ethnicity and social background of those involved. It also allowed comparisons to be made with quantitative data from research conducted elsewhere in Britain to check on the representativeness of the sample. Qualitative data produced by the focus groups complemented the survey data. It entailed more in-depth consideration of specific issues and provided insights that would not have been possible through the use of questionnaires alone.	

Research project web-sites

Web-sites provide researchers with a means of publicizing their work to a very wide audience and they have enormous potential for researchers in terms of advertising their work and making the findings widely available. In addition to this, research project web-sites can provide a form of public accountability and transparency that fits nicely with the growing emphasis on good research governance. They can be used, for example, to justify the need for the research by providing information on: the background to the research. Information can be presented which explains the potential benefits to be gained from undertaking the enquiry.

Research project web-sites can also address the issue of the *scientific integrity* of the research by making details about the nature of the research publicly available. The site can hold information about things such as:

- *research design*: Details of the strategy and methods employed in the investigation can be posted on the site, or visitors can be directed via a hyperlink to another page that has the relevant information.
- *researcher credentials*: The site can contain details about the researcher's expertise and competence to undertake the research.
- *sponsorship*: The site can provide the opportunity to identify any sponsorship or conflict of interest that might impact on the impartiality of the research.

Trust in the research can be enhanced through appropriate use of a research project web-site. The site can be used, for instance, to provide assurances about *compliance with the law* – particularly with respect to data protection and intellectual property rights. They can contain a formal commitment on the part of the researcher covering things such as:

- *data security*: Measures taken to safeguard the data can be outlined and assurances can be given about the use of the data and their non-disclosure to third parties.
- *ownership of the data*: Issues relating to copyright and intellectual property rights can be addressed.

The propriety of the research can be reinforced when the research project web-site is used in relation to the protection of the participants' interests. Web-sites can cover things like:

- *informed consent*: Relevant information for prospective and current participants can be posted so that their consent, should they choose to give it, can be truly 'informed'. There can be hyperlinks to other pages and sites for anyone seeking further details.
- *anonymity*: The researchers can state their commitment to this principle and to provide necessary assurances to participants.
- *confidentiality*: As with anonymity, the research project web-site provides the opportunity to state a commitment to this principle and to specify actual safeguards that have been put in place.
- *privacy*: Respect for the privacy of participants is becoming an increasingly significant issue in research governance. It has become common practice to place a link to a *privacy policy* on commercial web-sites as a way of addressing the need for propriety in relation to data, and research project web-sites should similarly contain an explicit privacy policy relating to the project.

Guidelines for good practice

Accountability of research serves two purposes. In terms of the quality of research, it provides a means by which other researchers can evaluate the methods and the findings of a particular project. It addresses the need for credibility – convincing the readers of the research that its findings are based on good research practice and are worthy of being treated as superior to common sense when it comes to describing or explaining the thing that has been investigated. In terms of ethics, it provides a transparency to the process of research that benefits participants by allowing them an appropriate level of insight into the nature of the investigation. Accountability of research, then, is regarded as necessary from both a scientific and a moral standpoint and the following points of good practice can prove beneficial in these respects.

Keep good records

Accountability requires first and foremost that the researcher makes detailed records covering the whole process of the research. It is a basic discipline of good research that such records should be kept from the start. In order to provide an account of actions and decisions, particularly those taken at the early parts of research. The necessary detail and the nature of the researcher's thoughts at the early stages of the research cannot rely on the recall of memory at the final stages of writing up the research. In practice, the accuracy of any account will depend on being able to refer to records made *at the time*; relying on memory is not defensible. Such records should cover not only the methods of data collection but also the reasoning for making decisions about the choice of approach to the research and the analysis of the results.

The research data should be *catalogued and stored* in a safe place even after the research has been completed. In principle, the researcher should be able to produce the evidence to prove that the research actually took place. In principle, other researchers should be able to access the data to re-analyse it and, thereby, to check the conclusions drawn from the data. Depending on the specific area of research, records should be kept for at least five years after the completion of the project.

Provide an account of the research process that stands as a distinct, separate section of any report on the research

This might be a separate chapter in a dissertation, it might be a subsection of an article in an academic journal or it might be a footnote to a piece in a popular glossy magazine. Its size and the amount of detail will reflect the nature of the report and its readership. Normally, however, the account of the research appears under a distinct and separate heading that identifies it as the 'methods' section, the purpose of which is to bring together the various strands of the investigation so that the reader can see exactly how the research was undertaken. This is vital because it informs the readers' subsequent judgements about the quality of the investigation and its conclusions.

First describe what was done, then explain why it was done

For the purposes of clarity, what is required in the first place is a straightforward *statement of fact* about what has been done. Where possible, this should be separated from a discussion or defence of why it was done. A justification is certainly necessary but it generally helps to deal with the question of 'why?' *after* having dealt with the factual questions. It helps to deal with the matters of 'what?', 'who?', 'which?', 'how many?' and 'when?' first, and then to proceed to discuss the merits of the approach once the reader is in possession of the facts about what was actually done.

Acknowledging that different kinds of social research might call for adaptions and modifications, the 'core' items that underpin an account of empirical research generally address the following things.

There needs to be a clear and succinct list of the questions, issues or hypotheses the research has attempted to investigate

Research questions, issues or hypotheses need to be specified because they provide the basepoint from which to make judgements about the suitability of the approach that has been adopted. The research questions provide the objectives towards which the empirical investigation is targeted and the strategy/methods constitute the means for achieving answers to the research questions. Good research uses the most suitable means (strategy/methods) for achieving the objectives of the research (captured in the research questions).

Link up with **PURPOSE**

An explicit statement should be made about which strategy has been used to investigate the research question(s) (HOW)

The account needs a statement about the broad strategy that has been adopted to tackle the research questions(s). Surveys, case studies, experiments, action research and ethnography provide distinct starting blocks for research that carry their own assumptions, their own advantages and their own limitations when it comes to dealing with issues and problems of interest to social researchers. By stating which approach has been adopted, the researcher sets the stall out for what is to follow.

There should be a description of the method(s) used for collecting the data (HOW)

For social research this tends to involve the use of questionnaires, interviews, observation or documentary sources. Multi-method research involving the use of more than one method, valuable as a means of triangulation, calls for the researcher to spell out the range of methods employed in data collection and to link specific methods to specific types of data.

Precise details need to be given about the data that were collected (WHO, WHAT, HOW MANY)

Having described how the data were obtained, the account of the research can proceed to give exact details of who or what was included and what numbers were involved. It is generally good practice here to be very specific in terms of the numbers involved. The words 'some', 'many' or the like should be avoided because they are vague and send the wrong signals about the research. In this context, precise numbers are needed. 'About 50 interviews were conducted' is not as good as saying '52 interviews were conducted'.

A description of when and where the data were collected should be included (WHEN, WHERE)

With regard to details about when and where the data were collected, efforts should also be made to be precise about things such as the time of the research (month and year), the time-span during which the research was undertaken and the context within which it took place (location, circumstances).

The criteria for selecting the sources of data need to be specified (WHICH)

The research should focus on people, things or situations that have been chosen in terms of their significance for the research questions. The criteria for choosing them are thus important. The account needs to describe how the sources of data were identified and how they were selected. For example, a survey approach will tend to collect data from a sample drawn from a broader population that is relevant to the issues being investigated. This calls for a brief explanation of how the sample was selected (sampling frame, sampling method), how contact was established (post, phone) and what measures were undertaken to encourage a good response rate. It is also good practice to refer to technical names if they apply (e.g. to specify whether the sampling was random or nonprobability, whether the sampling was systematic, quota, etc.). If data were collected by interviews, it would be important to specify whether they were unstructured, semi-structured or structured interviews.

There should be a justification for the choice of strategy, methods and analytic techniques used – an explanation of why they are appropriate under the circumstances (WHY)

As was suggested earlier in this chapter, justifying the chosen approach to the research involves substantiating the claims that the strategy and methods fit the needs of the research question, that the approach has a logical coherence to it and, importantly, the pragmatic point that the approach actually adopted was better than – or no worse than – the alternatives. It also requires that the research operates within a code of ethics.

It is good practice to include a statement within any report on the research about its methodological limitations

Without destroying the credibility of the whole investigation, there needs to be some acknowledgement of the limitations of the research which derive from the theories and underlying assumptions of the approach and that result from the strategies and methods used – the design of the study. Such a statement is often required under the specific heading of 'limitations', following practice in the more 'scientific' journals. The limitations, alternatively, can be broached in the methods section when discussing the choice of the methods and strategies. The principle, none the less, is that the researcher should demonstrate an awareness of the boundaries to the research and what it is reasonable to conclude on the basis of the investigation.

Develop a web-site devoted to the research project

Basic web-sites are easy to manage and cheap to maintain. They can improve the transparency of the research process by making details of the project publicly available. They can equally prove beneficial from a research ethics point of view by including things like a privacy policy and an ethics statement relating to research data.

Further reading

Denscombe, M. (2007) *The Good Research Guide: For Small-scale Social Research Projects*, 3rd edn. Buckingham: Open University Press, Chapter 15.

Lincoln, Y. and Guba, E. (1985) *Naturalistic Enquiry*. Newbury Park, CA: Sage, Chapters 11 and 13.

Murray, N. and Hughes, G. (2008) *Writing Up Your University Assignments and Research Projects*. Maidenhead: Open University Press.

Murray, R. and Moore, S. (2006) *The Handbook of Academic Writing: A Fresh Approach*. Maidenhead: Open University Press.

Checklist for ACCOUNTABILITY

When considering the accountability of the research you should feel confident about answering 'yes' to the following questions: ✔

1 Have sufficient details been given about:
The kind of data that were collected? ☐
The amount of data involved? ☐
When and where the data were collected? ☐

2 Has the rationale for selecting items of data been explained (e.g. how data sources were identified; what sampling procedures were used)? ☐

3 Has the choice of research approach (strategy, methods, analysis) been justified in relation to:
The research questions? ☐
Possible alternative approaches? ☐
Ethical considerations? ☐

4 Have methodological limitations been acknowledged in terms of:
The underlying assumptions of the approach? ☐
The breadth of coverage? ☐
The depth of detail? ☐
Objectivity? ☐

5 Has the account of the research been adapted to suit the specific readership? ☐

6 Have relevant details of the research been made publicly available via the Internet (perhaps using a dedicated research project web-site)? ☐

7 Have notes been kept of the research process and the crucial decisions affecting the research? ☐

8 Have data and research records been formally documented and stored securely for later reference? ☐

© M. Denscombe, *Ground Rules for Social Research*. Open University Press.

V

FINDINGS

10

GENERALIZATIONS

Ground rule:	**Research should produce findings from which generalizations can be made**
Question:	Do the findings from this specific piece of research apply more generally to other comparable situations?
Answers:	Either: the research is based on a sample of people, events or data that are representative of the wider population (*generalizability*).
	Or: sufficient information is given about the characteristics of the sample or the cases used in the research for judgements to be made about the extent to which findings can be expected to apply more widely (*transferability*).
	Or: the people, events or data included in the research have been chosen because of their particular characteristics and the belief that these characteristics will be helpful for generating and developing theories (*theory relevance*).

A generalization involves drawing some conclusion about a whole group or category of things on the basis of information drawn from particular instances or examples. On the basis of what is found to exist in a relatively few instances or examples, propositions are made about the nature and qualities of the whole class.

Social researchers tend to be concerned with generalizations for two reasons. The first centres on the *empirical* matter of how far the characteristics of the people, events or data chosen for the study are to be found elsewhere throughout the class of thing being studied. Researchers usually wish to feel confident that their findings have been based on samples that are either *representative* of, or have *particular characteristics* that are significant for the analysis of, the broader class of thing being investigated. The second reason centres on the researcher's wish to produce generalized knowledge in the form of *theories*. In this case, the suitability of the people, events or data chosen for the study depends on how their traits meet the needs of producing, testing or developing theories. The concern with generalizations relates to the way findings from specific pieces of research lend themselves to the development of propositions that work very widely – possibly universally – and that contribute to establishing rules or theories about the workings of social phenomena.

These two kinds of concern with making generalizations, it should be stressed, are not mutually exclusive. Nor are they without their critics. As we shall see, there are differing versions of how researchers can extrapolate from their particular findings to more generalized classes of things. And, there is some controversy about how far social researchers should be concerned with striving to develop 'grand' theories and universal laws. There is even a line of argument that rejects the idea that generalizations are necessary at all. Such controversies and criticisms bear testimony to the contested nature of social research. But, having acknowledged this, it is important to recognize also that generalizations:

- continue to be a crucial aspect of good research for all but a small minority of those operating under the umbrella of 'social research';
- can be justified in different ways depending on the nature of the particular research and its underlying assumptions;
- need to be incorporated into the rationale for the research.

Criteria for the selection of samples and case studies

For both quantitative researchers and qualitative researchers there is the same underlying issue when it comes to the credibility of their generalizations. Whether using a sample or a case study, the *criteria for selection* are the crucial starting point when it comes to generalizations.

In essence, the selection of the items to be included in the study needs to be done on a logical basis – a basis that allows generalizations from the data to be defended as reasonable and justifiable – and within social research there are broadly two approaches to this matter. One way is to go for a *representative sample*. This tends to be favoured by relatively large-scale survey research using quantitative data and a positivistic approach. The alternative is to select the items for study on the basis of their *particular characteristics*. Smaller-scale research involving case studies, qualitative data and an interpretivist approach tend to rely on this.

Box 10.1 Generalizations	
The key issue	**Things to be considered**
Do the findings from the research apply elsewhere?	• Have the *criteria for selection* of the people, events or data been described and justified? • Reflecting the criteria for selection, have an adequate *number* and appropriate *diversity* of people, events or data been included in the research? • Does the description of the sample or cases used in the research allow comparisons with others of their type?

Generalizations from a representative sample

Social research rarely covers each and every instance of the particular phenomenon that is being investigated. To do so would cost too much and would take too long. Instead, research tends to focus on a reduced number of instances of the thing under investigation. It investigates a sample or it investigates specific cases. The moment it does so, however, it confronts a fundamental question: *to what extent do the findings from the sample or case apply to other instances that were not included in the study?*

Research that is based on a representative sample addresses this question using the logic that the instances actually used in the research share the same key characteristics as the full set – the total, the 'population'. But instead of investigating all parts of 'the cake' the research concentrates on just 'one slice'. Provided that the slice does indeed share the same general characteristics as the whole cake, it follows that the findings from the sample should match the findings that would have emerged had the researcher actually managed to research the whole thing.

To be representative, samples need to do the following:

• cover *all relevant types*;
• have these types *in proportion* to the volumes found in the whole population.

To illustrate this point, consider the possibility of studying the nature of health education in schools. Assuming that a study of all schools in the country would be too expensive and time-consuming, the researcher might wish to base the data collection on a subset of the total. To be representative of the whole population this subset would need to include examples of all types. This would mean including:

- large schools, medium-sized schools, small schools;
- urban schools, suburban schools, small town schools, rural schools;
- middle-class schools, working-class schools;
- private schools, local authority schools.

The numbers in each category would need to be in proportion to those found in the whole population. So, for instance, having defined what constitutes 'large', 'medium' and 'small' schools in terms of pupils on the school roll, the *representative* sample would select numbers in each category to balance the proportions in the total population.

> **Key point**
> A representative sample includes a balanced cross-section of all of the relevant instances. This justifies generalizing from the findings of the sample.

There are essentially two ways to achieve this representativeness. First, there is the use of *random samples*. Provided that the units included (people, observations, etc.) in the research are sufficiently large in number and are chosen on a genuinely random basis, the end result ought to be representative of the total population from which they were drawn. True, the sample is always likely to vary slightly from the total population, but the difference is statistically calculable in terms of its extent and the likelihood of it occurring. It is not appropriate at this point to delve into the theory of sampling and sampling error and the reader should consult other sources for further information on the technical aspects of this. The point at present concerns the principle, and the principle is one that lies close to the heart of quantitative research using large-scale samples. It is the principle of random selection and the way that, when coupled with large numbers of units for study, this can provide the basis for representativeness.

Second, there is the selection of samples by *quotas*. On the basis of attributes of the population which are already known, the researcher can select samples deliberately to include all the relevant types and to cover these types in proportion to their profile in the total population. This is particularly useful when, for whatever reason, there are not the kind of large numbers needed to ensure representativeness through random selection. Continuing with the example of the schools-based research, the researcher could use existing national statistics covering the size of schools, the proportions that are state-funded and the location in schools in urban/rural settings to establish quotas – targets for the number of schools to be included within each category – such that the final overall profile of schools used in the research matches that are to be found nationwide. Having got a target figure for each sub-group of schools, the researcher can then set about filling the quotas. When doing so, schools enter the sample not on the basis of some random selection but on the basis of deliberate selection by the researcher who chooses the schools because of their particular characteristics and the way these characteristics match the criteria for each sub-group of schools. Once the quota is filled, of course, schools will also get rejected from the sample on the basis of their specific characteristics.

In the case of both random and quota samples, researchers are in a position to generalize from their findings because their research uses data drawn from a representative sample – a sample that on statistical grounds can be shown to cover *all* relevant types, and include these types in direct proportion to the volumes found in the whole population. However, it is not always easy for researchers to obtain a sample that qualifies as 'representative' according to these strict criteria. For one thing, it demands that we know relevant details about the whole population. These details are not always available. It demands that the research will include sufficient numbers to cover all relevant types. This is not always possible. It demands that we can get access to exactly the types of instances we require in exactly the proportions needed. This is not always feasible. As a result, social researchers frequently rely on a less stringent version of representativeness in which the principle remains the same but the rigour of selection of the sample is relaxed somewhat. The principle is still that the instances used for the research allow the findings from the research to be extrapolated to other instances not included in the research. However, in light of the difficulties just outlined, the researcher does not claim that the sample necessarily meets all the criteria of representativeness. Rather, the claim is that the instances used for research are 'typical'.

In this context, the word 'typical' carries with it some notion of being standard, of being normal, of being usual. It *suggests* that any findings from the sample will apply elsewhere because the instances included in the sample have no particularly unusual characteristics that mark them out from the rest.

Now, while claims to conducting research on 'typical' instances certainly retain the need to identify key features relevant to the investigation (in the previous example, things like the size and location of the school), the sample might not include *all* of the relevant categories. It might just focus on the main one. Nor will the sample necessarily include the categories in strict proportion to the whole population. The claim to generalizability, however, persists through the emphasis on:

- including the *main* type; and
- achieving *some balance* of the numbers in each category.

Generalizations from examples chosen for their particular qualities

It is quite reasonable for social researchers to shun the idea of using a large sample as the source of their data and, instead, to prefer to focus their sights on a limited number of instances – possibly just one – of the thing in question. A case study approach is the obvious example here. Researchers can make the strategic decision to concentrate their investigation on one or a few cases in order to allow greater depth to their research, more attention to the dynamics of the situation, better insights that come from a detailed knowledge and understanding of a specific example. It is qualitative researchers who tend to favour this strategy.

Resources generally dictate that the focus in depth that is necessary for the collection of qualitative data is paid for at the expense of a breadth of enquiry that involves large numbers. A corollary of this is that there is almost no chance of getting a sample that is large enough and widespread enough to satisfy the criteria for being representative, in a statistical sense, of the whole 'population'. The selection, instead, tends to rely on a more purposeful process in which *examples are chosen for their particular qualities* – as opposed to being chosen with no regard for their individual traits (random) or being chosen with respect to some general category (quota). There are, broadly speaking, four grounds on which cases might be chosen to reflect their particular qualities.

First, researchers can justify generalizations from their case study (or small sample) if they can establish that the instance included in the research was *typical of other instances*. The basis for the generalization is that whatever was found in the one instance actually studied was likely to appear in other instances because there was nothing unusual, nothing special, about the case that was investigated. It was, in effect, the same as the rest and so the findings should apply elsewhere to other instances that were not studied. Of course, the task confronting researchers here is to establish that the case studied was indeed typical of others. To do this, they need to demonstrate that there is an extent of similarity between the case and the rest that warrants such generalizations, and this calls for some comparison between the features of the case and those found in other cases.

Second, at the opposite end of the spectrum, social researchers can opt to focus on instances that are anything but representative or typical. *'Extreme' instances* may be selected deliberately because they have certain qualities that exaggerate the influence of a particular factor that is of interest to the researchers. Following the illustration of drugs education in schools, researchers might opt to focus on instances which are extreme in terms of things like the prevalence of drug use among pupils in the school. They might deliberately focus on one or a few case studies of schools that they know to have a high incidence of drug use to see how these schools deal with the matter. The logic, here, is that things might be visible in these circumstances simply because the situation is extreme or special, and that these might be impossible to detect in more 'watered down' instances. *Things become visible here that would remain hidden under typical circumstances.*

Generalizations from such findings use the rationale that there is something to be learned from these extreme instances; that what is found under these circumstances still has relevance for the more routine and ordinary instances. It can suggest the way things might develop if typical instances start to shift towards the special or extreme. If schools detect an increase in drug use among pupils, their patterns of drug education might logically develop towards that which has already been found in the special case study schools. Alternatively, the special/extreme example might act to alert us to factors that would otherwise have remained hidden under the typical circumstances. What was detected in the extreme instance should be looked for in the typical.

Third, researchers might decide to focus on instances which would appear to present a *least likely scenario* in terms of the theory or proposition they are investigating. Following the commitment to testing theories to destruction and challenging existing theories or suppositions through attempting to 'falsify' them, there is a clear logic to choosing instances that might be expected to 'go against the grain' and prove the theory wrong.

Link up with **PROOF**

Fourth, the selection of a case might reflect the fact that it constitutes an event or situation that is a *special case* – a one-off or extremely rare occurrence. Researchers might find themselves with a chance of a lifetime to study an event or situation that commands attention as something special. It is almost certain that such events or situations are beyond the control of the researcher in the sense that he or she could not organize for them to happen, as in an experiment. The timing and the location of the event will be something to which the researcher responds rather than initiates.

 Caution

Choosing to look at special events obviously focuses attention on the unique or rare qualities of the item and would appear at first glance to operate on a very different agenda from research that chooses its people, events and/or data as normal, representative or typical. The purpose of the research is to account for the item in terms of its unique qualities. In turn, this would seem to suggest that when conducting this kind of investigation, the researcher is not really concerned with generalizations. However, this conclusion would be a little hasty and not strictly correct. When describing and explaining what is unique about the special case, the researcher inevitably

188 GROUND RULES FOR SOCIAL RESEARCH

needs to contrast the situation with aspects of more routine cases (representative, typical) and this involves some comparison with 'the general'. What makes the particular case 'special' can only be understood by way of contrast with what is more normal and more general.

Making comparisons

The degree to which the findings from the small number of events or cases being studied might be expected to apply elsewhere can be addressed by comparing and contrasting the nature of the specific units of study with the broader population of such units that exist. The in-depth, qualitative study of five schools, to pursue the example above, should include a contrast of these specific 'units' with schools in general. The size of the schools in terms of pupil intake, the catchment areas and their curriculum organization are factors on which information can be provided and then compared with the situation that occurs in the wider population of schools in the society. In this way, the specific small number being investigated can be contrasted with national averages and prevailing norms, with current policies or regional conditions, in a way that allows them to be identified as similar to, or different from, other schools. Armed with such information, it is possible to make some reasoned estimation of the extent to which the findings might be transferable to other situations.

Alternatively, the selection of instances for research can be based on their usefulness in terms of the contrast they offer with other instances chosen to be included in the research. The researcher can deliberately set out to select examples that provide a stark contrast with one another and that represent the widest variation possible within the thing being studied. The schools example, again, proves valuable since it is something that most people can relate to. The researcher could choose schools for inclusion in the research on the basis that they are very different in terms of key criteria, such as size and location. The logic is that the comparison of large with small, urban with rural, will identify similarities and differences that might not become as evident had they been chosen simply as typical examples. Choosing them to achieve a maximum variation allows the researcher to use the comparative method, controlling for key variables such as size and location, to see what other factors might appear to be linked with these.

Selection on the basis of comparison can be useful, in two particular ways. First, it can allow an element of 'triangulation' between alternatives. The researcher, here, is able to see how a certain thing works in two or more very different settings. Second, it is useful where the research design is emergent. Where the researcher selects cases as part of an unfolding path of discovery, like a detective following a lead, then the idea that has emerged from the one example can be compared with the next example, which might be consciously chosen as one that is different.

Generalizability and transferability

When it comes to the grounds for making generalizations from research find-ings, there is a distinction to be made between the notions of *generalizability* and *transferability*. Both terms convey the idea of applying the findings from particular pieces of research more broadly beyond the bounds of the actual people, events, data, etc. actually used in the investigation. Generalizability, however, is a quality of the findings that is measurable, testable and checkable, and tends to be associated with quantitative and more positivistic styles of research. Contrasting with this, transferability is a more intuitive process in which the relevance of the specific research findings to other events, people or data is imagined rather than actually demonstrated. In a strict sense, most small-scale and/or qualitative research concerns itself with the transferability of findings rather than their generalizability.

Transferability is a process in which the researcher and the readers *infer* how the findings might relate to other situations. They literally 'transfer' the results from the research situation to other situations. The transferability of the findings relies on information being provided about the people, events or data being studied – information that is sufficiently detailed to allow an informed judgement about how far and how well the findings map on to other situations. There needs to be information on the people, events and/or data, their key characteristics and how these compare with others of their type. It is the duty of the researcher to provide such relevant information about the situation, and enough of it, so that its wider relevance can be perceived.

The term *thick description* is often used in this context. According to Geertz (1973), a thick description is an account of a situation that manages to capture the many facets, the various angles and the multiple levels that comprise the complex reality of social life. Its quality is to convey enough detail so that the readers can imagine themselves 'being there' and participating in the situation, and also to unravel the many layers of meaning that tend to surround social phenomena. Whereas a 'thin' description might depict things in a relatively simple fashion in terms of one perspective, one set of meanings, one angle on things, a 'thick' description goes further.

The researcher plays a key role in providing the necessary information, but the readers of the research also play a crucial role when it comes to the trans-ferability of findings. Part of the researcher's role is to interpret and evaluate the findings – but the readers of the research are not passive recipients who merely soak up the analysis presented by the researcher. To a greater or lesser extent, especially when qualitative research uses case studies and ethnograph-ies, the readers themselves engage in interpreting and evaluating the findings. They themselves imaginatively transfer the findings to other situations, rely-ing on their own knowledge and values in doing so.

Box 10.2 Generalizability and transferability explained

What is 'generalizability'?

It is the *methodological* application of findings from one set of data, one piece of research, to other instances of the phenomenon. It is something done on the basis of statistical tests, 'scientific' rigour, systematic checking, etc. and tends to be associated with positivistic kinds of research and the use of quantitative data.

What is 'transferability'?

It is the *imaginative* application of findings to other settings. It is something done in an informal, personal and creative fashion. It is the process carried out by readers of research when they infer from what they read and 'transfer' the result to other situations. The more information they have about the original research, the better informed their inferences will be. This kind of generalization tends to be associated with interpretative kinds of research and the use of qualitative data.

Idiographic research

There is an argument put forward by some interpretive researchers that there is no need to address the matter of generalizing from the specific and particular features of the unique thing that is portrayed by the research. Generalizations, they argue, are not part of the agenda for this style of research. The point of their research is to identify things that are unique and peculiar to the thing they are studying. Theirs is *'idiographic* research', whose purpose is openly and explicitly to focus on the specifics of a particular case and how these reflect the localized context (Denzin and Lincoln 1994). As Smith argues, those engaged in idiographic research tend to focus on specific locations (an organization, a community, an event, a time period in history) and to concern themselves with the relationships and processes occurring within those settings. 'They do not attempt to invest their explanations with the capacity to generalize beyond the events or states of affairs for which they were devised' (1998: 345). *Generalizing is simply not part of the research agenda for idiographic research.*

Stake illustrates this line of reasoning when he argues that:

> The real business of a case study is particularization, not generalization. We take a particular case and come to know it well, not primarily as to how it is different from others but what it is, what it does. There is an emphasis

on uniqueness, and that implies knowledge of others that the case is different from, but the first emphasis is on understanding the case itself.

(1995: 8)

This, however, is a minority viewpoint. Without getting embroiled in the subtleties and intricacies of the debate, it is far safer for the non-established researcher to take on board the point that Williams (2000) makes: that interpretive researchers inevitably engage in some form of generalization, *whether or not they like to admit it*.

Theory relevance

Some researchers argue that the key to making generalizations does not actually depend on the absolute numbers of items studied or the degree to which they are representative of the whole population (e.g. Glaser and Strauss 1967; Lincoln and Guba 1985). They defend the use of small numbers in research on the basis that what is important is the extent to which the examples chosen for study are relevant in terms of theory, rather than representative of the whole population from which they have been selected. Such researchers, generally qualitative researchers, retain a commitment to the principle of generalizability. Lincoln and Guba (1985), for example, promote the idea that findings should apply in other contexts – much in line with the notion of external reliability used with quantitative research. However, in qualitative research, they argue, the criterion for generalizations shifts from the idea of being representative in terms of the traits of the population to being representative in terms of the key features of a theory.

Generalizations from case studies often fit into this category. When used as a pilot study or exploratory investigation, a case study can suggest possible concepts and theories that can be checked out subsequently in other situations to see if these concepts and theories work more widely. Equally, case studies can be used as a test-bed for concepts and theories. Researchers can take ideas developed elsewhere (by other researchers, in other locations) and check whether they work in the specific circumstances of the case being researched. Either way, the issue of generalization is dealt with in terms of the 'theory relevance' of the case. In the former, it is a matter of *generating theory*, in the latter, it is a matter of *theory testing*. And what matters crucially for the researcher is how well the specific case study exhibits traits that match the theory.

So, for example, a study of the behaviour of officials in a social security office might be based on one case study and this case study might be justified as appropriate not in terms of how well it fits the pattern of social security offices nationwide but in terms of the theory of bureaucracy which is relevant to the study. To the extent that it maps on to the theory of bureaucracy and bureaucratic behaviour, it is a suitable site for investigation. Theories and conceptual frameworks provide the criteria, generally available and universally recognized, that allow researchers to appreciate the significance of the case being studied (in this case its significance in relation to a theory of bureaucratic behaviour) and which allow researchers and readers to *transfer* the findings to other situations. The theory provides the basis for transporting findings and conclusions from setting to setting because the theory provides explicit and logical premises underlying the findings and conclusions of the study – a common language through which to interpret things.

Link up with **PROOF**

How far can you generalize?

Generalizations allow researchers to make statements about matters above and beyond what they have actually found through their empirical investigations. From their study of particular instances of a phenomenon they can move towards more *universal* statements about the phenomenon that apply in all situation at all times. Their research findings can be generalized into theories. As Layder points out:

> Theorizing involves the ability to move from the concrete and particular (detailed observations or factual information) to more general and abstract concerns and ideas – that is, to shift to a concentration on the more general characteristics of the things one observes. This, in turn, involves a process of generalizing which requires the application of the same principles, standards and criteria across a broad range of situations and examples rather than limiting oneself to describing the details of particular situations, events or examples.
>
> (1998: 100)

In principle, then, it might seem that there are no limits to how far researchers can generalize from their findings, other than arriving at the ultimate generalization – universal theories that cover every instance. Researchers might hope to achieve in the social world what has been achieved in the natural and physical sciences by things like Einstein's theory of relativity and Darwin's theory of evolution.

Attempts to emulate the natural and physical sciences, however, have been subjected to telling criticism in recent times and it would be rather naïve in the twenty-first century to treat generalizations in social research as part of a process moving towards developing grand theories. Social researchers have become rather wary about the suggestion that they can, or should, attempt to generalize to this upper limit and, in recent decades, there has been a tendency to adopt a far more modest vision of how far it is possible and desirable to generalize on the basis of research findings. The main reason for this is that the quest for general laws, models and abstract theories very much reflects the aims of *positivistic* research and its efforts to uncover the regularities that are presumed to exist in the world. In the words of Lincoln and Guba (1985: 111), this 'oozes determinism, and seems to place the entire world at the feet of those persons who can unlock its deepest and most pervasive generalities'. Critics of positivism have argued that explanations of the social world which take the form of universals and grand theory vastly oversimplify matters. A broad spectrum of approaches, including postmodernists, social constructionists and other interpretivists, have become allied in their scepticism about the prospect of producing grand theories. The social world, they argue, is:

- highly complex;
- multifaceted;
- reflexive in nature.

Grand theories cannot hope to represent such a world. Instead, the social researcher can only hope to engage in trying to portray relatively small bits of the world, and to do so in a way that acknowledges the complexities, even the contradictions and enigmas, that constitute the social world.

One outcome of this critique has been an additional sensitivity on the part of social researchers to the matter of making generalizations and a tendency to operate at a lower level of generality. Aware of the limitations to how far it is justifiable to generalize about matters in the social world, there has been a shift towards attempting to tackle phenomena that are less complex, more bounded, possibly more localized, and to use theories that might apply to this specific phenomenon. To illustrate the point, rather than attempting to produce a general theory of teaching – a theory that would explain teaching in all locations in all schools for all people at all times – researchers will tend to feel more comfortable focusing on the more manageable task of explaining, for example, supply (locum) teaching in secondary schools in rural locations in a particular society, in relation to a specific period of time. The explanatory variables would be restricted by focusing on a subset of teachers (supply teachers), a subset of schools (rural locations), one society (e.g. the UK, the USA) and a given time-span (e.g. the last decade).

It is important to recognize, however, that social researchers have not actually abandoned efforts to generalize from their findings. They continue to search for statements about broader classes of things which, though they might not claim to be universals, nevertheless provide some theoretical insight into how and why things work as they do. Researchers still engage in some level of theorizing. While being very sensitive to the limitations to theorizing within the social sciences, their investigations usually involve some pursuit of explanations that involve generalizing across situations and some attempt to contribute to knowledge by seeking to locate specific items (data from observation, experiences, etc.) within a broader framework that provides a better understanding of the way such items are interrelated.

Guidelines for good practice

Generalizations are a necessary and inevitable aspect of good research. The vast majority of social researchers – positivists, critical realists, pragmatists and interpretivists – acknowledge that generalizing beyond what they have actually found forms a fundamental and unavoidable feature of what they do in research activity. Acknowledging this point, there are certain practices that should be adopted.

Explicit attention needs to be given to the rationale for generalizations based on the research data

There needs to be some discussion of the bases on which generalizations can been made from the research. Across the range of disciplines and approaches that can be incorporated into the realms of social research, it is only a small minority who would argue that their research can or should ignore this issue.

Generalizations based on the representativeness of the data need to be explained and justified in relation to the sampling strategy used

They are concerned with the *generalizability* of the findings. They must demonstrate that the process of selecting the sample was likely to cover the whole range of relevant types, and include the types in proportion to the volumes found in the whole population.

With the use of case studies and smaller samples, where a 'representative' sample is not claimed, sufficient detail needs to be given about the nature of the units that are studied and the process of their selection

Here, the concern is with the *transferability* of the findings. Social researchers who generalize on these grounds, mainly interpretivists, must supply what is often called a 'thick description' with sufficient detail to make things 'come alive' for the reader.

Research that uses case studies can justify generalizations made on the basis of its findings by striving to ensure the representativeness of the data collected within the case

When distributing questionnaires, when identifying suitable people to inter-view, when deciding which events to observe, when selecting which docu-ments to analyse, researchers can be guided by principles of sampling and representativeness that are the same as those used in large-scale surveys. They can aim to include all relevant categories and ensure sufficient coverage of situations and events to justify claims that, within the case(s) being studied, the data are representative.

Generalizations need to be made cautiously and with careful attention being paid to the inherent limitations of making generalizations about phenomena that are extremely complex

In accounts of the research, there needs to be a clear acknowledgement of factors that inhibit the prospects of making generalizations. This point is all too easily overlooked, or treated as a weakness of the research. It should be remembered, though, that good research explicitly recognizes its own limitations, and the matter of generalizability is exactly one point where it is important to recognize such limitations.

Further reading

Blaikie, N. (2000) *Designing Social Research: The Logic of Anticipation*. Cambridge: Polity Press, Chapters 6 and 7.

Denscombe, M. (2007) *The Good Research Guide: For Small-scale Social Research Projects*, 3rd edn. Buckingham: Open University Press, Chapters 1 and 2.

Lincoln, Y. and Guba, E. (1985) *Naturalistic Enquiry*. Newbury Park, CA: Sage, Chapter 5.

Stake, R. (1995) *The Art of Case Study Research*. Thousand Oaks, CA: Sage, Chapters 3 and 5.

Williams, M. (2000) Interpretivism and generalization, *Sociology*: 34(2): 209–24.

Checklist for GENERALIZATIONS

With respect to generalizations based on the research you should feel confident about answering 'yes' to the following questions: ☑

1 Have the findings been considered in terms of one of the following:
Their generalizability to wider populations? ☐
Their transferability to comparable situations or events? ☐
Their significance for generating or developing theories? ☐

2 Has the selection of the people/items from whom data were collected been explained in terms of one of the following criteria:
Complete coverage of research population? ☐
Representative sample? ☐
Typical instance(s)? ☐
Extreme example(s)? ☐
Least likely instance(s)? ☐
Special case or instance of particular relevance? ☐

3 Bearing in mind the criteria for selection, have an adequate *number* and appropriate *diversity* of people, events or data been included to warrant generalizations from the research? ☐

4 Is there an explicit acknowledgement of any limitations affecting the extent to which findings from the specific research can be generalized? ☐

5 If generalizations are based on the transferability of findings, have these been facilitated by the provision of a 'thick description'? ☐

6 If generalizations are being made on the basis of small numbers, have these been justified by:
A contrast with the wider population? ☐
A comparison with other cases? ☐
Sampling within cases? ☐
Their relevance to theory? ☐

© M. Denscombe, *Ground Rules for Social Research*. Open University Press.

11

ORIGINALITY

Ground rule: **Research should contribute something new to knowledge**

Questions: What is original about the research?

What did the research find out that was not already known?

Answers: The research is significantly different from previous studies in one or more ways.

There is at least one element of originality contained within the choice of topic, in the methods of investigation or in the analysis undertaken.

The original contribution is apparent in the aims of the research, is explained in the literature review and is discussed in the conclusions to the research.

There are cynics who argue that there is nothing new in life and that everything has been said or done before in some way or another. Without agreeing with the point, their opinion is one that researchers need to bear in mind. All too often things are presented as original that are actually nothing more than old ideas and old practices recycled to appear as though they are new and, quite rightly, researchers should be prepared to face the basic, common-sense question: *What did you find out that we did not already know?* This question provides a challenge to researchers that they can neither neglect nor dismiss lightly. It is a fundamental question that needs to be addressed because, with the notable exception of investigations that purposely replicate a previous study to check its findings, the idea of doing 'research' implicitly carries with it the idea of doing something new, of moving into uncharted territory, of boldly going where no one has gone before.

New knowledge

The most obvious way in which research can claim to involve originality is by producing new knowledge. This approach to originality owes much to the (positivistic) building-block vision of science in which the aim is to expand what is already known about the social world by conducting research that develops or extends the existing knowledge-base of facts and theories.

There is an appealing logic to this vision of originality and it is fair to say that some equation between the notions of 'originality' and 'new knowledge' has become embedded as received wisdom about good research to which almost all disciplines and approaches would subscribe in some way or other. There are, though, some significant practical problems faced by researchers who would wish to push back the frontiers of knowledge on this basis. These problems arise because *the building-block approach operates on the premise that existing knowledge should provide the starting point from which to launch any investigation*. This might, at first glance, appear to be logical and obvious. In practice, however, things are not quite so straightforward.

Knowledge in advance

In principle, to extend existing knowledge, research ought to be built upon the cutting edge of existing knowledge. The aims of the research, and its design, should reflect the best and most up-to-date thinking. This means that the researcher needs to be fully conversant with all the latest information before he or she specifies what is to be investigated and how it will be researched. There is a practical difficulty here in the sense that gaining the necessary command of the existing state-of-the-art knowledge needs to be a task under-taken *in advance* of any empirical investigation. In practice, most research projects allow for some learning *en route* – principally through the literature review. The review of existing knowledge, in fact, tends to be completed during the project rather than before it begins. This does not mean that researchers start from a position of ignorance on the topic of investigation but it does mean that their starting position is usually one that gets developed and refined during the process of the overall project.

Link up with **ACCOUNTABILITY**

Consensus of opinion

The building-block approach implies that there is one definitive and agreed position from which to launch the investigation. In the social sciences, with their different disciplines and alternative perspectives, this is hardly likely to be the case in practice. A review of the literature will almost inevitably provide a range of possible starting points rather than one unequivocal position.

Information overload

There is a presumption that the researcher has the ability and resources to gather and assimilate the vast amounts of information that already exist on a topic. The point of the literature review, after all, is to inform the researcher about what is already known on the subject so that this knowledge can be used as a launch pad for an investigation that takes things further and moves into uncharted territory. But with developments in information and communication technologies this places a heavy burden on researchers in terms of their accumulation of information from databases and bibliographic sources electronically available on a global scale. The relative ease with which it is now possible to collect published results from relevant research is, indeed, a mixed blessing. Presuming that the researcher can gain access to all the information and has the necessary resources to obtain it, there is then the problem that the researcher is likely to be faced with a huge volume of material. Even acknowledged experts in their fields might find the task of reading and understanding everything written on the topic a bit of a daunting task. The prospects of the project researcher or newcomer to the field having the time or ability to cope with it all are not good – unless, that is, they are selective in their choice of sources and their reading. In practice, researchers (whether experts or not) have to be selective in the information they use as the basis for their investigation, but this coping strategy inevitably invites the possibility that the researcher will miss some knowledge that currently exists and which might have been important as a starting point for the research.

Discovery

The development of new knowledge is a complicated process. It involves a way of understanding things, and the task of contributing something new in this respect is generally beyond the scope of any one piece of research and any individual researcher. Especially for small-scale researchers and newcomers, it might seem highly ambitious to suppose that their investigation might actually change what we know about a subject, our understanding of what it is and how it works. And there is, of course, good sense to such caution. In practice, particularly in the social sciences, the occasions of 'breakthrough discoveries' are extremely rare.

Link up with **PROOF**

Originality as 'difference'

The idea of originality as the production of new knowledge, then, might have the appeal of a straightforward logic behind it but, in practice, it creates demands that are very difficult to meet. As a consequence, the criteria for originality normally applied are much more limited. Recognizing the difficulty of adding knowledge, the research community tends to ask, instead, in what respects the current research is *different* from previous research. This might be a new angle on the topic, a new twist to the methods or a new conclusion based on the findings. In whatever respect, and however minor, the research needs to be clear about what is new and what is different in the investigation which, in this sense, makes it unique and moves things on from where they used to be. The idea of originality, then, is not just concerned with ground-breaking outcomes of the findings but involves something that can be evident in various aspects of the research process – something which distinguishes this investigation from others that have preceded it.

> **Key point**
>
> Originality tends to refer to 'difference' rather than 'contribution to knowledge'.

 Caution

The quest for originality through 'difference' does not invite eccentricity. Being different, in itself, is not enough to qualify the research on the grounds of originality. The new elements need to be *constructively* different. Claims to originality on the basis of being 'different' need to demonstrate that the ways in which the research is different are:

- linked to established practices;
- relevant to the progress of knowledge.

Difference relates to previous topics, designs, methods or analyses, not the inclusion of some crazy, 'off the wall' ideas that bear no relationship to conventional practice.

New topic

The element of originality in research can derive from the choice of subject matter that is investigated. In effect, the researcher can meet the demand for originality through choosing a new topic – one that has not previously been studied.

At one level this might seem a very difficult thing to do because social researchers have probably exhausted all the possibilities of new things to be studied that fall within the realms of social science. Psychology, economics, sociology, education, health studies, business studies, etc. cover a wide range of topics but there have been a vast number of people engaged in studies over a long period. It might seem a fair bet that, between them, earlier researchers are likely to have left no stone unturned, no virgin territory waiting to be researched for the very first time.

The prospects of being able to identify a whole new area for research, then, may not be good. However, this does not eliminate the possibility of staking a claim to originality through the study of a new topic. What it means is that if a topic is to be 'new', it needs to be a very much more narrowly defined area of study. To illustrate the point, we can use the example of an investigation into absenteeism from school. The researcher will not be able to claim the research has an element of originality because it intends to investigate the area of 'absenteeism from school' or 'truancy'. Other researchers will have got there first. A literature search will quickly reinforce this point. There is, however, the possibility of conducting original research if the researcher can identify some more narrowly focused topic within the broader area. If the study is of 'absenteeism amongst 12-year-old girls in Newtown', then there is a far greater chance that no one has investigated it before. The investigation of absenteeism is not original, but the study of absenteeism among a specific age group and a specific sex in a specific location is much more likely to provide a 'new topic'.

New method

As with the choice of a new topic, there is practically no chance of using a method of investigation that is entirely new. The development of the disciplines that make up the social sciences has involved a strong focus on methods and the basic ground work has been undertaken already. It is pretty unlikely that some entirely new method to rival the existing ones (questionnaires, interviews, observation, etc.) will be invented by the researcher and used as the basis for claiming originality. Again, however, where the research involves a development of specific features of a broader method or where it uses methods in an innovative way to investigate a topic, claims to originality through the use of methods become credible.

An example might best serve to illustrate this point. The example is real (see Denscombe 1995). It concerns an intriguing and novel approach to the use of group interviewing. The researcher, Bob Bennett, was interested in the attitudes of school pupils to dance and dancing. He used a brief question-naire to find out which pupils were broadly well disposed to dancing and which were 'anti-dancing'. He was conscious that gender was a significant factor both in terms of the pupils' attitudes to dance and, importantly, in terms of how it might affect the interaction between himself and the male/female pupils on this topic. As a teacher at the school he was able to set up the group interviews in a novel fashion which attempted to address the issue of the way gender might influence what was said and what was understood during the group interviews. At any one time during the group interviews there were six people present. There was the researcher, and there was a South Asian female colleague who was present as a co-researcher to try to counterbalance any 'bias' that might result from the fact that the researcher was a White male. Alongside the two adult researchers were two pupils (one male and one female) who had been chosen because they held positive attitudes to dance. They acted as advocates of dance. The other two members of the group interview were pupils who held negative attitudes to dance. These were two females, then two males, two females, two males, and so on.

This constituted a novel application of the group interview technique in that it paid particular attention to the impact of the researcher's gender and ethnicity, and attempted to control for its effect. It used quasi-experimental controls within the group interviews to get views from female 'dance-negatives' and male 'dance-negatives'. It engineered a confrontational situation in which those with negative attitudes to dance had their views challenged by the 'dance-positive' pupils, who effectively acted as surrogate interviewers. The research, then, used a derivation of the group interview method but, in this instance, it involved controls and a confrontational approach which marked it out as something new and something different from the mainstream.

 Caution

It is worth stressing that attempting to achieve originality on methodological grounds is rather ambitious and challenging and might not be recommended to the newcomer or the project researcher. Other than those with the nerve to be an 'intrepid explorer' and those prepared to have their findings 'rubbished' by readers who might be unconvinced about the value of the new method, researchers might be advised to tread with caution when it comes to using a new method. It is not a particularly safe or easy way to lay claims to originality.

New information

The acquisition of new information is another way in which the social researcher can lay claims to originality. As ever, however, we need to be quite precise about what we mean by this. The term *information* suggests the notion of 'useful facts'. A railway timetable, for example, contains lots of information – useful facts about the schedule of trains running from one location to another. A telephone directory, likewise, provides an illustration of what we mean by 'information' in the sense that it lists subscribers and their addresses.

The information is normally categorized and ordered in some way to make it useful. The railway timetable will be arranged according to the times and destinations of the trains. The telephone directory will be arranged alphabetically. Without the information being organized in some such fashion, their use would be very difficult and their value, as information, wholly undermined.

In the realms of social research, the collection of information can be a crucial part of the investigation. For example, the investigation into absenteeism from school might well start by gathering information about the proportion of the school student population that is absent from school each day, and then perhaps some further information about what kinds of pupil are most likely to be absent. The information base, then, might take the form of facts about 'the size of the problem' and who is most affected (males/females, ethnic origins, city/rural, working-class/middle-class, etc.), organized on the basis of particular localities.

As a basis for claiming originality for the research, though, the production of such new information needs to satisfy certain conditions.

- The researcher needs to have demonstrated that the specific information does not already exist. Obviously, yet vitally, there is no justification in research terms for duplicating information that already exists.
- The data need to have been collected in a systematic way using appropriate research methods. From the research point of view, the adequacy of the new information rests not just on the fact that such information has never been collected before, but also on its having been gathered in a rigorous way in line with accepted research practices.

Box 11.1 Originality	
The key issue	**Things to be considered**
Is it possible to produce research that has something genuinely new to say?	• In what respects is the research different from previous studies on the topic? • Does the research provide new information? • Does the research explain something in a new way? • Is there some new approach to understanding existing data? • In what ways do the findings build upon what was already known? • Is it clear which aspects of the research are new and which are drawn from other people's work?

New analysis

For more advanced social research it is necessary to go beyond a straight-forward description of the information. The point is that new information has a limited value as a stand-alone outcome from research. It might tell us something new, and something useful that we did not already know. The new information might be the outcome of good research procedures and thus be regarded as accurate information. But, by its very nature, such new information is concerned with the question 'what' rather than the question 'why'. To pursue the example of absenteeism from school, the facts collected and organized about the amount of absenteeism that exists and the social groups who tend to be most involved will provide information that describes the situation. Such information is a necessary component of good social research. However, in its own right, such new information does nothing to explain *why* the absenteeism occurs or *why* certain groups might be more affected than others.

Explaining why things are the way they are is at the heart of more advanced research, and it is at this point that research becomes involved with *knowledge*, as distinct from information. *Knowledge places information within a broader set of ideas and theories that allow the researcher to make sense of the facts.* Knowledge involves a way of understanding the information by seeing it as part of a system of thought – a system that allows the researcher to link the information to other events, to intervene and make changes, possibly even to make pre-dictions about future developments. Knowledge requires the researcher to explain the information that has been collected in terms of a broader system of ideas and theories because it is only in the context of such ideas and theories that the researcher can begin to identify the significance of the facts and attempt to exercise some influence on events.

A range of possibilities opens up to researchers in terms of their analyses of the data – possibilities that can be used to make the research different and, in this sense, original. In practice there is likely to be some overlap between these but, in essence, originality can be claimed on one or more of the following grounds:

- *Analysis to make sense of new data.* The raw data can be shaped by the use of established theories, models or analytic frameworks. The theory makes sense of them and gives them meaning. In this sense the analysis is 'theory-driven', which means that from the researcher's point of view, the key task is fitting the data to the theory – not vice versa. The originality, here, stems from the newly collected information rather than the means for analysing it.
- *Analysis to get a new perspective on a topic.* Analysis can be undertaken

with the express intention of getting a new perspective on the topic. In this case, the information itself does not need to be new. Indeed, it might well be secondary source data. The element of originality, however, comes from the researcher's choice of the particular theory, model or analytic framework to be used and the underlying assumption that it has not previously been used in relation to the topic. It involves applying a theory or approach in a way that has not been previously done to shed new light on the topic.

- *Analysis to fine-tune or develop an established theory.* Newly collected information can be used by researchers to fine-tune or develop an established theory, model or analytic framework. The originality, in this case, stems from the nature of the newly collected information and, of course, the end-product is improved knowledge that comes from the research.
- *Analysis to test or challenge an established theory.* Newly collected information can be used by researchers to test or challenge an established theory, model or analytic framework. The originality, in this case, stems from the nature of the newly collected information and, of course, its suitability as a test of the specific theory. Sometimes the research will be set up with the explicit intention of testing a theory. At other times, the challenge can develop as a result of the collection of new data that seem to reveal some inadequacies in the existing explanations. Either way, the new information can be used to contribute towards the development of alternative and better explanations. Originality, here, stems from the use of new data to show weaknesses in the current beliefs.
- *Analysis for theory generation.* Data can be used inductively to generate new theory. In the spirit of 'grounded theory' the task facing the researcher in the analysis of the data is that of looking for themes, links and relationships within the data that suggest the bases of some theory or framework that applies more generally. The originality of the research depends not only on the nature of the data that are collected but also on the end-product – the new theory generated on the basis of the data.

Box 11.2 Some possibilities for an original analysis	
Established theory →	used to analyse new data
Established theory →	applied to new circumstances (e.g. data to which it has not been applied before)
New data →	used for a critique of an established theory, model, etc.
New data →	used to refine or confirm an established theory, model, etc.
New data →	used to generate a new theory, model, etc.

Plagiarism and false claims to originality

Plagiarism involves the use of other people's work – their ideas or their words – without due acknowledgement. It involves presenting other people's work as though it was the researcher's own. At its worst, this can mean taking published accounts of research produced by another person, replacing the author's name with your own, and then claiming ownership of the work. This is the theft of intellectual property, and it is fraudulent. It is totally unacceptable practice at a legal and ethical level.

At a different level, the issue of plagiarism can arise in relation to use of other people's ideas and words *as a contribution* to a piece of new research being conducted by a researcher. This is of direct relevance to the whole question of originality in research and is not concerned just with blatant and fraudulent attempts to steal another person's work in its entirety. Instead, it is concerned with questions about which parts of research have been originated by the researcher himself/herself and which have been derived from the works of others.

> *Key point*
> **Plagiarism is intellectual theft and academic fraud. It is one of the worst things that a researcher can do.**

Ideas, theories and information

The principle operating here is that researchers should acknowledge the source of ideas and words that they 'borrow' from others in the course of their own research, and thus distinguish between the ideas and words that belong to them – which are original – and those whose origins lie with some other person or some other source. In practice, of course, it might be impossible for the researcher to trace the origins of all the ideas that accumulate and combine to form the thinking behind a piece of research, let alone cite all the sources in any report on the research. In practice, therefore, it is the spirit of the principle that researchers tend to abide by more than some literal application of the rule. Researchers may not be able to identify the origins of all their ideas – but they can, and should, acknowledge the sources of the *main, relevant* theories and information that underpin their research. This, of course, requires the researcher to be able to discern which are the most significant sources as far as their research is concerned – the crucial signposts to others about the origins of the ideas. It calls for the ability to sift through the many sources gathered through the literature search and choose which among the many are vital ones that have shaped the thinking behind the research and which warrant 'due acknowledgement'.

> **Key point**
> It may not be possible to cite all the sources of ideas, theories and information that shape a piece of research. It is essential, however, that the significant sources are acknowledged by the researcher.

Words

The temptation to use another person's words can be great. The author might express matters with a clarity that the researcher might feel he or she cannot hope to surpass. In such a case it is acceptable to use a brief extract provided that two conditions are met:

- the words are kept faithful to the original;
- the exact source of the words is given (including page numbers).

If extracts are taken from sources, word for word, the researcher's notes should make this very clear, and include details of the page of the sources from which the extract was taken. The way to avoid plagiarism, then, is to ensure that clear records are kept of the sources of ideas and words that the researcher might subsequently wish to use in his or her own work so that these ideas and words can be properly attributed to the people who originated them.

Link up with **ACCOUNTABILITY**

 Caution

Plagiarism is easy to do – but it is also becoming easier to detect. The temptation to plagiarize can be great because the Internet and text editing technologies make it easy to copy extracts; for example, through downloading material from web-sites or scanning in pages from books. There is no doubt that new information and communication technologies make plagiarism easier – but the intellectual crime remains as serious as ever. And, importantly, simple Google searches and the use of specialized software makes plagiarism easier to detect.

Guidelines for good practice

Originality is a core ingredient of good research. Apart from those relatively rare occasions when research sets out to check previous research findings through replication, social researchers are expected to demonstrate that their investigation contains an element of originality and to give some consideration to how this element of originality can allow a contribution, however small, to existing knowledge. To meet this expectation there are six elements of good practice that can help.

Always bear in mind the question: 'What is original about this research?'

A constant awareness of the question and its significance ought to be part of the mind-set for conducting research – part and parcel of the mentality with which researchers approach their task. As well as being good practice, it will prepare researchers for the question when it is posed by those who read and evaluate the research.

Provide an explicit account of what is original in the research

The originality of the research needs to be made clear to the reader. It is important that any account of the research clearly identifies those aspects of the research that mark it out as different from what has gone before. It is one of those items that need to be written about with particular care in order to pre-empt and combat any cynicism from readers of the research about whether it was worthwhile undertaking the investigation in the first place. The elements of originality should be

- apparent in the aims of the research;
- explained in the literature review;
- discussed in the conclusions to the research.

Acknowledge that originality tends to mean 'difference' rather than 'a new contribution to knowledge'

The spirit of building upon what has gone before and of contributing something new that will advance our understanding of the thing in question is one that permeates almost all social research. However, as we have seen, the astute researcher will realize that the possibility of any single piece of research making a contribution to knowledge is one that needs to be treated with caution. Rather than make extravagant claims, it is better to focus more modestly on establishing that the research has originality in the sense that it is 'constructively different' from what has gone before. That is, it is different – but in a way that helps to move things forward.

Be clear about which aspects of the investigation involve originality

Researchers should appreciate that originality does not need to be evident in every aspect of the research and should know precisely which component(s) of the research contain the constructive difference:

- the choice of topic;
- the relationship to existing research and knowledge in the area;
- the methodology;
- the analysis;
- the findings.

Recognize that the idea of advancing knowledge operates in a 'contested domain'

Social researchers cannot please all the people all the time. They need to make choices about what they research and how they undertake the investigation because there is rarely, if ever, a single undisputed starting point from which to begin. Existing knowledge on the topic they intend to investigate generally involves disputed areas and a lack of consensus.

Always avoid plagiarism

It is essential to acknowledge explicitly the origins of the ideas and information that have been used. It is absolutely vital to avoid using other people's contributions, especially their specific words, without attributing them to the originator. Failing to acknowledge the originator or ideas and information invites allegations of plagiarism. It can be construed as intellectual theft and academic fraud. If it is done intentionally, that is exactly what it is. If it is done unintentionally, that is still no excuse.

Further reading

Cryer, P. (2006) *The Research Student's Guide to Success*, 3rd edn. Maidenhead: Open University Press, Chapters 19 and 20.

Feyerabend, P.K. (1975) *Against Method: Outline of an Anarchistic Theory of Knowledge*. London: New Left Books.

Neville, C. (2007) *The Complete Guide to Referencing and Avoiding Plagiarism*. Maidenhead: Open University Press.

Checklist for ORIGINALITY

When considering the originality of the research you should feel confident about answering 'yes' to the following questions: ☑

1   Does the research differ from previous studies in at least one of the following ways:
Provide additional or new information on a particular topic? ☐
Involve the application of research methods in some original and appropriate way? ☐
Help to generate a theory, model or analytic framework? ☐
Apply established theories, models or analytic frameworks to new data? ☐
Test an existing theory, model or analytic framework in new circumstances? ☐
Provide a critique of existing theories, models or analytic frameworks? ☐

2   Does the literature review assure us that the same research has not already been undertaken elsewhere? ☐

3   Has the element of originality been made clear and obvious in:
The aims of the research? ☐
The literature review? ☐
The conclusions drawn from the research? ☐

4   Does the research avoid plagiarism by:
Producing ideas in the author's own words? ☐
Acknowledging the sources of information used by the author to support his/her ideas? ☐
Referencing the sources in a proper manner? ☐

© M. Denscombe, *Ground Rules for Social Research*. Open University Press.

12

PROOF

Ground rule: **Researchers need to be cautious about claims based on their findings**

Questions: How can you prove you are right?

How can researchers prove that their explanations are better than common sense?

Answers: Evidence has been provided to support the arguments put forward by the research. This evidence is suitably substantial and has been collected in a rigorous and systematic way.

Conclusions drawn from the research are appropriately cautious, reflecting the 'provisional' nature of theories and the difficulty of identifying simple cause–effect relationships.

Alternative theories and competing explanations have been taken into consideration.

The notion of 'proof' has some distinct connotations when used by social researchers. First, it refers to something that is achieved rather than something that is 'given'. Proof does not depend on edicts – truths handed down from higher authorities. The proof of a point cannot depend on referring to religious laws, nor can it appeal to beliefs handed down from generation to generation as tradition. Whatever the virtues of the truths contained in religion or tradition, they do not provide the bases on which social researchers, operating within a neo-scientific framework, can work towards establishing the truth of their findings. Proof is never a matter of faith as far as social researchers are concerned. Proof is always *the product of enquiry*.

Second, proof for social researchers cannot rely on the logic and rationale of an argument unless this is corroborated by *empirical evidence*. Armchair theorizing might allow someone to devise an enormously complicated, rationally coherent theory about how things work but it might exist on a plane quite removed from the everyday social world. It might be completely out of touch with reality. There is, therefore, an assumption that the proof of any such theory would rest on seeing how it works in practice. Its proof, or disproof, depends on getting empirical evidence to back it up.

Third, proof relies on evidence that has some calculable qualities. Broadly speaking, the kind of evidence to which researchers can appeal is evidence that lends itself to being measured and calculated in some form or other. This does not rule out proof based on abstract ideas and concepts. It does not restrict proof to only those things that can be touched, seen, weighed and measured. Psychologists, for example, devote a good deal of attention to calculating things like feelings, ideas, attitudes and emotions. What it does rule out is proof which appeals to metaphysical concepts. It rules out claims based on grand, high-level, philosophical notions such as 'human nature', 'the meaning of life', 'the essence of being' – things that do not lend themselves to observation and measurement. Such things are beyond proof in the conventional research sense.

Fourth, as far as social research is concerned, the idea of proof presumes that evidence has been collected in a rigorous, systematic and accountable fashion. In this sense it differs from some alternatives like *personal experience* or *common sense*, which, though they might share the belief in evidence as the basis for signalling what is true and real about the world, rely on relatively few facts, probably accumulated in a rather haphazard way. Although it might be quite reasonable during everyday conversation for someone to argue 'In my experience . . .' or 'According to this expert writing in a magazine . . .', these do not provide sufficiently systematic forms of enquiry to qualify as proof when it comes to social research.

Box 12.1 Proof	
The key issue	**Things to be considered**
On what basis can researchers claim their findings to be true?	• Has suitable evidence been used to support conclusions? • Have efforts been made to 'test' the propositions and theories used in the research? • Are conclusions cautious and do they avoid making unwarranted claims on the basis of the evidence?

Verification (proof that appeals to the evidence)

When someone asks the question 'How can you prove that?' researchers might well answer something along the lines of 'Look at the evidence.' From a research point of view, this is quite a reasonable thing to say. Although there are some caveats that need to be made on the point, it is fair to say that social researchers in general would subscribe to the view that any attempt to provide proof requires the researcher to *demonstrate* the truth of what is being claimed with reference to evidence based on what happens out there in the social world.

There is an elementary point about social research to be made here. *Proof requires that the ideas and explanations put forward by researchers need to be supported with reference to empirical evidence.* Initially, this point might seem to be drawn from positivistic research, empiricist approaches or research that operates with inductive logic, and there might be a temptation to regard verification as something whose relevance is restricted to these types of social research. This, however, would be a mistake. It applies to other styles of social research as well. Interpretive approaches, grounded theory and the use of qualitative data, equally, require the researcher to supply proof in the form of evidence that involves the use of empirical data (Marshall and Rossman 2006). The appeal to evidence has a fundamental role within all (social) research. What qualifies as 'evidence' might vary between styles of research, but the need for research to verify its claims with reference to empirical evidence remains constant.

 Caution

Empirical evidence may not provide all the answers. Some realms of knowledge do not place the same kind of reliance on empirical evidence. For instance:

- religion and spiritual faith;
- sorcery, witchcraft, magic;
- aesthetics, art, fashion, beauty;
- mathematics;
- political ideology, prejudice.

In such areas, proof, if it is needed, is to be found in a system of ideas and beliefs whose truth and whose reality exist independently, in their own right. They rely on faith, rational logic or matters of judgement as the basis of arguing what is right and what is wrong in terms of the way we understand the world, with appeals to material evidence taking, at most, second place. This does not necessarily make them inferior kinds of understanding. There are certain issues they can address, problems they can answer, that social research cannot handle so well – things like the quality of beauty, the meaning of life, the feeling of love.

Falsification (research can only support theories, never prove them)

There is an attractive simplicity to notion that researchers can prove their ideas are right by producing evidence that supports and confirms these ideas. However, as a principle guiding the way social researchers can prove their arguments, verification has some problems – problems that have seen it refined through the principle of *falsification*. This approach to the relationship between evidence and proof is generally attributed to Karl Popper (1902–92). He argued that appeals to the evidence can never actually guarantee that a theory is right. The available evidence can only confirm that the theory is right . . . so far. Each new confirmation, useful though it might be in bolstering our confidence in the theory, cannot actually *prove* that the theory is true. Subsequent observations might refute the original theory and consign it to the rubbish bin of ex-theories that worked for a time but were eventually found to be wrong. Theories like 'the world is flat', or the 'sun revolves around the Earth' were assumed to be true for a long time but eventually shown to be false. In this respect, all theories, *all knowledge, must remain 'provisional'* because it is possible that at some time in the future what we know today might be found to be wrong.

Following Popper's ([1959] 2002) approach, the idea of proof has been transformed. Evidence can never prove that a theory is right, absolutely and for all time. The best that evidence can ever hope to achieve is to provide *corroboration* for a theory, for the time being. Theories, however valid and worthwhile they appear to be at the moment, could be shown to be false at any time in the future and, no matter how many times the theory has been corroborated by events to date, there remains the prospect that just one new event could show the theory to be inadequate.

> Corroboration gives only the comfort that the theory has been tested and survived the test, that even after the most impressive corroborations of predictions it has only achieved the status of 'not yet disconfirmed'. This . . . is far from the status of 'being true'.
>
> (Cook and Campbell 1979: 20)

Testing theories (in circumstances where they are least likely to hold true)

Falsification not only embodies the principle that theories are always open to being refuted, it also carries with it the idea that researchers should actively seek to test theories in circumstances where they are most likely to be refuted. Crotty makes the point that:

> An advance in science is not a matter of scientists making a discovery and then proving it to be right. It is a matter of scientists making a guess and then finding themselves unable to prove the guess wrong, *despite strenuous efforts to do so.*
>
> (Crotty 2003: 31)

Rather than trying to prove the theory right, the task is to try to prove the theory wrong. The theory needs to be 'tested to destruction' by seeing if it works in 'least likely' conditions. If a theory is found to hold true under these adverse circumstances, then there is more chance that the theory is a good one.

 Caution

There is an important corollary to this. Any theory or proposition that falls within the realms of social research ought to take the form of something that lends itself, in principle, to being disproved. It should be, in this sense, *falsifiable*. This does not mean that it will be found to be inadequate when tested, only that the nature of the theory/proposition is such that it is possible that it might be found to be wrong.

Link up with **PURPOSE**

Robust theories (theories that withstand efforts to disprove them)

Although, in principle, theories must be capable of being falsified, in practice, some theories will be confirmed time and again over a period of time, to the point where they can be used for practical purposes as though they were absolutely true. They become sufficiently established for people not to worry about whether they will hold true. Instead, people can work on the assumption that, since the theory has worked so consistently in the past, there is every reason to believe that it will work this time.

> **Key point**
> The amount of confidence and trust that can be placed in a theory depends on its ability to withstand concerted efforts to disprove it.

The more a theory can withstand ingenious attempts to find situations in which it does not work, the more *robust* it is. This is an important point. It provides the means for distinguishing between various theories in terms of how good they are and for evaluating them as superior or inferior. Using the criterion of robustness, confidence in theories will accord with:

- how thoroughly and repeatedly efforts to refute them have been conducted, and failed;
- how many times they have been confirmed and shown to work;
- how well they have stood the test of time.

Limits to falsification (a reluctance to abandon established theories)

The principle of falsification has become embedded in contemporary research. However, when it comes to testing theories, researchers would not normally ditch a theory simply on the basis of one piece of research that produced findings that would seem to contradict the predictions of the theory. No *single* piece of contra-evidence is treated as a sufficient basis for refuting an established theory.

There are a number of reasons for this. The first of these is that *the evidence itself might be wrong*. In the words of Chalmers (1999: 87), 'When observation and experiment provide evidence that conflicts with the predictions of some law or theory, it may be the evidence which is at fault rather than the law or theory.' It could result from a bad research design. The evidence would need to be checked through other research before accepting that it deserved to be treated as genuine and worthy of serious consideration as potentially falsifying the theory.

Second, the *findings might be a quirk* – an exception to the rule that does not qualify as something that refutes the general theory. Again, the status of the contra-evidence itself comes into question and, before the theory is abandoned, further scrutiny of the evidence is required. Even if the contra-evidence is found to be genuine, it might be so exceptional that, rather than the theory being abandoned altogether, all that is called for is some tweaking of the theory to accommodate the new findings.

Third, where a theory predicts that certain things will occur and this is not borne out by a single observation, the reason might be to do with the nature of the phenomenon rather than a failing of the theory. In particular, theories that explain the likelihood or *probability* of some event occurring cannot be considered to have been disproved if, on one instance, the evidence does not support the theory. For example, the case of one heavy smoker who reaches the age of 75 without suffering from lung cancer or heart disease does not serve to invalidate the theory that tobacco smoking causes these illnesses. In terms of probability, this remains the case.

One-offs, then, do not provide a sufficient basis for falsification in the real world of research. The research community needs more than this. Before an established theory is abandoned, the research community will need to be assured that:

- the contra-evidence is genuine and based on sound research practice;
- the contra-evidence occurs repeatedly and can be produced regularly and consistently by a variety of researchers;
- the contra-evidence cannot be accommodated within the existing theory.

In practice, the refutation of any theory tends to involve the *accumulation of a body of evidence* that the existing theory does not work. More than this, the theory needs to be shown to be failing in certain vital ways that cannot be overcome by some fine-tuning of the existing theory. Researchers need to feel that there is something fundamentally wrong with the existing theory before it gets jettisoned. And this is the crucial point that lies behind criticisms of the one-off falsification idea. A lot of time, energy and money will have been invested in the existing theory and researchers will not abandon it lightly. There are commercial reasons, political reasons, and career reasons why researchers should wish to cling to existing theories rather than ditch them at the first sign of trouble. The ideas of Thomas Kuhn (1970) are regarded as significant here. He argued that in the real world of research there is an unwillingness to abandon an existing theory unless the new contra-evidence is considered particularly important in terms of its implications. Its importance depends on the extent to which it does the following:

- challenges some of the core tenets and beliefs of the existing theory (that it cannot be dealt with by refining or adapting the existing theory);
- gives rise to a new theory that not only explains the new finding but also serves to provide an adequate explanation of those things explained by the existing (old) theory.

There is an analogy here with computer software. Existing software, for example, for browsing the Internet, might be found to be good enough for certain purposes, but in need of development in specific areas. The browser software is unlikely to be abandoned immediately because it might be possible to improve the existing program to include the desired new features as an updated version of the original package. However, there might come a time when it is no longer possible to keep fine-tuning the original software and when, to produce the necessary new advance in the browser software, some completely redesigned and fundamentally new software is needed. The important point, however, is this. The advances that this new software contains cannot be at the expense of the earlier features. It cannot leave a great void. It needs to include these as well as adding the new features. So it is that any new theory cannot disregard what is already known, but needs to provide an explanation for this as well as providing new insights.

Causation (significant contributing factors rather than a single causal factor)

Causation is a surprisingly complex notion and the researcher – especially the small-scale project researcher – needs to tread carefully when it comes to matters of proof about causal relationships. Moving beyond superficial and simplistic notions of causation, researchers must be sensitive to the difficulties involved and, consequently, be quite cautious about any claims they might make on the basis of their investigation.

A causal relationship involves more than just a link between certain factors. Research might reveal, for instance, a link:

- when one thing happens and another follows, and this sequence occurs time and again;
- when two things always occur together – regularly, when one happens, the other also happens;
- when two things vary in relation to one another – when one increases, the other increases, or when one increases, the other decreases.

However, it is vital that careful consideration is given to the nature of any links that are reported as findings from the investigation. The reason for this is that observed links can result from three very different situations. They can be:

- *Coincidence*. The fact that they coincide need not imply that there is any real underlying connection between them.
- *Correlation*. In this case, the link between factors results from some genuine connection between them, but there is no evidence about which factor

is the determining one – the one that influences the others. The factors simply 'co-relate'. There could even be a third factor that interlinks the two.

- *Cause*. There is some evidence, in this case, about the direction of the link, with one factor being shown to be the *independent variable* that has a definite effect on other *dependent variables*.

If researchers wish to speak of the causes of a social phenomenon, they need to demonstrate that the links that have been observed are something more than pure coincidence. Pure coincidence has no place in social research. What would be the point of reporting that two or more factors appeared to coincide but that this was due to sheer chance or perhaps the result of some other factor unconnected with the aims of the research? It is very unlikely to contribute to an understanding of the phenomenon.

Social researchers, then, need to provide some convincing argument that any observed link reflects a genuine, underlying relationship between the factors. In addition to this, they need to be quite clear about whether the reported link has the status of a correlation or of a cause. There is a huge difference in social research between showing that two things correlate and showing that one factor *causes* the other. If an observed link is presented as a correlation, there is no suggestion about which factor is the independent variable that 'causes' the others, or which factors are the dependent variables that are, in a sense, subordinate to the causal factor. However, where research points to a causal relationship, it explicitly differentiates between such dependent and independent variables.

When researchers look for the cause of a phenomenon, they set out to do two things. First, they try to pinpoint with precision the factor that seems to be responsible for producing the phenomenon. The aim is to isolate the factor from others which might be close to it, similar to it, overlapping with it. Second, they attempt to prove that the factor is actually the *cause* of the phenomenon. To do this, the researcher needs to be able to demonstrate:

- that the factor is *directly responsible* for the phenomenon (rather than being somewhere down the line in a chain of events);
- that it is the *crucial factor* which gives rise to the phenomenon (rather than being one of a range of factors which could give rise to the same outcome).

Key point

When analysing and reporting observed links between factors, social researchers need to eliminate any that are based on pure *coincidence*, and then be very clear whether the remaining links are based on *cause* or *correlation*.

Multiple causes

The search for a simple cause–effect relationship faces particular difficulties in the social sciences. One reason for this is the complexity of the situation. This makes it difficult to extract one distinct and unique factor that will lead to an identical outcome on all occasions. There are so many factors at play in any given situation that social researchers are rarely in a position to isolate just one factor or to demonstrate that a factor always leads to the same outcome. Recognizing this, most social researchers are content to analyse phenomena in terms of multiple causality, acknowledging that the factor they have investigated may not be the only cause of the specific phenomenon. The more limited aspiration in such complex situations is to make a case that the factor that has been identified is *a significant contributor* to the phenomenon, albeit not the only cause. So, for example, it is possible to establish that social class is a causal factor affecting people's educational achievement. This does not depend on demonstrating that social class is the only factor affecting educational achievement. It is one among others, but it has a significant impact.

> **Key point**
> Good social research does not always depend on being able to identify one single causal factor that is responsible for a phenomenon. Given the complexity of social life, a more realistic ambition can be to show how a particular factor has a *significant* impact – recognizing that other factors may also have a role to play.

Uncertainty and probability

The idea of one factor causing another generally suggests that when the initial (causal) factor occurs, the other factor (effect) also occurs. However, while this holds true for much scientific research, there are occasions when the relationship between factors does not lend itself to being understood in simple A causes B terms. In molecular physics and microchemistry, as principal examples, the link between factors ceases to be 'determinate' and, instead, becomes a matter of 'probability'. The laws of science, in these cases, no longer rely on demonstrating that each and every time a cause occurs an effect will follow – that factor A (the cause) determines factor B (the effect). They rely instead on demonstrating that there is a strong probability that when factor A (the cause) occurs, it will lead to factor B (the effect). In other words, *a causal relationship is established through probability, not certainty* about the effect following the cause.

Likewise in the social sciences, it is acknowledged that, given the nature of the subject matter being investigated, things might be regarded as a cause even when they do not lead to a given outcome each and every time. To pursue the example given above, to establish that there is a causal relationship between social class and educational achievement it is not necessary to show that each and every person from a middle-class background does better than each and every person from a working-class background. For social research, the aim need only be to show that there is a greater *chance* of doing well in formal education if you come from a middle-class background (and, of course, that the link is more than just a coincidence or correlation).

> **Key point**
> In social research a causal link can be demonstrated through evidence of a high probability that one factor leads to another, without the need to show that it does so on every single occasion.

Link up with **CRITICAL REALISM**

Alternative theories

The falsification principle, referred to above, paves the way for a pragmatic position about theories and knowledge which shifts the notion of proof from whether knowledge is 'right' to whether it 'works'. There is the interesting possibility of having, coexisting alongside one another, two or more different theories that explain the same thing. Each could be robust enough to withstand testing in situations where it might not be expected to work. Each could work well enough to meet current requirements and could be *good enough for practical purposes*. Proof and disproof become matters of how *well* a theory works relative to alternative theories that exist. It is the job of social researchers to evaluate the alternatives in terms of how well they work and to judge theories as better or worse depending on how well they help our understanding of a particular phenomenon (Pawson and Tilley 1997).

Guidelines for good practice

When it comes to matters of proof, the researcher needs to tread the tightrope between, on the one hand, an approach that naïvely makes grand claims in terms of having presented proof and, on the other, an approach that responds to the fact that ultimate proof might be impossible by abandoning any serious attempt at all to try to support arguments or theories through evidence. To help the balance, there are certain things that can be done.

Do not assume that facts speak for themselves

Proof requires that the ideas and explanations put forward by researchers need to be supported with reference to evidence. Researchers need to *demonstrate* the truth of what is being claimed with reference to evidence based on what happens out there in the social world.

Be careful not to draw unwarranted conclusions from the evidence

There is always the danger that researchers might read too much into their findings and draw conclusions from them that go beyond what is really contained in the evidence. There can be the temptation to develop an idea too far relative to the evidence that is available. There is also the danger of being 'off target' when interpreting the meaning of the findings – reading into the data things that the impartial reader might be unable to discern. Good research takes care to avoid such possibilities by striving to do the following:

- be sure that any conclusions are based firmly on the evidence;
- show clearly how the evidence ties in with the theory, propositions or arguments being used by the researcher.

Show how the research accords with the principle of falsification

It is not just experimental or positivistic kinds of social research that need to reflect the principle of falsification. The spirit of falsification has come to permeate a broad spectrum of thought about the qualities of good research and can be found in a number of guises that can apply to exploratory research as well as experimental, qualitative research as much as quantitative, interpretive research as well as positivistic. It is important for the researcher to do the following:

- explain how the topic of the research lends itself to *falsifiable* propositions – statements based on the theory that could, in principle, be found to be wrong;
- show how the circumstances or design of the research *'test' the ideas* underlying the research, remembering the advantages for proof where theories can be 'tested to destruction' by seeing if they work under 'least likely' conditions.

Consider alternative explanations

In social research, theories compete with one another. It is not so much a matter of which theory is right and which theory is wrong, it is a question of what assumptions they operate on and how well they work. The criterion for judging them is how well they explain things, and this will reflect, in many ways, the values that lie behind them. Researchers, then, are not likely to be able to dismiss alternative theories as 'wrong' or irrelevant. Instead, they ought to contrast their own explanation against competing versions with the purpose of mounting an argument that their explanation is better than the others. It is important to remember, though, that better or worse explanations will be judged in relation to:

- the specific purposes of the investigation;
- the researcher's values;
- the relative merits of different kinds of social research, and whether there is a preference for quantitative rather than qualitative data, etc.

Link up with **OBJECTIVITY**

Be cautious about findings and what they 'prove'

The conclusions that are drawn on the basis of the research need to be quite cautious in the way they are expressed. As has been argued, the findings of research cannot ever 'prove' outright that any theory about the social world is right. The best they can do is to lend support to that theory and possibly to build on an accumulating body of evidence that makes the theory more robust and more likely to hold true across a variety of situations. It can bolster confidence that a particular way of understanding the social world works and is useful – but it cannot actually prove it outright. Nor can any individual piece of research ever realistically hope to disprove a theory or belief outright. So, in line with good science, *researchers need to be cautious about their claims.*

Researchers do not need to apologize for the fact that their individual findings have not produced a monumental leap forward in human understanding, especially those working on their own with low budgets, but they do need to acknowledge the fact in the way they present their conclusions and the way they make any claims on the basis of their findings. They should:

- avoid jumping to conclusions too quickly on insufficient data;
- be keen to avoid making extravagant claims that cannot be substantiated by their particular (one-off, small-scale) findings.

Recognize the limitations of the research

All research, in some respect or other, has its limitations. With respect to proof, the limitations relate to the extent to which the evidence produced by the research provides support for, or how far it goes towards refuting, theories and arguments considered in the research. This will depend on:

- the quality of the data;
- the extent to which the circumstances of the research provide a good test of the ideas.

It is highly unlikely to be a case of total support or refutation, and care needs to be taken to identify how far the evidence goes in either direction.

There is another sort of limitation that should be recognized – social research has boundaries. It does not provide the answers to everything, and should steer clear of areas where other realms of discourse are better placed to comment.

Acknowledge the provisional nature of knowledge

The concept of proof is fundamental to social research, yet it is also remarkably elusive. If there is one thing to be learned from science over the past centuries, it is that what we believe today to be 'proven fact' can well come to be regarded as a primitive belief in years to come. For the moment, the best that research can achieve in its quest for proof is to test out existing knowledge to see how robust it is, and to develop and check new theories where they are deemed necessary. This calls for an open-minded approach and an irreverence for existing theories. The enquiring mind of the researcher should retain a healthy scepticism about 'received wisdoms' and a constant willingness to question existing theories as part of a continual journey of discovery. Knowledge is provisional – the best available for the time being until better knowledge is produced. Researchers should demonstrate some sensitivity to the fact that their knowledge is the product of a certain time and a certain culture – embedded in a Western scientific frame of reference.

Avoid oversimplifying the complex causes of phenomena

The notion of a 'cause' is actually more complicated than it might at first appear. Social researchers need to take heed of this and tread carefully when writing about the causes of any phenomenon. In social research it is difficult to isolate one crucial variable and demonstrate that it causes another. Phenomena tend to be caused by more than one factor, and these factors are sometimes 'latent'. It is important, therefore, that researchers do not oversimplify matters and suggest that factor A causes factor B without taking into account the strong possibility that a number of other factors might well have some influence – factors that are too many or too subtle to control for the purposes of research. Researchers might be on safer ground if they talk in terms of factors having a significant impact on the phenomenon in question, as opposed to causing it.

Allow for the possibility of contradictions and uncertainty

It may not be possible to identify a simple and straightforward cause–effect relationship when studying a particular event or phenomenon. Yet there is a certain implicit pressure for researchers to produce findings that are neat and consistent – 'solid proof' and unequivocal support for the theory in question. Miles and Huberman (1994), though, warn about the dangers of 'oversimplifying' – rendering events, attitudes, etc. more patterned and coherent than they are. There is the danger of overlooking contradictory data and things that make the analysis messy: 'interpreting events as more patterned and congruent than they really are, lopping off the many loose ends of which social life is made' (Miles and Huberman 1994: 263).

Given the complex and sometimes paradoxical nature of the social world, good social research does not necessarily depend on being able to provide nice, neat, 'watertight' explanations. It is quite likely that findings and conclusions will be incomplete, will confront contradictions in the data and will contain an element of uncertainty. Researchers should bear in mind that analyses should not seek to gloss over the existence of uncertainty and contradictions in the phenomena in an effort to emulate a (simplistic) vision of causal relationships in the social world.

Further reading

Babbie, E. (2004) *The Practice of Social Research*, 10th edn. London: Thomson/ Wadsworth, Chapter 3.

Cook, T.D. and Campbell, D.T. (1979) *Quasi-experimentation: Design and Analysis Issues for Field Settings*. Chicago: Rand McNally, Chapter 1.

De Vaus, D.A. (2001) *Research Design in Social Research*. London: Sage, Chapter 1.

Feyerabend, P. (1975) *Against Method: Outline of an Anarchistic Theory of Knowledge*. London: New Left Books, Chapters 17–19.

May, T. (2001) *Social Research: Issues, Methods and Process*. Buckingham: Open University Press, Chapter 2.

Pawson, R. and Tilley, N. (1997) *Realistic Evaluation*. London: Sage, Chapters 2 and 3.

Popper, K. ([1959] 2002) *The Logic of Scientific Discovery*. London: Routledge, Chapters 3–8, 10.

Sayer, A. (1992) *Method in Social Science: A Realist Approach*, 2nd edn. London: Routledge, Chapters 2, 7, 8.

Walliman, N.S.R. (2005) *Your Research Project: A Step-By-Step Guide for the First-Time Researcher*, 2nd edn. London: Sage, Chapter 4.

Checklist for PROOF

When considering the matter of proof you should feel confident about answering 'yes' to the following questions: ☑

1 Does the research involve ideas or propositions that are, in principle, 'falsifiable'? ☐

2 Are the conclusions based firmly on the evidence? ☐

3 Are the conclusions appropriately cautious, avoiding any grand claims that cannot be substantiated by the findings? ☐

4 If the evidence is inconclusive or includes contradictions, have these been acknowledged and discussed rather than glossed over? ☐

5 Has serious consideration been given to alternative theories and competing explanations of the thing being studied? ☐

6 If the findings are unusual or unexpected has consideration been given to possible:
   Weaknesses in the methodology? ☐
   Problems with the theory? ☐

7 If the research is designed to 'test' specific ideas or theories, are these ideas or theories tested under 'least likely' conditions? ☐

8 Has due recognition been given to the limitations of the research (quality of data, research design, etc.)? ☐

9 Has the research avoided oversimplifying the causes of the phenomenon studied? ☐

© M. Denscombe, *Ground Rules for Social Research*. Open University Press.

References

Alvesson, M. (2002) *Postmodernism and Social Research*. Buckingham: Open University Press.

Babbie, E. (2004) *The Practice of Social Research*, 10th edn. London: Thomson/Wadsworth.

Bell, J. (2005) *Doing Your Research Project: A Guide for First-Time Researchers in Education, Health and Social Science*, 4th edn. Maidenhead: Open University Press.

Bhaskar, R. (1975) *A Realist Theory of Science*. Brighton: Harvester.

Bhaskar, R. (1979) *The Possibility of Naturalism*. Brighton: Harvester.

Bhaskar, R. (1986) *Scientific Realism and Human Emancipation*. London: Verso.

Blaikie, N. (2000) *Designing Social Research: The Logic of Anticipation*. Cambridge: Polity Press.

Blaikie, N. (2007) *Approaches to Social Enquiry*, 2nd edn. Cambridge: Polity Press.

Blaxter, L., Hughes, C. and Tight, M. (2006) *How to Research*. Maidenhead: Open University Press.

Bloor, M. (1997) Techniques of validation in qualitative research: a critical commentary, in G. Miller and R. Dingwall (eds) *Context and Method in Qualitative Research*. London: Sage.

Bryman, A. (1988) *Quantity and Quality in Social Research*. London: Unwin Hyman.

Bryman, A. (2006) Integrating quantitative and qualitative research: how is it done? *Qualitative Research*, 6(1): 97–113.

Bryman, A. (2007) Barriers to integrating quantitative and qualitative research, *Journal of Mixed Methods Research*, 1(1): 8–22.

Bulmer, M. (ed.) (1982) *Social Research Ethics*. London: Macmillan.

Burgess, R.G. (1984) *In the Field: An Introduction to Field Research*. London: Allen & Unwin.

Burrell, G. and Gibson, G. (1979) *Sociological Paradigms and Organizational Analysis*. London: Heinemann.

Carmines, E. and Zeller, R. (1979) *Reliability and Validity*. Beverly Hills, CA: Sage.

Chalmers, A.F. (1999) *What Is This Thing Called Science?* 2nd edn. Buckingham: Open University Press.

Cherryholmes, C.H. (1992) Notes on pragmatism and scientific realism, *Educational Researcher*, 14: 13–17.

Cook, T.D. and Campbell, D.T. (1979) *Quasi-experimentation: Design and Analysis Issues for Field Settings*. Chicago: Rand McNally.

Craig, G., Corden, A. and Thornton, P. (2000) *Safety in Social Research* (Social Research Update 29). Guildford: University of Surrey.

Creswell, J.W. (2007) *Qualitative Inquiry and Research Design: Choosing Among Five Traditions*, 2nd edn. Thousand Oaks, CA: Sage.

Creswell, J.W. (2009) *Research Design: Qualitative, Quantitative, and Mixed Methods Approaches*, 3rd edn. Thousand Oaks, CA: Sage.

Creswell, J.W. and Plano Clark, V.L. (2007) *Designing and Conducting Mixed Methods Research*. Thousand Oaks, CA: Sage.

Crotty, M. (2003) *The Foundations of Social Research: Meaning and Perspective in the Research Process*, 2nd edn. London: Sage.

Cryer, P. (2006) *The Research Student's Guide to Success*, 3rd edn. Maidenhead: Open University Press.

Denscombe, M. (1995) Explorations in group interviews: an evaluation of a reflexive and partisan approach, *British Educational Research Journal*, 21(2): 131–48.

Denscombe, M. (2007) *The Good Research Guide: For Small-scale Social Research Projects*, 3rd edn. Buckingham: Open University Press.

Denscombe, M. and Aubrook, L. (1992) The ethics of questionnaire research on pupils in schools: 'it's just another piece of schoolwork', *British Educational Research Journal*, 18(2): 113–31.

Denzin, N.K. and Lincoln, Y.S. (1994) *Handbook of Qualitative Research*. Thousand Oaks, CA: Sage.

De Vaus, D.A. (2001) *Research Design in Social Research*. London: Sage.

Dyson, S. and Brown, B. (2006) *Social Theory and Applied Health Research*. Maidenhead: Open University Press.

Feyerabend, P.K. (1975) *Against Method: Outline of an Anarchistic Theory of Knowledge*. London: New Left Books.

Fink, A. (2005) *Conducting Research Literature Reviews: From the Internet to Paper*. Thousand Oaks, CA: Sage.

Finlay, L. and Gough, B. (2003) *Reflexivity: A Practical Guide for Researchers in Health and Social Sciences*. Oxford: Blackwell.

Firebaugh, G. (2008) *Seven Rules for Social Research*. Princeton, NJ: Princeton University Press.

Geertz, C. (1973) Thick description: toward an interpretive theory of culture, in C. Geertz (ed.) *The Interpretation of Cultures*. New York: Basic Books.

Glaser, B. and Strauss, A. (1967) *The Discovery of Grounded Theory*. Chicago: Aldine.

Glaser, J., Dixit, J. and Green, D. (2002) Studying hate crime with the Internet: what makes racists advocate racial violence? *Journal of Social Issues*, 58(1): 177–93.

Gouldner, A. (1962) Anti-Minotaur: the myth of value-free sociology, *Social Problems*, 9: 199–213.

Green, J. and Browne, J. (2005) *Principles of Social Research*. Maidenhead: Open University Press.

Grix, J. (2004) *The Foundations of Research*. Basingstoke: Palgrave Macmillan.

Guignon, C.B. (1991) Pragmatism or hermeneutics? Epistemology after foundationalism, in D.R. Hiley, J.F. Boham and R. Shusterman (eds) *The Interpretive Turn: Philosophy, Science, Culture*. Ithaca: Cornell University Press, pp. 81–101.

Halfpenny, P. (1982) *Positivism and Sociology: Explaining Social Life*. London: Allen & Unwin.

Hammersley, M. (1987) Some notes on the terms 'validity' and 'reliability', *British Educational Research Journal*, 13(1): 73–81.

Hammersley, M. (1992) *What's Wrong with Ethnography? Methodological Explorations*. London: Routledge.

Hammersley, M. (1993) Research and 'anti-racism': the case of Peter Foster and his critics, *British Journal of Sociology*, 44: 429–48.

Hammersley, M. (2000) *Taking Sides in Social Research: Essays on Partisanship and Bias*. London: Routledge.

Hammersley, M. and Atkinson, P. (1983) *Ethnography: Principles in Practice*. London: Tavistock.

Hammersley, M. and Gomm, R. (1997) Bias in social research, *Sociological Research Online*, 2(1): 1–17. Available at http://www.socresonline.org.uk/2/1/2.html

Harding, S. (1992) After the neutrality ideal, *Social Research*, 59(3): 567–87.

Hart, C. (1998) *Doing a Literature Review: Releasing the Social Science Research Imagination*. London: Sage.

Haskell, T.L. (1990) Objectivity is not neutrality: rhetoric vs. practice in Peter Norvick's 'That Noble Dream', *History and Theory*, 29: 129–57.

Homan, R. (1991) *The Ethics of Social Research*. London: Longman.

Israel, M. and Hay, I. (2006) *Research Ethics for Social Scientists: Between Ethical Conduct and Regulatory Compliance*. London: Sage.

Johnson, R.B. and Onwuegbuzie, A.J. (2004) Mixed methods research: a research paradigm whose time has come. *Educational Researcher*, 33(7): 14–26.

Johnson, R.B., Onwuegbuzie, A.J. and Turner, L.A. (2007) Toward a definition of mixed methods research, *Journal of Mixed Methods Research*, 1(2), 112–33.

Kalof, L., Dan, A. and Dietz, T. (2008). *Essentials of Social Research*. Maidenhead: Open University Press.

Kimmel, A.J. (2007) *Ethical Issues in Behavioral Research: Basic and Applied Perspectives*. Oxford: Blackwell.

Kirk, J. and Miller, M. (1986) *Reliability and Validity in Qualitative Research*. Beverly Hills, CA: Sage.

Kuhn, T.S. (1970) *The Structure of Scientific Revolutions*, 2nd edn. Chicago: University of Chicago Press.

Layder, D. (1990) *The Realist Image in Social Science*. Basingstoke: Macmillan.

Layder, D. (1998) *Sociological Practice: Linking Theory and Social Research*. London: Sage.

LeCompte, M. and Goetz, J. (1982) Problems of reliability and validity in ethnographic research. *Review of Educational Research*, 52(1): 31–60.

Lee, R. (1993) *Doing Research on Sensitive Topics*. London: Sage.

Lee, R. (1995) *Dangerous Fieldwork*. Thousand Oaks, CA: Sage.

Leedy, P.D. and Ormrod, J.E. (2005) *Practical Research: Planning and Design*. Upper Saddle River, NJ: Prentice Hall.

Levin, P. (2007) *Skilful Time Management*. Maidenhead: Open University Press.

Lincoln, Y. and Guba, E. (1985) *Naturalistic Enquiry*. Newbury Park, CA: Sage.

Loue, S. (2000) *Textbook of Research Ethics: Theory and Practice*. New York: Kluwer Academic.

Marshall, C. and Rossman, G. (2006) *Designing Qualitative Research*, 4th edn. Thousand Oaks, CA: Sage.

Mason, J. (2002) *Qualitative Researching*. London: Sage.

Maxcy, S.J. (2003) Pragmatic threads in mixed methods research in the social sciences: the search for multiple modes of inquiry and the end of the philosophy of formalism, in A. Tashakkori and C. Teddlie (eds) *Handbook of Mixed Methods in Social and Behavioral Research*. Thousand Oaks, CA: Sage.

Maxwell, J.A. (2005) *Qualitative Research Design: An Interactive Approach*, 2nd edn. Thousand Oaks, CA: Sage.

May, T. (2001) *Social Research: Issues, Methods and Process*, 3rd edn. Buckingham: Open University Press.

Menges, R.J. (1973) Openness and honesty versus coercion and deception in psychological research. *American Psychologist*, 28: 1030–4.

Middleton, J., Gorard, S., Taylor, C. and Bannan-Ritland, B. (2006) *The 'Compleat' Design Experiment: from Soup to Nuts*. York: Dept. of Educational Studies, University of York.

Miles, M. and Huberman, A. (1994) *Qualitative Data Analysis*. Thousand Oaks, CA: Sage.

Morgan, D. L. (2007) Paradigms lost and pragmatism regained: methodological implications of combining qualitative and quantitative methods. *Journal of Mixed Methods Research*, 1(1): 48–76.

Murray, N. and Hughes, G. (2008) *Writing Up Your University Assignments and Research Projects*. Maidenhead: Open University Press.

Murray, R. and Moore, S. (2006) *The Handbook of Academic Writing: A Fresh Approach*. Maidenhead: Open University Press.

Myrdal, G. (1969) *Objectivity in Social Research*. New York: Pantheon Books.

Neville, C. (2007) *The Complete Guide to Referencing and Avoiding Plagiarism*. Maidenhead: Open University Press.

Oliver, P. (2003) *The Student's Guide to Research Ethics*. Maidenhead: Open University Press.

Pawson, R. (2006) *Evidence-based Policy: A Realist Perspective*. London: Sage.

Pawson, R. and Tilley, N. (1997) *Realistic Evaluation*. London: Sage.

Peirce, C.S., Hartshorne, C. and Weiss, P. (1931) *Collected Papers*. Cambridge, MA: Harvard University Press.

Popper, K. ([1959] 2002) *The Logic of Scientific Discovery*. London: Routledge.

Punch, M. (1986) *The Politics and Ethics of Fieldwork*. Beverly Hills, CA: Sage.

Ridley, D.D. (2008) *The Literature Review: A Step-by-Step Guide for Students*. London: Sage.

Rorty, R. (1991) *Objectivity, Relativism, and Truth:* Volume 1: *Philosophical Papers*, Cambridge: Cambridge University Press.

Rumsey, S. (2008) *How to Find Information*, 2nd edn. Maidenhead: Open University Press.

Sayer, A. (1992) *Method in Social Science: A Realist Approach*, 2nd edn. London: Routledge.

Sayer, A. (2000) *Realism and Social Science*. Thousand Oaks, CA: Sage.

Schutz, A. (1964) The stranger: an essay in social psychology, in A. Schutz (ed.) *Collected Papers*, Volume II. The Hague: Martinus Nijhoff.

Seale, C. (1999) *The Quality of Qualitative Research*. London: Sage.

Seale, C. (2007) *Qualitative Research Practice*. London: Sage.

Silverman, D. (1998) Qualitative/quantitative, in C. Jenks (ed.) *Core Sociological Dichotomies*. London: Sage.

Silverman, D. (2006) *Interpreting Qualitative Data: Methods for Analyzing Talk, Text and Interaction*, 3rd edn. Thousand Oaks, CA: Sage.

Silverman, D. (2005) *Doing Qualitative Research: A Practical Handbook*, 2nd edn. Thousand Oaks, CA: Sage.

Smith, M.J. (1998) *Social Science in Question*. London: Sage/Open University.

Social Research Association (2003) *Ethical Guidelines*. http://www.the-sra.org.uk/ethical.htm

Stake, R. (1995) *The Art of Case Study Research*. Thousand Oaks, CA: Sage.

Tashakkori, A. and Teddlie, C. (1998) *Mixed Methodology: Combining Qualitative and Quantitative Approaches*. Thousand Oaks, CA: Sage.

Tashakkori, A. and Teddlie, C. (eds) (2003) *Handbook of Mixed Methods in Social and Behavioral Research*. Thousand Oaks, CA: Sage.

Thompson, S. (1996) *Paying Respondents and Informants* (Social Research Update 14). Guildford: University of Surrey.

Walliman, N.S.R. (2005) *Your Research Project: A Step-By-Step Guide for the First-Time Researcher*, 2nd edn. London: Sage.

White, P. (2009) *Developing Research Questions*. Basingstoke: Macmillan.

Williams, M. (2000) Interpretivism and generalization, *Sociology*: 34(2), 209–24.

Yin, R.K. (2008) *Case Study Research: Design and Methods* 4th edn. Thousand Oaks, CA: Sage.

Index

Related books from Open University Press
Purchase from www.openup.co.uk or order through your local bookseller

THE GOOD RESEARCH GUIDE
FOR SMALL-SCALE RESEARCH PROJECTS
Third Edition

Martyn Denscombe

As a best-selling introductory book on the basics of social research, *The Good Research Guide* provides an accessible yet comprehensive introduction to the main approaches to social research and the methods most commonly used by researchers in the social sciences.

This edition has been updated to account for recent developments in the field such as:

- The emergence of mixed methods approaches
- Increased use of internet research
- More frequent use of methods such as triangulation and focus groups
- Developments in research ethics

Written for anyone undertaking a small-scale research project, either as part of an academic course or as part of their professional development, this book provides:

- A clear, straightforward introduction to data collection methods and data analysis
- Explanations of the key decisions researchers need to take, with practical advice on how to make appropriate decisions
- Essential checklists to guide good practice

This book is perfect for the first-time researcher looking for guidance on the issues they should consider and traps they should avoid when embarking on a social research project.

Contents

2007   360pp

978–0–335–22022–9 (Paperback)

USING STATISTICS
A GENTLE INTRODUCTION

Gordon Rugg

IF YOU'RE ENCOUNTERING STATISTICS FOR THE FIRST TIME, AND WANT A READABLE, SUPPORTIVE INTRODUCTION, THEN THIS IS THE BOOK FOR YOU.

There are plenty of excellent stats books in the world, but very few of them are entertaining reading. One result is that many students are deterred by stats. But this book is different.

Written in an informal style, it guides the reader gently through the field from the simplest descriptive statistics to multidimensional approaches. It's written in an accessible way, with few calculations and fewer equations, for readers from a broad set of academic disciplines ranging from archaeology to zoology.

There are numerous illustrative examples that guide the reader through:

- How to answer various types of research question
- How to use different forms of analysis
- The strengths and weaknesses of particular methods
- Methods that may be useful but that don't usually appear in statistics books

In this way, the book's emphasis is on understanding how statistics can be used to help answer research questions, rather than on the minute details of particular statistical tests.

Using Statistics is key reading for students who are looking for help with quantitative projects, but would like a qualitative introduction that takes them gently through the process.

Contents:
Introduction – Some introductory concepts - Descriptive statistics: A first encounter - Measurement theory - Descriptive statistics revisited - Knowledge representation - Beyond description : Answering "so what?" questions, and the role of inferential statistics - Inferential statistics - Probability theory and inferential statistics - Parametric versus non-parametric statistics - Non-parametric statistics – Correlations - Parametric statistics - Bigger questions: Multidimensional statistics - Appendices, references and further reading

2007 152pp

ISBN-13: 978–0–335–22218–6 (ISBN-10: 033–5–22218–8) Paperback
ISBN-13: 978–0–335–22219–3 (ISBN-10: 033–5–22219–6) Hardback

WRITING UP YOUR UNIVERSITY ASSIGNMENTS AND RESEARCH PROJECTS
A PRACTICAL HANDBOOK

Neil Murray and Geraldine Hughes

- What is good academic writing?
- How should I present my written work?
- How can I improve my written work?

Academic writing can be a daunting prospect for new undergraduates and postgraduates alike, regardless of whether they are home or overseas students. This accessible book provides them/students with all they need to know to produce excellent written work.

Based on their many years of experience, the authors have structured the book so as to build students' confidence in their own writing ability whilst at the same time respecting conventional ideas of what is, and what is not, acceptable in the academic domain. To reinforce student learning, the material is presented using a wealth of clear examples, hands-on tasks with answers, and logical sequences that build on earlier chapters. The first two sections of the book address the preparation and writing of assignments and research projects, while the third provides a useful toolkit containing reference materials on areas including punctuation, grammar and academic terminology.

The book includes numerous tips and insights and comprehensively covers issues such as:

- Reading around a new topic
- The need for coherence and how to achieve it
- Structure and organisation
- Plagiarism, quoting and citing sources
- The main sections of a typical research project
- Writing style
- Finding your own voice
- Examiner expectations

Contents

2008   256pp

978–0–335–22717–4 (Paperback)   978–0–335–22718–1 (Hardback)